The WarRoom Guide to Competitive Intelligence

The WarRoom Guide to Competitive Intelligence

Steven M. Shaker

Mark P. Gembicki

McGraw-Hill

New York   San Francisco   Washington, D.C.   Auckland   Bogotá
Caracas   Lisbon   London   Madrid   Mexico City   Milan
Montreal   New Delhi   San Juan   Singapore
Sydney   Tokyo   Toronto

Library of Congress Cataloging-in-Publication Data

Shaker, Steven M.
    The WarRoom guide to competitive intelligence / Steven M. Shaker,
Mark P. Gembicki.
        p.   cm.
    Includes index.
    ISBN 0-07-058057-X
    1. Business intelligence.   2. Competition.   I. Gembicki, Mark P.
II. Title.
HD38.7.S48   1998
658.4'7—dc21   98-49540
                                                                          CIP

McGraw-Hill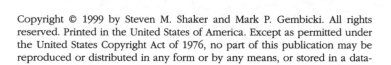

A Division of The McGraw-Hill Companies

    2 3 4 5 6 7 8 9 0   AGM/AGM   9 0 3 2 1 0 9

ISBN 0-07-058057-X

*The editing supervisor for this book was Jane Palmieri, and the production
supervisor was Tina Cameron. It was set in Garamond by Renee Lipton of
McGraw-Hill's Professional Book Group composition unit.*

Printed and bound by Quebecor/Martinsburg.

McGraw-Hill books are available at special quantity discounts to use as
premiums and sales promotions, or for use in corporate training programs.
For more information, please write to the Director of Special Sales, McGraw-
Hill, 11 West 19th Street, New York, NY 10011. Or contact your local
bookstore.

Contents

Part 3 How to Protect Your Company

Introduction

Maximizing the "flow and control" of information is key to competitiveness, whether it is on the battlefield, the campaign trail, or in the marketplace. An organization's ability to compete will in large part be determined on how well it collects, analyzes, disseminates, and safeguards information. Most corporations treat and organize the functions of competitive intelligence, decision-making, and security as separate and distinct activities. It is our philosophy and management approach at WarRoom to integrate these areas. One cannot be done well without performing the others effectively. Figure I-1 displays the weblike integration of these areas.

During the cold war, the strategic triad of manned bombers, intercontinental ballistic missiles, and submarine-launched ballistic missiles were synergistic and supportive. One element helped to protect and reinforce the other two. The overall strength and defense of the country was far greater than just the sum total of the strategic arms. Likewise, the competitiveness of today's organization can be enhanced by the integration of competitive intelligence, security safeguards, and decision-support within a war room framework. This book is devoted to achieving this totality and synergy. It introduces innovative yet "real-world" techniques for collecting, processing, and managing vital information.

We the authors are engaged in making the transformation for corporations from "seat-of-the-pants" to knowledge-based comprehension and decision-making. In part, this is achieved from our conversion of board rooms into war rooms, a technique and process which we have pioneered, and one with which you the readers will become fully acquainted in this book. *The WarRoom Guide to Competitive Intelligence* is designed for senior executives, managers, and people with future aspirations for corporate leadership positions, who are also conscious of the need to be more competitive and secure.

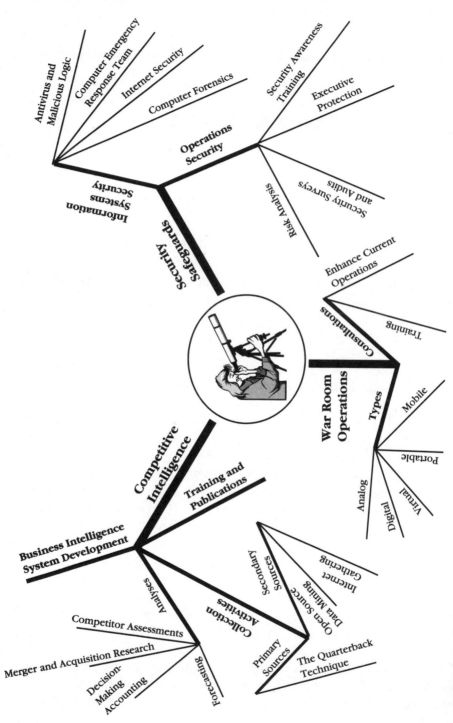

Figure I-1. The competitive intelligence, decision-making, security "web" calls for an integrated war room approach.

Upon reading this book, you will become "armed and fused" to set up your own competitive intelligence organization. You will understand the fundamentals of intelligence and the importance of identifying the requirements (what you need to know) which impact your key decision-making. You will learn how to institute a real-world system which is built around the conduct of an intelligence-gathering operation. You will be prepared for the dramatically changing information age business world by setting into motion some state-of-the-art competitive intelligence techniques and processes. You will also know what steps you need to take to protect the "keys to the kingdom" by safeguarding your information.

Steven M. Shaker

Mark P. Gembicki

Acknowledgments

A number of individuals have been instrumental in the development of this book from its embryonic concept to its evolution into a polished work. We owe a special thanks to our literary agents Laura Belt and Lisa Swayne from Adler & Robin who found us an exceptional publisher. The staff at McGraw-Hill have been wonderful, including Mary Glenn, who not only greatly enhanced the book's organization, but also "cracked the whip" when necessary to move it along, and Jane Palmieri, for making the editing process quite painless for us and for tolerating our last-minute changes. We especially want to thank our families for their understanding and support.

What Is
Competitive Intelligence?

1

The Intelligent Organization

One day a decade and a half ago, a young man sat in the plush offices of a Fortune 100 corporation located in the Midwest. He had become accustomed to talking with individuals with considerable seniority over him, who were making salaries ten times his. Yet these executives treated him with great respect and often entrusted him with some of their company's most sensitive information. The reason is that through this young man, just a few years out of graduate school, they were fulfilling what they perceived was their patriotic duty. They were informing senior decision-makers in Washington of foreign developments and activities they learned about through their business transactions, things which also impacted the interests of the nation.

What the young man heard that day astounded him. It wasn't of real interest to the intelligence community analysts he served, but he was shocked that the information he learned from one senior executive in one office was the very same material sought by another key executive located a floor away. Soon he learned that this was common. There was no real mechanism or system to facilitate the collection of information for business decision-making. Piles of information of obvious strategic and tactical value were being obtained by these individuals every day, but no one was assembling it, pulling it together, and getting it to others who could use it.

Moreover, this young intelligence officer soon found that the lack of a systematic and focused approach to handling key information was not unique to this corporation. The other companies he dealt with—be they giants, midsized, or "mom and pop" operations—all lacked a coherent means for collecting, analyzing, and disseminating information. A fundamental flaw seemed to exist in corporate America: The culture at large and MBA programs in particular were neglecting an essential ingredient to effective management. This shortcoming existed at the same time the information technology revolution was taking off and people were just beginning to grapple with how to harness its power. It also became clear that some of the same intelligence processes and techniques used by government, although often implemented in a very unique and secretive fashion, could be of immense benefit to businesses.

The young man enjoyed his work and believed he was making a positive contribution to his country, but now he knew he could also make a difference in the business world. The kernel of thought had been planted, which led to a professional transformation. With others who had come to similar conclusions, he embarked on a mission to cultivate and transform the way businesses handle information.

What Is Competitive Intelligence?

Intelligence is often called the second oldest profession. It has existed since the dawn of civilization. Sun Tzu and many other ancient warriors realized it was a fundamental part of generalship and essential to the art of war. Sun Tzu wrote

> ...what enables the wise commander to strike and conquer, and achieve things beyond the reach of ordinary men, is fore-knowledge. Now this foreknowledge cannot be elicited from spirits; it cannot be obtained inductively from experience, nor by any deductive calculation. Knowledge of the enemy's dispositions can only be obtained from other men.[1]

Intelligence, however, also has been an integral part of commercial and nonmilitary institutions. It was, and remains today, an important element in the activities of the Catholic Church.[2] It was also critical to the success experienced by the British East India Company and other early commercial ventures. Only recently, however, in the past decade, has intelligence become an organized, systematic activity worthy of its own recognized unit or organization within the corporation.

Generally speaking, *intelligence* is a compilation and analysis of data and information provided by any and every source, human or otherwise, that has foresight and can render an insightful picture of intentions, capabilities, or activities, as well as their possible implications and consequences. *Competitive intelligence (CI)* is intelligence specifically adapted to the commercial world. It is a systematic, ongoing business process to ethically and legally gather intelligence on targets such as customers, competitors, adversaries, personnel, technologies, and the total business environment. It is provided by any and all sources. Once acquired, the objective is to disseminate tactical and strategic CI to decision-makers at all levels in a visually effective, timely, and secure manner. CI differs from government intelligence for several reasons. The foremost is that CI adheres to certain business standards and ethics that are not practiced by national intelligence organizations. In part, CI cannot be gathered under the guise of diplomatic immunity or enjoy the patriotic impunity that enables one to ignore the laws and regulations of others. More to the point, in many cases illegal and unethical conduct is just bad business. The negative ramifications and public relations of getting caught doing something bad far outweigh any of the benefits derived. The Society of Competitive Intelligence Professionals (SCIP), the leading association of competitive intelligence practitioners, promotes an exemplary code of ethics well worth adhering to.[3] It is as follows:

- To continually strive to increase respect and recognition for the profession.
- To pursue one's duties with zeal and diligence while maintaining the highest degree of professionalism and avoiding all unethical practices.
- To faithfully adhere to and abide by one's company's policies, objectives, and guidelines.
- To comply with all applicable laws.
- To accurately disclose all relevant information, including one's identity and organization, prior to all interviews.

- To fully respect all requests for confidentiality of information.
- To promote and encourage full compliance with these ethical standards within one's company, with third-party contractors, and within the entire profession.

Our experience in the areas of business, government, technology, intelligence, and security has enabled us to enhance the CI process so it can be used by amateurs and professionals alike, with the same relative degree of success and effectiveness. It is the smart and legal way to conduct business and increase organizational security. Over the years, we have extracted and fine-tuned some of the more intriguing government intelligence processing and visualization techniques and adapted these to the competitive commercial environment. The result is an array of techniques that involve not only the attention naturally to be focused on competitors or adversaries but also gathering intelligence on customers, emerging technologies, and other factors in the overall business environment.

In the United States much of the impetus for competitive intelligence occurred in the mid-1980s when U.S. businesses were being clobbered in the marketplace by the Japanese. As the head of the Japanese Ministry of International Trade and Industry (MITI) so aptly posed it in a 1985 press conference:

> Japan was defeated in World War II partly due to the superior intelligence network and strategy developed by the American government....Why can't American businessmen develop the same kind of superior intelligence and strategy to cope with Japan today and be victorious? Most Japanese don't understand why American businessmen cannot win this war.

Stepping up to the need to counter the Japanese, a number of American executives began to assemble experts from government intelligence to assist them in their commercial engagements. One such pioneer was Robert Galvin, the former CEO of Motorola and now Chairman of the Executive Committee of Motorola. In the early 1980s, in addition to his corporate responsibilities, Galvin served as an adviser to the President's Foreign Intelligence Advisory Board (PFIAB). PFIAB, started in 1956 by President Eisenhower, provides advice to the President concerning the quality and adequacy of intelligence collection, analysis, estimates, and operations. The

PFIAB serves as an independent source of advice on the effectiveness of the intelligence community in meeting the needs of the nation, and how well it is preparing for the future. The Advisory Board consists of senior officials in government, industry and academia.[4] Galvin was impressed with the systematic process by which information was obtained, assessed, and disseminated. He began to ponder how such a system could function within a corporate model, so he decided to set up an intelligence process within Motorola. Realizing that such concepts and approaches would be foreign to most MBAs and business executives, he hired senior government intelligence officer Jan Herring, the National Intelligence Officer (NIO) for Science and Technology. Herring brought in some other agency talent, including a former CIA operations officer specializing in collection from domestic business and academic sources. Together they helped to set in place an intelligence organization patterned after the U.S. government model but fine-tuned for the business world. As in any such undertaking, there were trials and tribulations, but in general the organization proved extremely beneficial to Motorola and helped the company to reassert its competitive position with the Japanese. Herring went on to become a vice president with The Futures Group and introduced his business intelligence model and approach to numerous companies, including NutraSweet, General Dynamics, Phillips Petroleum, Amoco, and Southwestern Bell.

Herring and others like him made this transition from the governmental arena, and working with people from such traditional business disciplines as market research, strategic planning, marketing, financial analysis, and security, began to evolve competitive intelligence into its own profession and discipline. CI does not replace these other areas, but it reinforces and supports the ongoing decision-making required in these functions and that needed by CEOs, CFOs, CIOs, and other key managers.

Most executives make their decisions the same way everyone else does. They use some knowledge and a great deal of "gut instinct." Intuition is not bad; in fact, in many cases it has been a determining factor for success. Leaders in many fields have achieved their status in part through their innate intuitive abilities. Figure 1-1 illustrates this decision-making paradigm and the role intuition and knowledge play in decisions. Both intuition and knowledge are influenced by past experiences, although intuition occurs more at the subconscious

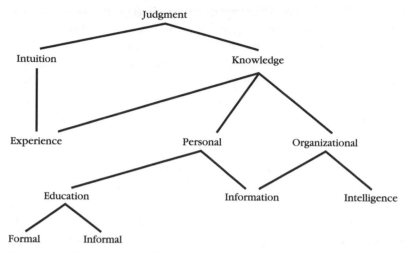

Figure 1-1. The role of intelligence in the typical decision-making paradigm.

level. Knowledge is derived from both the decision-maker's personal understanding as well as what he obtains from within the organization. Personal knowledge comes from both formal and informal education. Formal education includes what the executive learned in school, perhaps while getting her MBA, as well as her involvement in various seminars and professional training programs. Informal education, including "on the job training" and insight gained through one's own readings and observations, often proves more useful. Organizations have typically provided their executives with a lot of information and very little intelligence. A preferable approach is to enhance the decision-making process by furnishing the executive with more intelligence and less information and data. It's not necessary to eliminate intuition but rather to provide the best possible knowledge to use in conjunction with a "seasoned" intuition.

During stable periods in which little change is occurring and the environment is relatively constant, the executive's decision-making can rely chiefly on past experience. What worked before will likely work in the future, because the same business environment exists. In periods of dynamic change, however, one's past experience does not always suffice. There may not be a common frame of reference in which to judge events and circumstances. In periods of great change, thcrcforc, decision makers need more outside support. They need an intelligence mechanism that can produce on an ongoing basis information that provides foreknowledge of things to come.

The old adage that knowledge is power has never been more true than in today's complex and fast-paced international business environment. Success for every business, whether it's a one-person operation or a Fortune 500 corporation, increasingly depends on a timely awareness by key executives of the rapidly changing events impacting their organizations. Yet in most corporate settings, executives consistently work with massive amounts of raw data, small amounts of value-added information derived from analysis, and very little intelligence. Competitive intelligence reverses this traditional trend toward data and information and redirects it toward *actionable* intelligence. Figure 1-2 shows the hierarchy of information. The foundation of the pyramid is *data,* which is by far the largest block of information. Data consists of the most basic of information. It often is quantitative in nature and is readily available to the public through publications and on-line Web sites and databases. The other, higher levels of information are built upon this underlying data. The next level above data is *information.* Information refers to data which has been analyzed and therefore has some added value for business people. At the pinnacle of the pyramid is *intelligence.* Intelligence is information that enables a key executive to make a decision because it provides a degree of foresight of things to come that could impact

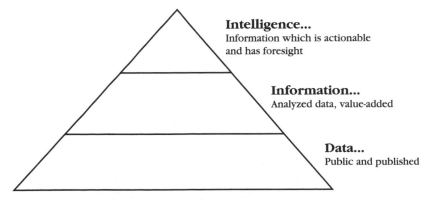

Figure 1-2. The information hierarchy; all information is not created equal.

Most managers have...
- Massive amounts of data and public information
- Small amounts of value-added information
- Very little intelligence

The focus of competitive intelligence is to reengineer the organization infrastructure so that the senior management works primarily with intelligence.

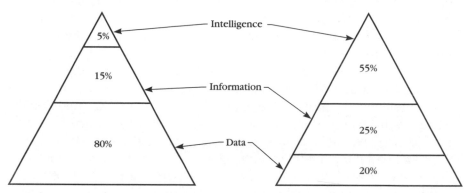

Figure 1-3. Reengineering the decision-making process from seat-of-the-pants to intelligence-based.

the company. It requires the executive to take some sort of action in response to the intelligence received, hence it is *actionable*.

Figure 1-3 illustrates the goal of reengineering the decision-making process from a "seat-of-the-pants approach" to one based on intelligence.

Two primary instruments are critical to transforming the organizational infrastructure so that senior management is working primarily with intelligence. The "Quarterback" operation is the means for rallying and focusing the organization. The "war room" methodology optimizes the knowledge-base and facilitates decision-making.

CI Today

Although a relatively new field, competitive intelligence is one of the most vibrant and fastest growing business disciplines. Corporations today reflect the full spectrum of competitive intelligence activities. At the low end are companies involved in ad hoc, reactive collection efforts. The extent of their efforts revolves around reading newspapers and conducting on-line searches. At the other end, illustrating the practices of the most aggressive and progressive organizations, are fully institutionalized competitive intelligence operations with dedicated staffs and substantial budgets. Clearly, most corporations represent the low end of the range, but those creating truly functional organizations are growing dramatically and represent some of the most competitive Fortune 500, mid-sized, and entrepreneurial-based corporations.

In 1990 SCIP had 1500 members. There were 200 attendees at their 1990 annual conference. By 1998 SCIP's membership had swelled to more than 6000, and more than 2000 individuals attended their 1998 annual conference.

The Futures Group (TFG), one of the preeminent consulting companies in CI, conducts a periodic survey examining the state of competitive intelligence in corporations.[5] The latest survey, Ostriches & Eagles 1997, to which 101 American firms responded, found that 60 percent of the companies responding had an organized business intelligence (BI)[6] system. This is a 2 percent increase over the survey conducted two years earlier. The companies surveyed represented a number of industries, including aerospace, consumer products, financial services, information products and services, and pharmaceuticals. Two-thirds of these companies had revenues of over $1 billion, and 28 percent had over $10 billion.

Those with BI systems rated the overall quality of their intelligence gathering at 6.4 on a scale of 10. Companies without a formal BI organization rated their ability to collect intelligence at 5.5. It is interesting that consumer products companies were most confident in the capability of their intelligence work and rated their intelligence systems at 6.4 (on a scale of 10) for effectiveness versus a norm of 6.1. The industry that gave itself the lowest rating was aerospace, which came in at 5.6 (on a scale of 10) for effectiveness versus a norm of 6.1. This low rating could be due to several factors. The aerospace companies have a high percentage of former military officers in their ranks. Many of these individuals have been exposed to military intelligence, so they may have a higher expectation for what intelligence should accomplish. There is also a tendency on the part of some former military officers to either overly characterize and present their commercial activities in military terms or underutilize techniques and approaches that are transferable from the military to the commercial world. Using the terms *war room* and *intelligence* in a commercial sense irks some of them.

The ways companies chose to evaluate their BI systems were interesting as well. "Actions taken" was scored by 67 percent of the respondents. "Market share changes" and "meeting financial goals" were each cited by 49 percent.

In this and a previous year's survey, Microsoft and Motorola were seen by the other companies as having the best corporate intelligence programs. They are therefore characterized as "eagles." The "ostriches" are the 17 percent of respondents who did not think other companies used competitive intelligence against them.

Surprisingly, nine out of ten companies indicated that the publications they read, e.g., newspapers, trade press, and industry newsletters, were the primary source of the information they obtained. The Internet, company employees, and suppliers and customers were credited with providing useful intelligence to 82 percent of the respondents. Industry conferences were cited by 80 percent, industry experts were given by 79 percent, and commercial databases were listed by 70 percent.

When asked the most valuable sources of information, 37 percent of the respondents indicated that it was suppliers and customers. Thirty-five percent stated that it was the publications they read. (Of those with a formalized BI program, 45 percent indicated that the publications they read provided the most valuable sources of information.) The next most-cited sources of important information were company employees (26 percent), industry experts (25 percent), and the Internet (24 percent). Industry conferences were only listed by 18 percent and commercial databases by 16 percent of respondents. These findings reveal that although CI has made significant strides over the past decade, the mechanisms, processes, and techniques used are still in their infancy and remain unsophisticated. The very low use of employees and conferences for obtaining worthwhile intelligence is proof enough of the lack of organized and sophisticated mechanisms to do so. Even companies with an established CI program are unlikely to develop a significant source structure within their organizations. The overreliance on publications indicates that most CI organizations are built on a "company library" model, albeit with the added feature that someone reads and reports on what gets collected. On a positive note, CI trainers can rejoice that there is still a great deal to teach and disseminate, and still room to exercise a significant influence with techniques like the Quarterback.

A major criticism, then, of the current state of competitive intelligence is that it is often looked at as a separate activity that feeds into executive decision-making and action and that ends when the intelligence has been delivered. Part of this problem may be due to an overreliance on the U.S. government intelligence model, where intelligence is collected and analyzed by the intelligence community and then disseminated to executive branch decision-makers. A major purpose of this model is to keep intelligence separate and distinct from policy-making so that intelligence is not politicized and the intelligence apparatus does not intrude upon our democratic decision-making processes. Those who focus on this model often think of intelligence as "providing actionable information to the decision-making." This implies that the information is so important that it requires decision-making to entail an action.

It is a major contention of this book, however, that in many business decisions and executive actions, intelligence must play an integral and ongoing role. Intelligence must be woven throughout many business processes. An emphasis on issues management as the actionable side of competitive intelligence amplifies on this approach, and it is further described in the next chapter, Information Warfare.

2

Information Warfare

*Communications without intelligence
is noise; intelligence without
communications is irrelevant.*
GENERAL ALFRED M. GREY, USMC

*...attaining one hundred victories in
one hundred battles is not the
pinnacle of excellence. Subjugating
the enemy's army without fighting is
the true pinnacle of excellence.*
SUN TZU
The Art of War

Like a samurai outfitted with a sword, knife, and other tools of
combat, the modern business executive is also equipped for warfare.
Contemporary weaponry comes in the form of personal notebooks,
pagers, cellular phones, electronic organizers, and other information
technologies and products. The modern fortress, the office, includes
the Internet and intranet networks of computers, electronic whiteboards, and numerous other IT systems. In this so-called information
age, people who can manage this flow gain a strategic and tactical
advantage over their competitors. Information warfare involves
achieving and maintaining this information advantage over
competitors. *Information warfare* is the offensive and defensive use

15

of information and information systems to exploit, corrupt, or destroy an adversary's information and information system while protecting one's own.

The terminology of information warfare has its roots in military operations. Recent military doctrine has added a fifth dimension, *info-sphere,* to the traditional battle-space arenas of land, sea, air, and space. The military considers this info-sphere as a place where primary battles will be waged in the future.

Winn Schwartau, a noted pioneer on the subject of information warfare, has developed a schemata consisting of three classes.[7] Class 1 regards personal information warfare and encompasses electronic attacks against an individual's privacy. In the past, spying on an individual to gain access to personal records might involve planting miniature microphones, concealing cameras, and wiretapping. Although these tactics are still in use, it is more likely that the same information (e.g., credit history, financial transactions, video rentals, library books, prescriptions, credit card purchases, criminal records) is now maintained in myriad databases. Obtaining these digital records through on-line means and defending against such penetrations constitutes the "battleground" for this class of information warfare.

Schwartau's second class is that of corporate information warfare. This involves the use of information and associated technology by corporations to help them outcompete competitors. This class not only concerns intelligence gathering—through both traditional and electronic means—but also involves leveraging this information to influence outcomes and events. Examples of Schwartau's second class include:

- A pharmaceutical company spreading misinformation that the use of a competitor's drug has side effects, including the possibility of its being a carcinogen. They recommend that doctors stop pre-scribing the drug until further research is conducted.

- A U.S. manufacturer buying its subassemblies and components from abroad, assembling much of the product overseas, but only packaging it in America. Nevertheless, the company tries to posi-tion itself with a "buy American" strategy and portray its competi-tors as foreign.

- A company's intelligence unit learning of the package of incentives that a competitor is offering a foreign government in order to win a competition to set up a new plant in their country. The company underbids its competitor and plants articles by friendly journalists describing how the competitor has failed to live up to commitments to other countries.

Schwartau's third class is global information warfare. Class 3 activities are directed toward or against entire industries, nations, and global economic forces. Although the first and third classes of information warfare can impact corporations, it is the second class that entails the proactive use of intelligence in business.

Myron L. Cramer's paper, "The Information Revolution: Its Current and Future Consequences—Information Warfare," further refines corporate information warfare into five elements: information collection, protection, denial, management, and transport. An organization's information warfare strategy, although perhaps not articulated as such, is how it chooses to implement and prioritize these elements. This in turn will impact its competitive position.

Cramer uses *information collection* in the same way that we use intelligence collection. Information includes the entry points for information into an organization from internal and external sources. This information responds to the organization's needs relative to planning its activities, executing its plans, monitoring its progress, and reporting its results. The overall value of the information is related to its quantity (completeness), quality (accuracy), and timeliness.

Information protection involves safeguarding the information once it has been collected by an organization. This means preventing or mitigating two kinds of threats, *information compromise* and *information destruction*. Information compromise happens when a competitor gains access to an organization's proprietary data. Information destruction is the loss of data or access to data that stems from a hostile attack by a competitor.

Information that is valued and sought by a competitor can include market projections, planned acquisitions, new product development plans, technical data, customer lists, personnel files, and financial data. Information does not have to be classified as proprietary or sensitive to have value to a competitor. For example, the travel schedule and itinerary of key executives may tip off an impending merger, acquisition, partnership, or other business deal. Protecting against information compromise can include both *operations security* and *counterintelligence.* These are described in depth in Chapter 10.

Information destruction by a competitor is rare, but it has happened. Such attacks are improper, unethical, and in most cases illegal. Attacks can take several forms; computer viruses, worms, Trojan horses, and logic bombs are examples of attacks against a company's computer system. A *virus* is a code fragment that copies itself into a larger program and modifies that program. It executes only when its host program begins to run. The virus then replicates itself, infecting other programs as it reproduces. Not only can a virus shut down a single PC it has infected, it can also cause massive failure of a network of computers. Such was the case when a virus caused the system crash of an AT&T long-distance switching system on January 15, 1990.

Worms are independent programs that reproduce by copying themselves full-blown from one computer to another, over a network. Unlike viruses, worms do not modify other programs. Rather than simply destroying data like viruses do, worms can cause the loss of communication by eating up resources and spreading through the networks.

A *Trojan horse* is a code fragment that hides inside a program and performs a disguised function. It is often used to disguise a virus or a worm. A *logic bomb* is a type of Trojan horse used to release a virus, worm, or other attack agent. It can be either an independent program or a piece of code that has been planted by a system developer or programmer.

Information protection is defensive in nature. A more aggressive posture in safeguarding one's information is to go on the offensive against the competitor's or adversary's collection systems. *Information denial* is one such measure. This can take the form of direct attacks on the competitors' collection system, or providing misinformation or deception to mislead the competitor.

The same methods that a competitor uses for information destruction (viruses, worms, Trojan horses, etc.) can be used by a company to disable an information collection system, although it would probably be illegal and unethical. Misinformation involves providing false information to the competitor's collection systems so that they will make faulty decisions based on erroneous information. Cramer provides several examples of misinformation. A company might receive information that a competitor is about to unveil a new product. Although the company does not have a comparable product, it issues its own press release describing its superior, though fictional, product. Thinking it has lost its market lead, the competitor puts its development efforts elsewhere. Even after the competitor brings its product to market, its lead can be effectively lost since some potential customers may have delayed their purchases waiting for the fictitious product from the other company.

Cramer also includes information management and information transport as crucial elements of information warfare. His main premise is that a competitive advantage can be gained from the improved management of information and from the enhanced efficiency of its transport.

How an organization balances and mixes these information warfare elements determines its overall information warfare strategy. Cramer attributes specific information warfare orientations to companies in which a single information warfare element is dominant. A *defensive orientation,* for example, characterizes an organization that emphasizes information protection and has in place significant access control and limited external system interconnections. Such a strategy might be taken by a dominant market leader that is trying to contain emerging adversaries which may attack the leader in an effort to change the current situation.

An *offensive orientation* is ascribed to an organization that is bent on attacking the market leader through information destruction, or to an organization that is exercising information denial by attacking its competitor's collection systems. A *quantity orientation* is exemplified by an organization that places its emphasis on information transport. It depends on the sheer volume and timeliness of its data to make attacks impractical. This posture works best with organizations that disseminate their information widely, little of which information is sensitive. A *quality orientation* is characterized by an organization that focuses on information management. Such a company gains its advantage by managing its information needs better than its competitors. It makes better use of less information and optimizes its use of modest protection.

The final orientation is that of the "sponge" organization. Here, the emphasis is on information collection. Such companies gain their competitive advantage by saving on research and product development; they bring products and services to market based upon the innovations of others.

Cramer suggests that the optimal strategy for an organization can be derived from the use of game theory. He, Schwartau, and other pioneers in information warfare have made an important contribution to the field of competitive intelligence: They help demonstrate that intelligence feeds and is woven into the larger context of gamesmanship between companies, often shaping perceptions and outcomes.

Issues Management

Using intelligence to optimize the process of and techniques for influencing perceptions and issues can take many forms. It may, as mentioned above, take the form of misinformation, where an erroneous understanding is promoted to achieve some strategic advantage. In most cases, however, the truth is not so clear; it's not black and white. In many cases, problems, issues, and solutions can be looked at from many angles and through many perceptual lenses. That is where the process of *issues management* comes in, to present the view that is most beneficial to the organization. Issues management is a highly effective tactic of information warfare. It involves the proactive use of competitive intelligence to support activities that influence and shape the issues and perceptions of external actors that, in turn, impact a product or program. It also involves using competitive intelligence interactively and tactically in conjunction with other corporate functions, including marketing, public relations, and strategic planning.

An issues management methodology can significantly influence the authorship, publication, and dissemination of essential information which supports the desired goals and purposes of any organization seeking to enhance its competitive position. Issues management entails a four-step process which follows a logical sequence of events to ensure effective visibility and coverage for the image being presented and perception being sought.

Step 1. Potential-Customer Accounting Analysis

Step 1 identifies the key individuals and/or organizations who will make or influence the selection or purchase process, i.e., those who choose an organization's goods or services. It includes determining their perceptions of the organization and its products and services. It identifies their position and level of influence (who sways their opinion and who else do their opinions sway) and salience (how important is this to them). The same or a similar approach can be used to determine the perception these key people have of the competition or options other than those offered by the organization seeking to improve.

Step 2. Issue exposure

Step 2 determines how to change perceptions that are negative and reinforce those which are positive. It selects those areas that are sought for maximum exposure and those areas in which exposure should be limited.

Step 3. Targeting and Prioritizing Media

This step determines which publications and media would have the greatest influence on the key decision-makers who impact the selection of the product or service. It then prioritizes the most beneficial media, develops an advertising campaign, and orchestrates the authorship of favorable press for the target products and services.

Step 4. Communications Plan

The fourth step involves creating a database of key journalists and media organizations, as well as procedures on how to most effectively submit and disseminate press releases and information to them. The database includes mail and e-mail addresses and phone and fax numbers. The communications plan also details several alternative approaches and scenarios for orchestrating a press conference. This enables a proactive approach to disseminating information, particularly in periods of crisis management.

Figure 2-1 provides an overview of the steps associated with issues management.

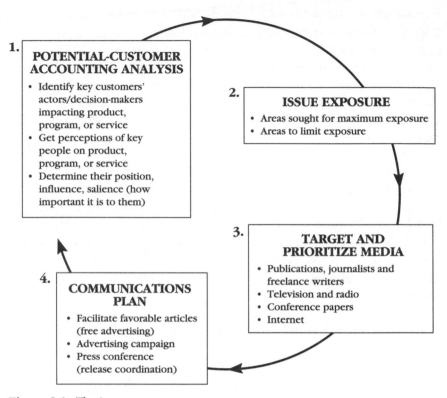

Figure 2-1. The issues management process.

The Media Management Tool: An Example of Issues Management

Competitive intelligence is essential in determining key external actors and decision-makers impacting the purchase of a product or service, along with their perception of the vendor organization and its products. CI is also used in selecting the media, publications, and journalists who would have the greatest impact on the decision-makers. Once an issues management campaign is implemented, CI also helps to monitor progress and assess the level of success.

The Web holds great potential for the future of competitive pursuits, whether in business or politics. The issues management approach just detailed has been introduced by Intelligent Automation, Inc. (IAI), a developer of state-of-the-art Internet and Web technologies. IAI has marketed this approach with Market Visions, Inc. (MVI), a political and advocacy campaign consulting and strategic planning company. Together IAI and MVI have been able to provide innovative tools and techniques to their clients that enable them to outcompete their opposition on the campaign trail. IAI has developed a "media management tool" that introduces a new political Web site paradigm, one in which the Web site and associated Internet technology is used as a device for issues management. IAI is also applying it to business-related issues management. Chapter 8 further describes this innovation and its utility in collecting and disseminating intelligence through cyber means.

In a political context, in addition to the standard features geared toward the general electorate and the cyber brigade of volunteers, a primary focus of IAI's Web site is to influence the media and their coverage and portrayal of events, day by day. Although the number of Americans who regularly surf the Net for information is growing exponentially, still only a minority of individuals use it as their primary information source. For the near-term, the mass media, mainly television and radio, will continue to be the primary means to convey messages and sway votes.

The 1997 Media in Cyberspace Study conducted by Columbia University professor Steven S. Ross and public relations executive Don Middleberg revealed that 93 percent of journalists use on-line services and the Internet.[8] The study indicated that many journalists go on-line to get their story ideas, and they use the Web for gathering images and other material. When researching a story, most reporters first try to reach a source, but their next action is to "surf the net."

The optimal use of the Web site, therefore, is not to directly influence the general electorate but rather to reach the electorate indirectly by influencing the media in their coverage and providing aggressive issues advocacy and rapid response capability. IAI has achieved this capability. Their media management system has the ability to manage e-mail lists and create direct mailers. With these, specific journalists can be alerted to events as they occur, moment to moment, on an ongoing basis. For instance, if the opposition states a particular position, journalists can be alerted within minutes regarding the flaws and inconsistencies in that argument. Specifically, an e-mail message goes out to a journalist. It contains an essential few paragraphs countering the opposition position. At the bottom of every e-mail is a link to the candidate's campaign Web site. Upon selecting the link, the journalist is drawn into the campaign Web site issue sheet that relates directly to the topic in question. The issue sheet contains various links to editorials, media clips, etc., that substantiate the client candidate's position and repudiate the opposition. Issue sheets are created day by day, issue by issue, aggressively interacting with the media and helping to shape the course of the campaign.

This media management tool incorporates other tools, among them an integrated tool for creating press releases, whereby campaign staff can compose the text of a release, including associated universal resource locators (URLs). IAI has also developed a proprietary technology called Cool Links that makes it possible to capture a profile of a person visiting the site, e.g., whether he or she represents the general electorate, contributors, volunteers, or media, and tailor the content the individual sees depending on that profile.

IAI's media management tool is now being adapted for a novel business application. It is aiding the producers of new television shows to entice prospective viewers. Hollywood blockbuster movies and television shows can be previewed and marketed on the Internet well in advance of their launch dates. By themselves, these Web sites have little draw. Their real utility comes from synergy with other media and advertising which contain the Web site addresses. Using multiple media strategically, in tandem with each other, creates far greater visibility and awareness than can be obtained from separate media campaigns. More information on the media management tool can be found at the Web site http://www.i-a-i.com.

3

From Battlefield
to Board Room

The shock waves emanating from the Oklahoma City blast damaged a number of building foundations. Among the most visible was the structural harm to the Murrah Federal complex and adjoining buildings. Less overt but also devastating was the impact on America's sense of security and self-image. The World Trade Center bombing had cracked the window to the outside world by showing that America could not be isolated from foreign-inspired terrorism. Oklahoma City, however, shattered the mirror reflecting our own souls by showing that a massive evil can be directed against Americans by their own countrymen.

Following the explosion, with the first rays of light filtering through the dust and television broadcasts revealing images of torn buildings and bodies, an expert team of FBI agents set up a command post in a nearby hotel. With only the basic materials—butcher board paper, magic markers, and tape—the bureau agents began amassing myriad bits of information. Sheets upon sheets were placed on the walls. After hours, and then days of "eyeballing" the handwritten data, members of the team were able to deduce clues. Data became information and information was transformed into operational intelligence. Eventually, the dedication and determination of some of America's best led to the arrest of some of our worst.

Gang warfare has escalated throughout our urban centers, causing many state and local officials to try new tactics and approaches to combat this societal epidemic. In Connecticut, state and local prosecutors have assembled a war room in which color pictures of gang members are displayed on a massive bulletin board. The gang members' photos are positioned in a pyramid according to their role and status within the gang. Other data is displayed that helps the prosecutors build and present racketeering cases.[9]

A major component to our strategic triad (i.e., competitive intelligence, security safeguards, and executive decision support) for winning the economic wars is the development and implementation of facilities for optimal decision-making. This we call "war rooms." General Norman Schwartzkopf used a war room when he planned and implemented an end run around the Iraqi front lines and routed Saddam Hussein's acclaimed Republican Guard. James Carville had one when he mapped out Bill Clinton's strategy to win the electoral college from President Bush. Now, smart strategic planners, marketing executives, and competitive intelligence professionals are using them as they vie for market share.

Maximizing the flow and control of information is key to competitiveness, whether the field of competition is a battlefield, the marketplace, or the campaign trail. An innovative tool and approach to planning and managing information and intelligence in such intense, time-sensitive environments is the war room. The war room concept calls for infusing and embedding information technology into the area where major information and intelligence collection, analysis, dissemination, and decision-making is occurring (e.g., a boardroom can become a war room). In their simplest form war rooms consist of foam or magnetic boards mounted on the walls of a room used for strategy sessions. In more sophisticated approaches, they are rooms with four walls of black-lighted ground-glass screens or similar type displays, including holograms, onto which computer-generated data can be projected. The displays permit a person to see all aspects of a decision-making process simultaneously and holistically, be it competitive intelligence, merger and acquisition research, strategic planning, program management, whatever. War rooms integrate the functions of data mining; automated text retrieval; rapid search, discover, and analysis; visualization; and simulation used in corporate "war games"/scenario planning, strategic and tactical decision-making, and operations.

The war room provides an environment in which marketing and competitive intelligence managers, analysts, collectors, and other team members supporting a competitive intelligence program can interact with intelligence and with each other. This interactive planning and decision-making occurs in a facilitated meeting that takes advantage of the additional ideas that can be generated using a "groupware" approach. Automated facilitation of this interaction ensures capturing the synergistic ideas that evolve, tracks the business intelligence process, and archives relevant information. Large boards or screen displays project the information and intelligence that the group utilizes and generates in a logical format, ensuring that all necessary information is available for both reference and inclusion. Information technology enhances the planning effort. In addition to the facility itself and associated information technology, people complete the makeup of the room and, in fact, are its most important component. Each war room environment consists of several task-specific work groups where users form self-directed work teams to solve problems or address issues. Each war room is also ergonomically designed to "bring out the best" in each team member.

The war room employs a process in which the collection and analysis of information, data, or intelligence in varying media formats is reproducible by its users. The preservation of information is not therefore jeopardized by an overreliance on the expertise of the person who performed the collection and analysis. If the analyst should disappear, a substantial learning curve is not required to reproduce system results.

Information systems security, which encompasses operations security and physical security in addition to computer security, seeks to prevent hackers from penetrating the war room. Basic security countermeasures are not enough when a commercial venture relies on the output of a war room.

Military War Rooms

For many years certain organizations have experimented with the use of special rooms or facilities to assist in their decision-making. The military has been in the forefront of this approach. Rooms used to develop tactics and grand strategies have been depicted in numerous movies and documentaries.[10]

Through World War II and into the 1960s, these rooms concentrated on game tables with miniature flags and models representing force disposition and movement. With the advent of modern communications and near-real-time reconnaissance and intelligence, these rooms have been refocused to concentrate on command and control rather than long-range planning and strategy formulation. It has been in the military research and development and acquisition arenas, the business side of warfare, that war rooms have seen the most progress and innovation for decision-making.

During Desert Storm General Schwartzkopf became a celebrity as his briefings to the news media were televised around the world. He was shown in his tent pointing to assorted maps. Although highly successful in his public relations efforts, there were those who were embarrassed that in the 1990s an American general was operating his command from a tent. To develop a hi-tech war room, the Defense Advanced Research Projects Agency (DARPA) contracted with SAIC Corporation to build a state-of-the-art modular command and control facility which could be quickly installed in the field. Called the Enterprise Room, it is located at DARPA's Arlington, Virginia, headquarters. It's no accident that one has the feel of being on board a futuristic starship. SAIC hired the set designer/architect involved in one of the *Star Trek* movies to help design the layout of the room. The room is about 60 by 60 feet, and most everything is in a shiny black. It has a central control platform. Most of the structures within the room are modular and are octagon-shaped. A large G-shaped desk faces the rear projection screen. It is bigger than most swimming pools. Everything is connected by optical fiber, and there are no visible wires. The facility is designed so that it can be quickly disassembled and reassembled in the field. Most of the technology developed for its use includes secure command and control. When asked what decision-support tools were being used within the facility to assist in decision-making, the answer was none. It seemed its most fruitful use to date has been in watching Sunday football.

For more than a century the military has often referred to the facility where major battles are planned and war game scenarios waged as a war room. These practices and approaches, however, did not penetrate the mainstream business world. The cyberneticist Stafford Beer proposed in 1975 that computer technology could enable the development of an "opsroom," in which real-time information is laid out graphically to provide foresight to its users and facilitate immediate, quality decisions. Beer provided preliminary designs that combined an individual's information processing capability (brain), group dynamics, and ergonomics.[11]

Beer exhibits a great deal of foresight in his operations center ideas and notions, some of which resemble the war room approach. Beer describes the use of iconic representations, a forerunner to what we at WarRoom call *visualizations*. Beer, however, perpetuates some unscientific misconceptions. For instance, his opsroom includes seven chairs, since he considers seven to be the maximum number for a creative group. Beer also perceived his opsroom primarily as a tool for government economic planners. He did not realize its potential for the commercial world.

Political and Governmental War Rooms

A successful Presidential campaign and its subsequent depiction in the movie *The War Room* began to popularize the term *war room* and its status as the special place within an organization where major decisions are made.[12] During the 1990 campaign, a war room was set up to gather as much intelligence, or to use political jargon, "opposition research," as possible on President Bush's campaign, with an emphasis on "issues management." This involved trying to anticipate what stories reporters were working on, shape those which were positive, and kill or dampen damaging stories. Brainstorming sessions on how to respond to stories that could not be curtailed or diluted occurred within the confines of the war room.[13]

Following the election, the war room concept became institutionalized within the White House and was seen as a place where Presidential aides could meet to work on achieving a single goal. War rooms were implemented for health care reform, the North Atlantic Free Trade Agreement (NAFTA), and reinventing government.[14] The respective war rooms were staffed with representatives of every White House department, whose mission in part was to coordinate efforts to communicate with lobbyists, members of Congress, and the American public.[15]

The concept spread to cabinet departments, with other agencies developing their own war rooms. Agriculture Secretary Mike Espy assembled a 10-person coordinating team working out of a war room to develop an action plan for Midwest flood recovery efforts during the summer of 1993.[16] The Department of Defense has instituted the largest collection of war rooms. The Defense Advanced Research Projects Agency has used war rooms in their strategic planning and investment decision-making related to counter-proliferation, "operations other than war," and assistance to law enforcement. The Navy Department has used a mine-countermeasures war room and an Industrial Outreach Program war room. Several Navy labs and acquisition organizations have set up war rooms on finding new opportunities and dual-use applications.

Traditional problems associated with planning for large-scale programs and activities include the inability to visualize or comprehend the complex interrelationships associated with the planning process, the inability to identify and prioritize needs, insufficient information about related activities, and absent or unfocused investment strategies.

One particular defense acquisition war room in whose design and implementation we as authors were instrumental was the Navy's Dual-Use Industrial Outreach Program. Many factors had to be considered. Working in conjunction with Global Associates, Ltd., an Arlington, Virginia, defense contractor, a war room was developed to provide the means to break complex problems down into comprehensible parts. It promoted structured dialogue and brainstorming of issues within each part, identified interrelationships, established program concepts, and tracked the evolution of a system. This method enabled the "web" of Navy dual-use program interrelationships to be clearly identified and visually displayed to enhance comprehension. The planners used the Navy dual-use war room to trace programmatic decisions to their original requirements and to focus the investment strategy to produce the greatest gains. It enabled the program manager and planners to see where program shortfalls existed, and it identified new cost-effective solutions.

Another project with Global was to assist the Defense Advanced Research Projects Agency (DARPA) with a war room to provide a technology forecast and assessment of weapons of mass destruction and a technology investment strategy plan for their counter-proliferation program. The counter-proliferation strategic planning process was a structured method used to develop an investment plan that was based on a series of needs and boundary conditions such as funding constraints, technical limitations, and time constraints.

By 1996 the Clinton campaign had improved on its earlier version and used it to target key locales and populations with selected advertising. Their war room was crucial to anticipate and parry Dole's thrusts and attacks and outmaneuver him on the campaign trail. Dole's campaign also put together a rapid response operation working from its own war room. Like the Clinton war room, its purpose was to "trump" the opponent's words on any issue and make sure the Dole side got more attention on TV and in the newspapers. The Dole campaign, however, did not optimize its facility to wage the electoral war as did the Clinton-Gore team. As a result, it never gained the same level of impact in day-to-day campaign decision-making.

Advocacy and lobbyist groups have also begun to develop war rooms to develop strategy and tactics, impact campaigns, and ultimately influence legislation. In 1996 the National Federation of Independent Business (NFIB) converted itself from being just a lobby dedicated to changing laws in favor of its members in small business to becoming a powerful electoral force seeking to elect members who would support NFIB-endorsed legislation. At the core of this transformation was a war room setup in the NFIB offices. The war room consisted of a windowless chamber crammed with files on every race, thick polling books, calendars of NFIB events, and a 4- by 6-foot map of congressional districts. The map was color-coded: blue for major involvement and red for involvement.[17]

From Board Room to War Room

Corporations have also begun to focus on competition-related planning, business intelligence gathering, and program implementation efforts using war rooms. In an all-out concerted effort to sell more Taurus automobiles, Ford set up a war room in the Renaissance Center office tower in Detroit. An intelligence command and control effort was orchestrated from which Ford operators worked phone banks and computers in concert with dealerships around the country. The result was more than twice as many Tauruses sold.[18] During an intense deal-making session forging a strategic alliance between telecommunications giants MCI and British Telecommunications PLC, MCI set up a war room in a London hotel room to track negotiations and their legal ramifications.[19] More recently, in January of 1996, MCI won in a federal auction the country's last remaining license for direct broadcast satellite TV systems. The company's chief strategists camped outside the auction headquarters in a bus which had been transformed into a mobile war room. In addition to strategizing in real time, they were able to communicate with their bidders at the auction site using scrambled wireless telephones. Their major logistical problem was keeping the parking meter filled with quarters.[20]

Prior to being absorbed by another utility, Gulf States Utility in Beaumont, Texas, had a computerized war room situated behind bulletproof glass. Their war room used computer screens to monitor and display the prices at which neighboring utilities offered to sell electricity. When the price was right, the war room researchers alerted management, who made the decisions to purchase or not.[21]

At first glance, Public Storage's conference room, located in Glendale, California, appears to be simply a nicely furnished conference room. However, when the shades are drawn and lights dimmed, it is transformed into a war room resembling something in a spy novel. The PS officials can access myriad databases about their competition and other market information, which is filtered into their strategic planning and decision-making. The war room is credited by company executives with aiding their rapid climb to become the nation's largest ministorage warehouse firm and with obtaining more than $2 billion in assets. The fierce competition for a dwindling supply of potential business made strategic planning and competitor intelligence of core importance for success. The war room was an outgrowth of the aggressive management style of Public Storage's president, B. Wayne Hughes, and the imagination of Sheryl du Roy, its director of the research group and war room coordinator. The war room enabled Ms. du Roy's research staff to keep alert for new sites for storage facilities, track the competitors in a particular locale, and link potential investors with the storage facility opportunities.[22]

At the heart of the PS war room were two computer systems, which worked in tandem. They produced a synergistic effect whose output was greater than the sum value of both systems. One system maintained extensive demographic data and elaborate maps. PS researchers were able to research any area in the country and get a good feel for socioeconomics, residents of the area, types of businesses, and buying patterns and preferences. This information was correlated and projected on full-color maps. The second system maintained an extensive competitor database.

The Verrex Corporation, based in Mountainside, New Jersey, has manufactured and sold their Decision Center to a number of companies located in Germany and the United States. Among the purchasers was the Medical College of Ohio. Costing from $125,000 to $200,000, the system consists of a large octagonal table with an octagonal cutout in the center housing various monitors. The system is basically a turnkey, multimedia conferencing system, complete with table, lights, chairs, cameras, and monitors. Unfortunately, not one decision-support tool has been integrated within the system. All the focus was on communications, none on facilitating team-based decision-making.

The use of war rooms is not exclusive to large corporations. David Falk, the sports agent to such superstars as Michael Jordan, Alonzo Mourning, and Patrick Ewing, has a war room located in his offices at the Pavilion in Chevy Chase, Maryland. At the eighth-floor headquarters of Falk Associates Management Enterprises (FAME) the inner sanctum war room consists of a mainframe, three laptops, and six telephone lines.[23] Most professional teams also run their draft choices out of war rooms.

Organizations that often find themselves in combat with big business also use war rooms. Local 25 of the Hotel Employees & Restaurant Employees International Union, which represents many of the workers in Washington's biggest hotels, used a war room in its attempt to unionize a major Hilton hotel located in the suburbs. Trina Scordo, a 25-year-old union organizer ran the downtown D.C. facility. Although located in a cramped and dingy wood-paneled space about 10 feet by 20 feet, it employed a systematic approach to utilizing the walls of the room. The main wall was covered with charts listing by department all of the 150 workers who were eligible to vote. On the first chart was a list of 98 individuals who had indicated their willingness to be represented by a union. Another column displayed checks among the names of the 125 persons who had received at least one "house call" from a union organizer. Next to the checked names were ratings from 1 to 4 representing the organizers' assessment of the individual's level of support. Ones were hard-core union supporters. Twos were considered pro union but not activists. Threes were doubters or fence-sitters. Fours were antiunion and typically slammed the door in the union organizer's face.[24]

Why the War Room

What all of these war rooms have in common, whether for political campaigns, advocacy causes, or competitor intelligence, is that they are associated with an intense, focused effort, in which a lot of people sift through data which impacts decision-making and necessitates certain actions. What is missing in most of these efforts, however, is an overall framework and disciplined approach to maximizing the operation of the war room and the flow of information.

As we have seen, many types or organizations engaged in very competitive pursuits, from warfare and corporate takeovers to union fights, have put in place war rooms to manage their activities. Most of these facilities are ad hoc developments and evolve with a lot of trial and error. Trends indicate that such rooms will proliferate, and an evolving science and art form for designing and implementing business war rooms is well under way.

In today's highly dynamic and competitive environment, great demands are being placed on key management decision-making. Key programs, projects, products, and services are faced with a number of critical decisions where the flow and control of information can impact plans, budget, and even survival. Decisions get scrutinized by numerous echelons of management. The seat-of-the-pants decision-making often characteristic of hierarchical, "rigid," vertical organizations is being replaced by a flatter, horizontal structure that utilizes teams of executives for key decision-making. Major decisions are increasingly being influenced and sometimes even made by these teams. As a result, some degree of individual accountability and impact is lost. The ability to justify decisions with a clear "logic train" and process is therefore essential to their ultimate implementation.

Technological support for well-informed, team-based decisions has been limited in the past. Traditional modes of conveying business information to teams—briefing books, projection of view graphs, even computer screens—are proving inadequate for comprehending the complex programs, relations, and processes involving the collection, analysis, and dissemination of key information. Since they are serial in nature, they enable the viewer to consume only one frame at a time. The beauty of the human mind is that it allows for parallel thinking. Although slow compared to the number-crunching prowess of the computer, the homo sapiens brain can examine multiple discrete bits of information simultaneously and form an array of linkages and connections. Thus thought can lead to learning, and additional thought can be transformed into creativity and inventiveness.

The Opportunity

The war room enables an entire process to be laid out in a framework which could never be captured on one screen or slide. It provides a format for individuals within the team to follow the whole process and logic train. It enables the linking of myriad data sets depicting a complex program or process.

A second benefit involves the explanation and advocacy of approaches and decisions that have been formulated. Senior corporate executives and middle management often find it difficult to articulate plans and generate support from other organizations and key decision-makers. The war room provides a solution to information glut and the visualization problem. It can help break down complex strategic planning, competitive intelligence, and other business processes, approaches, and planning into comprehensible parts. It can promote structured dialoguing and brainstorming. The most significant benefit of the war room is that the entire thought process behind a major activity, program, or project can be put into context.

The war room enables the competitive intelligence manager literally to walk other senior managers through the facility and process, facilitating their comprehension of the program's web of intricacies and helping to quickly establish program concepts. It also enables the staff to monitor and track activity on a real-time basis and determine measures of performance.

Multimedia rooms offer glittery presentations, but they neglect to incorporate a process to facilitate effective decision-making. Traditional command and control rooms focus on communications, but they also fail to incorporate an overall decision-making process and provide decision-support tools. The war room replaces these with a highly effective decision-making facility.

Groupware has proved an extremely valuable tool to aid teams in their decision-making. Groupware in itself, however, is limiting in that the process is serial by nature, and individuals view things differently. Much groupware is also based on eliminating dissension and automating the "Delphi" approach to decision-making. The Delphi technique, developed in the 1950s by Rand researchers Olaf Helmer and Norman Dalkey, rested on the premise that as a source of future speculation, a properly selected and questioned group of experts was superior to an individual technologist attempting to forecast by conjecture. This technique also was developed to overcome the weaknesses of the committee by using the individual judgments of a panel of experts working systematically and in concert, divorced from the distortions introduced by their personalities. Delphi attempts to eliminate these problems by using a questionnaire circulated to a panel of experts who are unaware of the identities of their fellow members.

Evidence supports the contention that Delphi studies result in gains in consensus, either through the rejection of extreme positions or by shifting the median as a consequence of specialty knowledge introduced by one or more panel members. There are some indications that in short-term forecasts, Delphi is too optimistic because of a tendency to underestimate development times. In the long term, Delphi may be too pessimistic because of the mind's inability to fully appreciate the effects of exponential growth.

There is a human dimension important to creativity and innovation that is hampered in the pursuit of eliminating group bias. The interaction of creative people is often personality-driven. Enthusiasm, energy, nonverbal expression (body language), and other factors are often the catalysts for creative thought between people. Many of us have been in group "brainstorming" sessions where the interaction seemed "to click," eliciting the best from each participant and resulting in a creative synergy. The challenge of the war room is to bring about the best structure so that the participants' creative thinking can be harnessed to offer innovative, novel concepts and solutions. Groupware can be a very useful tool within a war room setting if it is integrated well and does not dilute other important group processes.

The objective is to develop an optimized tool and forum to enable knowledge-based, team-based competitive intelligence gathering, comprehension, and distillation for key decision-makers. A complete war room consists of an integrated suite of "data mining," automated text retrieval, linkage, management, and analysis tools. Integrating all these elements into one seamless process yields superior results.

Visualized Intelligence

The ability to track and monitor activities, anticipate and forecast likely events, and quickly disseminate and comprehend intelligence is an essential asset to operating in today's time-sensitive environment. Although narrative information can be prepared in concise formats, the written word is still limited in its ability to portray the multidimensionality and density of information. The notion that one picture can represent a thousand words is probably an understatement in light of the latest data visualization techniques pioneered by Edward Tufte and other leading "visualization linguists." These individuals have advanced the art and science of utilizing graphics to visually display large quantities of information by the combined use of points, lines, a coordinate system, numbers, symbols, words, shadow, and color. All of these advances in visualization have been successfully applied to the collection, analysis, and dissemination of competitive intelligence.

An optimal integrated suite of competitive intelligence collection and analysis, management, and visualization systems enables management to:

- Establish a mechanism to record and track corporate intelligence requirements and responsibilities by individuals and organizations.

- "Mine" information and intelligence from databases, intranet and Internet, and from "open source" literature relating to competitors, customers, emerging technology, threats, and opportunities.

- Visually link this information, thus enabling individuals and teams of analysts to quickly ascertain the status of key activities and developments.

- Allow an analyst to zoom in on any link to examine information on a particular issue or concern in depth and in its entirety.

- Feed the collected information into various linked analytical tools to enable individuals and teams to assimilate, evaluate, and estimate findings.

- Allow teams to quickly prioritize and achieve group consensus.

- Furnish a mechanism for the quick conversion of findings into report formats.

- Provide for the secure and efficient dissemination of business intelligence reporting via the Internet and various intranets, as well as its placement at homepage/Web sites when appropriate.

- Provide for a quick "feedback" loop from corporate decision-makers and other program analysts by incorporating their follow-up questions into the initial intelligence requirements process.

How to Build a Competitive Intelligence Organization

4

The Competitive Intelligence Process

Even minutiae should have a place in
our collection, for things of seemingly
trifling nature, when enjoined with
others of a more serious cast, may lead
to valuable conclusion.

GENERAL GEORGE WASHINGTON

Collection, Analysis, and Dissemination

There is a difference in how the competitive intelligence process is viewed among certain CI theorists. This may in part be due to where their careers originated. Some with analytical backgrounds orient organizational structure and process around the analysis function, so analysts become the main gatekeepers. They believe that the analysts should oversee the development of all requirements, intelligence should be gathered under their direction, and all intelligence should be analyzed before being disseminated to decision-makers. They view the functions of collection and dissemination as subservient to that of analysis. Theorists from the collection side, as we are, hold the opinion that there is a great deal of intelligence which can be gathered and disseminated without going through a major analytical filter. They believe the analytical step often slows the dissemination of useful intelligence. This rivalry in orientation exists both in government and commercial intelligence. In reality, all elements of collection, analysis, and dissemination need to be integrated, coordinated, and well orchestrated. In general, one element should not be subservient to another unless a special need or project dictates it as such. Figure 4-1 shows the competitive intelligence process, which is circular in nature. Good intelligence should result in more questions being raised and a continuing need to collect, analyze, and disseminate. CI is ongoing, and as long as there are important decisions to be made, the process continues.

Effective intelligence is not collected in a vacuum. Trying to gather everything will result in obtaining very little of value. A program which is not focused will ultimately fail. The proper intelligence process begins with the identification and articulation of requirements. *Requirements* are those questions whose answers are needed to support effective decision-making. These serve as the catalyst for all subsequent activity. Generating requirements involves a subtle art of cultivating key executives and gaining their support. If done poorly, the method used in ascertaining the executive's information needs can turn the individual away from the CI program. Cultivating the intelligence user is just as important and demanding as eliciting information from the target, or source. For decision-makers to support a structured CI approach, they need to be convinced that they will benefit from it.

Requirements address an overarching question or need. They are qualitative in nature and can be responded to easily by the collector. These initial requirements are further refined into *essential elements of intelligence* (EEIs).[25] The EEIs are often more quantitative and respond to analytical criteria. There are many cases when the EEIs are not needed and the overall requirement suffices. The overall list of requirements should not be allowed to grow so large that it becomes unwieldy. About ten important requirements, each further refined into several EEIs, is a good number to work with.

Once this list of requirements and EEIs is generated, the next step is to determine who the individuals are who hold the answers to these questions. These are the *targets*, the custodians of information that responds to your requirements. If the requirements deal with a competitor, the most likely targets will be the competitor's management and employees. Occasionally, someone external to the

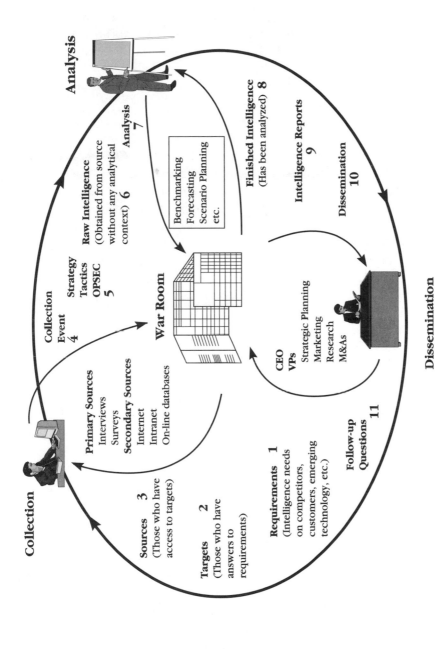

Figure 4-1. The competitive intelligence process.

competitor's company may truly be "in the know" and thus become a target. It is important to begin early to determine who these targets are. As one proceeds further into the CI process, additional targets will emerge, and some of those who may have been targeted originally will drop from the list. Perhaps you will know everything they know, or what they offer is of minimal value, or you are unable to get access to them.

Once targets have been identified, the key is to get access to them, find a way to interact, question them, and obtain intelligence. Gaining access occurs through the development of sources. *Sources* are those individuals who are used to interact with targets. They are used either because they currently have access to the targets or because it is believed they can develop a level of access. Many people within a corporation have connections—professional, educational, and personal ties—with their counterparts in competitor firms. They therefore have the wherewithal to pick up a phone and reach the target, and the target is likely to be responsive. In large part, success will depend on how the source elicits the desired information. It is the task of the CI collector who works with the source to come up with the best angle and tactics to broach a question.

All this can be somewhat confusing; many practitioners consider those who have answers to be the source of the intelligence. It is important, however, to make a distinction between sources and targets. This distinction must be made to enable the development of effective intelligence collection operations. Obtaining worthwhile intelligence is a very proactive activity. It requires a systematic search, similar to a weapon system acquiring a target and then homing in until it scores a direct hit.

Sources can come from within a company or be external to it. Internal sources are employees of the company. They are legally and, hopefully, emotionally bound to the welfare of the organization. There is a higher confidence level when entrusting sensitive information and activities to those who are affiliated with the company. External sources are those who are willing to obtain information for the company but are not employees. They can be consultants or vendors. Some may be in the pay of the company; others may have no financial relationship. An external source can be an industry analyst or business journalist who trades information with a corporate official. You find and cultivate ties to external sources from your internal sources. The topic of sources, both internal and external, is covered more extensively in Chapter 5 on the Quarterback.

Information sources can be further differentiated by whether they are primary or secondary. *Primary sources* include those who pick up information firsthand through their own discussions or interactions with the targets. *Secondary sources* have learned the intelligence secondhand. Someone else, a go-between, has relayed the information to the source. Although it still may be valuable, the level of confidence in the intelligence becomes degraded if it is arrived at through intermediaries. Secondary sources can also include information obtained through newsletters, journals, or on-line means. Such information, however, is likely to be at the lower levels of the pyramid (data or general information), rather than actionable intelligence.

To summarize, the organization develops intelligence requirements that it needs to make effective decisions. Individuals who are likely candidates for having the answers to these requirements are the targets. The way to get at these targets is through sources. The next stage in the process is to find an activity or to orchestrate a collection event where the source can gain access to and interact with the target. This may be as simple as a telephone call, but in most cases it requires much more planning and tactical effort. The Quarterback approach is one of the more refined and successful means in which to orchestrate these interactions.

Once the interaction occurs and intelligence is obtained by the source from the target, it must be processed. The collector debriefs the source as to what was learned. This intelligence is conveyed to an analyst as a sanity check. It is usually considered *raw intelligence* until it can be collaborated through other sources. In some cases, the intelligence has enough validity and importance that it will be disseminated to decision-makers immediately. For instance, if it is essential information relating to negotiations in progress over a merger, then it may be disseminated without collaboration. The intelligence report, however, should include a caveat that no other supportive intelligence has been obtained to date.

In many cases the collected intelligence responds directly to a requirement and does not require any special analysis to disseminate.

It may be integrated with other intelligence for future analysis, but due to the time sensitivity, it is sent as is. Some requirements, however, are complex, have no simple answer, and call for certain types of analytical techniques and efforts to arrive at an answer. These, in turn, require various clarifying needs and inputs (EEIs) which can be sent to collectors and ultimately to various sources. Intelligence that has been analyzed or has enough supportive information to make it credible is considered *finished intelligence*. Finished intelligence can be disseminated in various formats. The rapid progress in information technology has created many new and improved ways to process and convey information and intelligence. In general, intelligence reports should be prepared as executive briefs, no longer than a page. More in-depth background information should be available if the executive desires. If transmitted on-line or via e-mail, then hypertext links to other information and collaborative reports should be furnished.

The competitive intelligence process is quite complex and intricate. It involves:

- Developing and refining requirements and essential elements of intelligence (EEIs).

- Linking requirements to potential targets.

- Finding sources within the company and external to the company who can gain access to the targets.

- Briefing and developing sources to optimize their elicitation skills.

- Tracking events and activities and orchestrating interactions between sources and targets.

- Debriefing the sources after their interaction with the targets.

- Substantiating the raw intelligence with other intelligence.

- Developing an analytical framework in which to collect and synthesize intelligence.

- Disseminating intelligence through paper and electronic means.

- Obtaining feedback and follow-up questions from the decision-makers.

Managing this complexity of information, people activities, and interactions is extremely difficult. That is why it is best conducted within a war room setting, since the war room facility is designed to optimize the flow and control of information.

The Competitive Intelligence Collection Planning Process

Getting a handle on the competitive intelligence process requires development of a collection plan. The collection plan amounts to a structured, logical, sequential process for collecting intelligence, in which the results of one CI step feed into the conduct of the next task. Each step of the CI plan can stand alone as a useful element in the collection effort, but the synergistic value gained from completing all of the steps of the plan far exceeds simply the sum of its parts.

Figure 4-2 shows the CI collection plan methodology used by WarRoom. It mirrors the CI process but contains the initial information required to implement the collection effort. The plan incorporates certain innovative techniques and "trade craft" during the implementation of each step. The environmental scan approach, which we call EnviroScan, encompasses both primary and secondary sources of information. These include in-person, telephone, and e-mail interviews and "data mining" techniques ranging from library research to conducting searches on-line and through the Internet. State-of-the-art intelligent agents, robots, and metasearch engines are used to mine data from the Internet and various electronic databases. Collection activities culminate with the execution of more sophisticated trade craft operations, such as the Quarterback technique for gathering intelligence at conferences.

Collection Plan Guidance

Unless a CI unit has initiated and implemented several collection plans in the past, the effort does not come easy. Understanding the terminology, concept, and interactions requires a lot of questioning and discussion. The following white paper, entitled "CI Collection Plan Review," is an example of collection plan guidance that WarRoom provided to one of its clients. The names and identification information have been removed and appear as blanks.

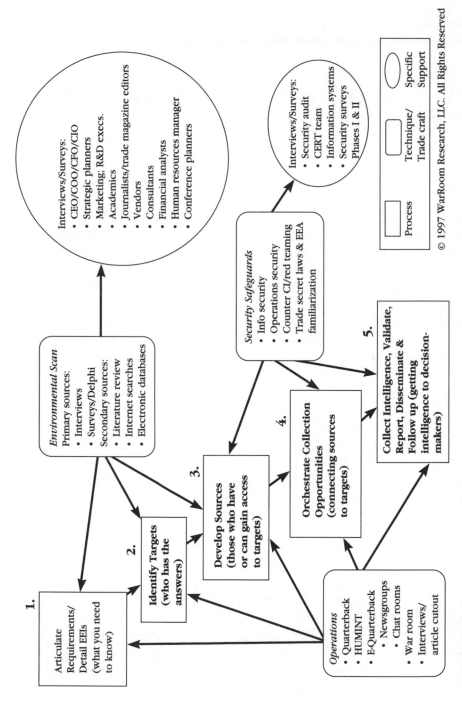

Figure 4-2. The five-step competitive intelligence collection plan and supporting processes.

Interviews/Surveys:
- CEO/COO/CFO/CIO
- Strategic planners
- Marketing; R&D execs.
- Academics
- Journalists/trade magazine editors
- Vendors
- Consultants
- Financial analysts
- Human resources manager
- Conference planners

Interviews/Surveys:
- Security audit
- CERT team
- Information systems
- Security surveys Phases I & II

Environmental Scan
Primary sources:
- Interviews
- Surveys/Delphi
Secondary sources:
- Literature review
- Internet searches
- Electronic databases

Security Safeguards
- Info security
- Operations security
- Counter CI/red teaming
- Trade secret laws & EEA familiarization

1.
Articulate Requirements/ Detail EEIs (what you need to know)

2.
Identify Targets (who has the answers)

3.
Develop Sources (those who have or can gain access to targets)

4.
Orchestrate Collection Opportunities (connecting sources to targets)

5.
Collect Intelligence, Validate, Report, Disseminate & Follow up (getting intelligence to decision-makers)

Operations
- Quarterback
- HUMINT
- E-Quarterback
  - Newsgroups
  - Chat rooms
- War room
- Interviews/ article cutout

Process

Technique/ Trade craft

Specific Support

CI Collection Plan Review

Prepared for _____ , Inc.

The following comments and recommendations represent our initial appraisal of the collection plan as gleaned from the contact and collection plan sheets furnished by _____ on March 10, _____.

1. Requirements

We believe that these requirements are well-stated and are at the right level of detail. They are qualitative in nature and can be easily responded to by the collector. We at WarRoom, however, refine the initial requirements into essential elements of intelligence (EEIs). The EEIs are often more quantitative and respond to analytical criteria. For example, your #2 requirement is: Who are the best _____ companies in _____. "Best" is a qualitative judgment that is appropriate for the initial requirement. The EEIs, however, should amplify on what "best" implies with certain select criteria. Criteria can relate to a level of performance, including revenue, profitability, cash flow, technology base, management culture, public's perception, etc. With a matrix of these criteria, you can benchmark acquisition candidates, compare their strengths and weaknesses, and come up with a prioritized list of target acquisitions.

2. Collection Plan Methodology

The collection plan sheets furnished to WarRoom Research (WRR) indicate that you have already developed a systematic and prioritized list of requirements, as well as identified internal and external sources who can furnish you with intelligence responding to these requirements. You also describe some preliminary findings and the collection approach used to gain this intelligence (i.e., visit, phone, vendor). This is a great beginning and already farther advanced than many CI programs. Our approach to the collection plan is similar, with a few added areas or tasks. Our requirements are at the same level of detail as those described in the sheets. They respond to an overarching question or need. If warranted, these are further refined into the EEIs. There are many cases when the EEIs are not needed and the overall requirement suffices. Our second step in the plan is to identify the targets who could answer these requirements. Our sources are those individuals who have access to these targets.

Much of the information related to prospective targets is obtained from an *environmental scan*. The environmental scan provides a systematic data collection methodology utilizing primary source (interviews and surveys) and secondary source (literature search, electronic database and Internet data mining) intelligence gathering approaches, as well as incorporating some innovative "third wave" techniques. We employ a combination of gathering techniques in order to obtain inputs from varied sources.

Once we identify the targets, we then cultivate the internal and external sources which have access to these targets. We develop the type of collection operation most suited for orchestrating an interaction between the source and the target. This can range from a simple phone call and interview to a more sophisticated Quarterback operation. Sophisticated and sensitive operations also require security safeguards, which are essential to our planning and implementation.

Immediately prior to an interaction between the source and target, the source should be briefed. The CI collector can provide him with the specific requirements and EEIs. As soon as possible following the interaction, while the information is still "fresh" in her mind, the source should be debriefed. If the information is credible and validated, then it can be provided as an intelligence report to the key decision-maker or integrated into a larger study or analysis. Good intelligence often leads to further questions and requests for additional information on the part of key decision-makers. A feedback loop should be structured so that these additional requirements/EEIs can be given to the source as follow-up questions for the next interaction between the source and target.

3. Acquisition War Room

Since much of your intelligence effort is focused on acquisition candidates, you may want to consider setting up a low-cost war room to monitor and track your acquisition efforts and the intelligence used to support your acquisition decision-making. All you require is a conference room where you can hang foam boards on the walls or place them on easels. These foam boards can use both narrative and visualization graphics to show the logic train of your acquisition process. The process could reflect

1. _____ strategic plan and vision for growth
2. The criteria for acquisition candidates
3. The intelligence requirements and their further refinement into EEIs
4. The CI targets who can answer these requirements
5. Internal _____ sources who can interact with the targets
6. External sources who can interact with the targets
7. The event or activity in which the source-target interaction is orchestrated
8. The intelligence gathered from the interaction
9. The intelligence dissemination and reaction of the intelligence user
10. Follow-up requirements and remaining intelligence gaps relating to the initial requirement
11. Overall progress of the acquisition

The war room proves to be a very effective means for tracking and monitoring your intelligence activities, as well as serving as an advocacy tool in which to explain and promote your efforts to upper management. Figure 4-3 displays a "straw man" version of what an acquisition intelligence war room might entail. Its actual design and layout would require in-depth consultation with _____.

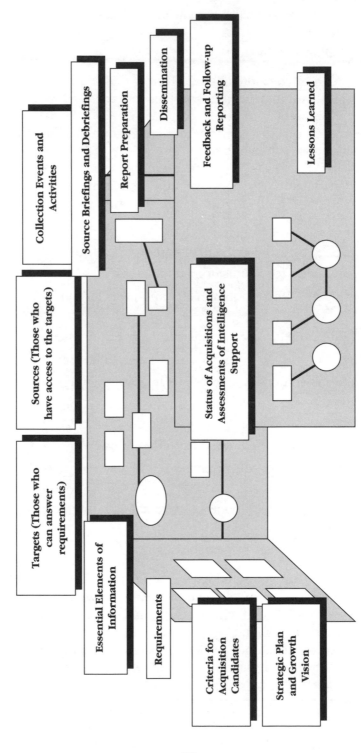

Figure 4-3. A straw man version of an acquisition intelligence war room.

The Benefits of the Environmental Scan

> To overcome the intelligent by folly is contrary to the natural order of things; to overcome the foolish by intelligence is in accord with the natural order. To overcome the intelligent by intelligence, however, is a matter of opportunity. There are three avenues of opportunity: events, trends, and conditions. When opportunities occur through events, you are unable to respond, you are not smart. When opportunities become active through a trend and yet you cannot make plans, you are not wise. When opportunities emerge through conditions but you cannot act on them, you are not bold. Those skilled in generalship always achieve their victories by taking advantage of opportunities. (Zhuge Liang, ca. 200 AD, *The Way of the General*)

There is a tendency on the part of some CI novices to run to their sources with the requirements as soon as they receive them, without "doing their homework." In certain time-sensitive situations, there may not be the opportunity or luxury to build a strong foundation of information prior to collecting intelligence. This, however, can have severe limitations and lead to major problems.

A strong foundation from which to obtain information about targets and to develop external sources is derived from our Environscan approach to environmental scanning. *Environmental scanning* is a widely accepted technique used to monitor the pulse of change in the external environment. It has been successfully applied to the political, economic, technological, and social arenas. Traditional environmental scanning approaches have certain things in common. They typically reflect the following generic components:

1. People and various resources to scan the print media (journals, magazines, newsletters, newspapers, etc.)

2. Preparing written abstracts from the resource articles

3. Drawing organizational implications from the trends and issues that are surfaced

4. Analyzing and prioritizing implications as to their strategic importance

The environmental scan initially utilizes a very broad approach to gathering information; it "spans the spectrum" of potentially useful information, including that related to prospective targets and sources. The information is then scanned in a more focused manner. A filter is used to scan the various primary and secondary sources of information.

The WarRoom collection methodology utilizes proven primary and secondary source information-gathering approaches to collection, as well as incorporating some innovative "third wave" techniques. A combination of gathering techniques is employed in order to obtain information inputs from several sources. This serves to substantiate, validate, and establish an accurate "level of confidence" in the collected information.

Information Source Targeting and Acquisition

Once you've determined the information desired, the next step is to "target" the information sources that can respond to these requirements. Information can be obtained from a combination of primary and secondary sources. Primary source gathering involves getting information directly from the organizations and individuals that originally compiled the information. Our collection team interviews key individuals and organizations through in-person meetings and phone conversations utilizing an interview question-naire. Our team typically prepares a survey/questionnaire form (in conjunction with the client), which is either faxed or sent by e-mail. We can also communicate directly to a number of "think tank" and research organizations worldwide through their Internet World Wide Web sites.

Use of Intelligence to Support Other Management Reporting

To be truly effective and meet the immediate needs of senior management, intelligence should have a stand-alone capability. However, intelligence also needs to be visible in the informational reporting for other applications and to support other business reporting. Seeing the importance of intelligence in an overall decision process sensitizes other managers to its value. If an R&D executive reviews an intelligence section in a report on a new product innovation, he may be more likely to consume and support regular intelligence reporting. If a public relations director sees the role intelligence can play in developing an effective media and issues management campaign, then that person is likely to be a contributor and supporter of the overall intelligence reporting.

The following two reports are examples of how intelligence can be woven into an overall assessment and evaluation. The first was prepared a number of years ago by coauthor Shaker and a colleague, George Kardulias, for a major aerospace company which was evaluating two other aerospace company programs. The output fed into the process of deciding whether the company should pursue a similar program.

This first report provides an effective framework for inserting intelligence and creating a desire on the part of the program officers for more intelligence involvement. The report is effectively laid out. It opens with an executive summary so that a senior executive can get the gist of the report without having to read all of it. It provides a very logical flow of information from development history and technology to economic and political factors. It describes the lessons learned and ends with a series of recommendations.

Aquila and Tacit Rainbow

**A Special Analysis of the Two Unmanned Air Vehicle Systems
Prepared for Company A***
November 30, 1990

Table of Contents

Executive Summary

AQUILA

Developmental History

Systems Integration

*For reasons of confidentiality, the company involved will be referred to as Company A, and the unmanned air vehicle being described will be referred to as System X.

Technology

Scheduling

Costing

Test and Evaluation

Political Factors, etc.

Lessons Learned

Parallels with System X

TACIT RAINBOW

Developmental History

Systems Integration

Technology

Scheduling

Costing

Test & Evaluation

Political Factors

Lessons Learned

Parallels with System X

Recommendations

Executive Summary

The Aquila program began development in the early 1970s and prior to its demise in 1988 had finally developed into a highly sophisticated drone able to assist high-tech weapons in finding and destroying hidden enemy targets. Aquila was pestered throughout its life cycle with budget cuts and program office mismanagement, which led Congress to cancel the program by cutting FY 1988 funding.

Starting out in the "black" [very secretive, highly compartmentalized] world, Tacit Rainbow had more luck than Aquila in the beginning but is in serious trouble now. Congress cut FY 1991 procurement funding (R&D is still intact) for the air-launched version due to program setbacks. The program is over budget and behind schedule and appears to be following in the footsteps of Aquila, with _____ projecting even further setbacks due to a change by Northrop in manufacturing plants. _____ estimates _____ Division is rapidly approaching an ideal window of opportunity to successfully market System X to DoD, especially for immediate use in the Persian Gulf. This report contains recommendations _____ feels would enhance System X's sales of _____ and has recommendations to avoid the pitfalls encountered by other programs. Furthermore, other markets are identified in the recommendations section of this report for which System X would be very competitive.

AQUILA

Developmental History

Aquila began in the early 1970s as a DARPA initiative to develop an "eye in the sky." The system was envisioned as furnishing reconnaissance to soldiers at an extremely low cost per unit of approximately $25K. The concept piqued the Army's interest, which eventually ordered the development of a miniature remotely piloted vehicle (mini-RPV) in 1974 to primarily identify and designate targets for U.S. Army artillery. Lockheed Missiles and Space Company (LMSC) of Sunnyvale, California, was awarded the Army contract to develop the mini-RPV, which came to be known as Aquila. Known briefly at first as Little r, the Aquila (Latin for eagle) was designated by the Army as the XMQM-105 program. Besides its primary fire support role, Aquila was to be used as a laser designator for a family of guided weapons, including Martin Marietta's Copperhead cannon-launched projectile, Rockwell's International Hellfire missile, and Hughes Aircraft's Maverick missile. The RPV was also to have some surveillance and intelligence gathering capability.

The prototype of the Aquila was powered by a $100 go-cart engine and cost only $100,000 when it first flew in December 1975. The Army awarded LMSC contracts for a target acquisition, designation, and aerial reconnaissance (TADAR) full-scale development program beginning on August 31, 1979. Under these contracts, Lockheed was to supply 28 XMQM-105 Aquila air vehicles (first flight July 1982), together with ground control stations (GCS), a remote ground terminal (RGT), hydraulic catapult launchers, Dornier net recovery units, payload subassemblies, maintenance shelters, training simulators, and training manuals. The Aquila program was transferred from LMSC at Sunnyvale, California, to Lockheed-Austin, Texas, in mid-July 1983.

According to Dr. Klaus Dannenberg, chief engineer of Lockheed's RPV programs, Aquila is really two programs: an earlier RPV technology development effort and a specific Aquila airframe project. Between 1975 and 1987, the U.S. Army spent more than $700 million on Aquila, with Lockheed pumping in another $125 million of its own. Some say the high cost is the result of Pentagon indecision, Congressional "on again, off again" funding, and Army demands for more capabilities to be added. First came a three-year technology-demonstration program, won by Lockheed. When the original program ended in 1978, Lockheed disbanded its team and the Army studied the reports. Funding was reinstated in 1979 and stopped again in 1981. So by late 1982, when Lockheed's skeleton staff was told that Congress wanted to restart the program, a lot of time and money had been lost.

Beset by technical problems and funding cuts since it entered into full-scale development in 1979, the Aquila program was radically restructured after an Army investigation in the summer of 1985. During 1985, an early operational capability Aquila system was fielded by the U.S. Army, operated by Army personnel in full-scale force-on-force exercises to develop operational techniques. At the end of 1985, the Army restructured the program to include a month-long capability demonstration in January 1986, and rescheduled the remainder of operational testing to November 1986. During the testing in January 1986, Aquila successfully demonstrated its capability to perform to its design specifications and was used to designate tank targets for live Copperhead antitank rounds fired from artillery howitzers. Other capabilities demonstrated included finding a target and determining its specific type, identity at specified ranges and conditions, locking on and tracking a moving target automatically, maintaining a laser spot on a moving target to provide a marker for laser guided munitions, retrieving the Aquila automatically, launching the Aquila at a central launching facility, passing it in flight to a forward facility, and reversing this process for recovery. The tests conducted in January 1986 were conducted at LMSC's expense. By 1986 the flyaway cost skyrocketed to $800,000 for each RPV, with Lockheed having received over $500 million by this time to perfect the vehicle.

By early 1986, 330 test flights of the Aquila had been completed: 306 were completely successful, 15 ended with parachute recoveries, and 9 crashed. Operational Test No. 2 (OT2), at Fort Hood, Texas, was completed by the U.S. Army in spring 1987. During this test period 310 flight hours were achieved in 143 flights, during which 20 Copperheads and more than 150 rounds of other types of ammunition were fired at the RPVs, and handoffs to other GCSs were made over ranges of up to 24 nautical miles (45 km; 28 miles). The U.S. Army's planned purchase included 376 air vehicles and 88 ground stations. It was hoped that a production go-ahead would be given in autumn 1987, but the proposed budget was again cut by the House Armed Services Committee (HASC).

Army OT2 at Fort Hood in early 1987 resulted in soldiers being able to find only 12% of moving targets and 23% of fixed targets using the Aquila television camera, compared with goals of 50% and 30% of the controlled targets, respectively.

But after the operators went through a 120-hour target detection and recognition course at Fort Huachuca, Arizona, and new software became available that automated most of the sensor and vehicle searching actions, performance rose. Over 90% of the moving vehicles were detected and over 80% of fixed. Uncamouflaged targets were detected in a force development test and experimentation (FDTE) exercise conducted at Fort Hood in October-November 1987, according to Lt. Col. Terry G. Johnson, deputy director of the target acquisition division at Fort Sill, Oklahoma.

The Aquila software broke search areas into 1km squares, kept track of areas that had already been searched, and automatically selected camera field of view, look angle, and aircraft altitude and waypoints, taking into account factors like the best viewing angle with respect to the sun.

The FDTE exercise was conducted with a visual spectrum black-and-white camera, but five later experimental flights with a forward-looking infrared (FLIR) camera convinced Army officials of Flir's value. "Flir is here to stay," Johnson said. "Part of the problem that we've had with Aquila is looking for targets that are camouflaged or hidden in foliage. If you can't see it with the naked eye, you can't see it with a black-and-white camera. With the Flir package, if you can get the heat source, you can accurately locate it."

Eighteen copperhead laser-seeking projectiles were fired at targets illuminated by Aquila's laser designator during the OT2 tests, and 14 of the rounds hit their targets. But these successes were not universally recognized in sufficient time to save the program.

In December 1987, the Senate Committee on Appropriation recommended the Aquila program be canceled for FY 1988. The committee deleted $179,448,000 requested by the Army for Aquila. The committee felt persistent failures in the field testing of this system eliminated the requirement for additional funds. Given the long record of problems and failures associated by the government to date, the committee urged the Army to consider termination of the Aquila. Those components of the system with merit were to be evaluated for applications on other remotely piloted and unmanned aerial vehicles. The Army made no move to protest the committee's recommendations and in early 1988 the Aquila procurement was permanently canceled.

As of July 1988, the Army had one operational RPV battery— the Delta Battery, comprising two Aquila systems and about 50 soldiers, attached to the 3rd Corps Artillery at Fort Sill. Delta Battery participated in the large-scale Fire Ex '88 artillery exercise at the Army Dugway Proving Ground, Utah, in mid-June 1988, where it served to correct artillery fire and provide targeting of air defense sites for the Air Force/General Dynamics FB-111 attack aircraft. Delta Battery conducted 12 flights in under two weeks and lost an aircraft on the 11th flight when an improper waypoint was typed in and the aircraft flew into a hill.

Systems Integration

The basic subsystems of Aquila include the airframe, power plant, launch and recovery, guidance and control, and the mission payload. The configuration of the airframe is that of a midmounted swept-wing tailless blended fuselage monoplane. The airframe built by the subcontractor, Hitco, emphasized a low observable composite consisting of molded and preimpregnated Kevlar epoxy laminates with graphite/epoxy laminates. The engine was a single Herbrandson dyad 280 B two-stroke flat-twin piston engine. Guidance and control was chiefly furnished by a flight control electronic package (FCEP) built by Lockheed. The ground station utilized a Norden GCS computer. In addition to the FCEP, a strap-down inertial sensor package built by Singer and called the attitude reference assembly (ARA), two air data transducers, three servo-actuators, and a new infrared source landing aid also assisted in guidance. Control is furnished through a jam resistant data link by a Harris Inc. modular integrated communication and navigation system (MICNS). This J-ban system provides command uplink telemetry and video downlinks and navigation of the Aquila relative to the ground station. The mission payload subsystem (MPS) is located in Aquila's lower forward fuselage. MPS consisted of a Westinghouse 3-axis stabilized daylight TV camera, which incorporated a laser range finder/designator, auto tracker, and three-fields-of-view optics. A stabilized, gimbal-mounted FLIR MPS was under development by Ford Aerospace when the program was canceled. A hydraulically actuated catapult built by All American Engineering was mounted on top of a five-ton truck for the launch mechanism. Recovery was furnished by a hydraulically deployed Dornier vertical ribbon net, raised on the back of a truck.

Technology

Aquila incorporated several demanding technological advancements that were meant to enhance its survivability in the high-threat war fighting environment forecasted for central Europe. These included improving the Aquila's already small radar signature (due to its inherently small size) by incorporating low observable technology. The low observable technology includes a composite airframe made of molded and preimpregnated Kevlar epoxy laminates with graphite/epoxy laminate that would absorb/muffle radar. Aquila also had an upward directed exhaust that would minimize IR signature and detection from below. Its jam-resistant data link featured a J-ban designed for command uplink telemetry and video downlinks and navigation of the RPV relative to the ground station. The data link was built by Harris Inc., and named the modular integrated communication and navigation system (MICNS). Harris's cost for this system escalated and its schedule significantly slipped, which was in turn blamed by Lockheed officials for causing many of the overall Aquila cost and scheduling difficulties. Maintaining the laser designator on target while the Aquila rolled, looped, and performed other aerobatics was a difficult technological undertaking, which was successfully accomplished. An area which was not adequately addressed until it was too late to save the program was in developing cuing aids on the monitor to assist the operator in locating and identifying targets.

Scheduling

Aquila's history of setbacks and technical problems lead to a project which lasted over 18 years and cost in excess of $750 million. The program as it is known today was initiated in 1974 when Lockheed Missiles and Space Company of Sunnyvale, California, was awarded an Army contract to develop Aquila. Development continued in a sputtering on-again, off-again manner depending on Congressional funding until the program funding was terminated for FY 1988. Even though Congress and the Army controlled the funding and program management and forced delays on LMSC's progress, LMSC received the brunt of the blame for the program setbacks and overruns.

Costing

The original DARPA "eye in the sky" concept of the early 1970s, which was the precursor to Aquila, was envisioned to be a throwaway system costing no more than $25K per unit. By the time Lockheed was chosen by the Army to build Aquila in 1979, each vehicle was estimated to cost about $100K. The ensuing "gold-plating" over the next decade lead to a nearly billion-dollar developmental effort by 1987 and a cost of between $800K and $1 million for each vehicle.

Test and Evaluation

On December 17, 1984, Aquila successfully demonstrated its ability to provide laser designation of a target for Copperhead artillery round. Prototype quality testing was performed from January through April 1985. In 1985, the U.S. Army fielded an early operational capability Aquila system in full-scale, force-on-force exercises to develop operational techniques. A month-long capability demonstration took place in January 1986, when Aquila successfully proved its ability to perform to design specifications and to designate tank targets for Copperhead rounds fired from artillery. Also demonstrated were its ability to find a target, determine specific type, to identify at specific ranges and conditions, to automatically lock and track a moving target, to maintain a laser spot on a moving target, and to launch and retrieve Aquila. By early 1986 some 330 test flights were undertaken, of which 306 were considered successful, while 15 ended up in parachute recoveries and 9 crashed. Operational Test 2 was conducted at Fort Hood from November 1986 through March 1987. One hundred forty-three flights were made totaling 310 hours. Twenty Copperheads and more than 150 rounds of other types of ammunition were fired at the RPVs, and handoffs were made to other ground control stations over ranges of up to 24 nautical miles. According to the Government Accounting Office (GAO), operators were only able to spot one out of five moving targets and one-third of the standing targets. Other failures included not being able to set up and launch the system in the allocated time. Following the test in December, a Pentagon Inspector General released a report stating that Lockheed officials illegally inflated the test scores. Lockheed officials denied this and countered that the Army was determined to test Aquila as arduously as possible, in ways well beyond the contractor's specifications. They claimed that this was done due to the Army's sensitivity to criticism of other systems' past OT failures, and to the powerful pressures from Aquila's critics.

Political Factors and Key Decision-Makers Impacting Aquila

Advocates of a program, if they feel they have been misled or "burned," can become the harshest critics. Such was the case of Congress, which had been the catalyst behind Aquila ever since a 1980 GAO report claiming how RPVs could save lives and dollars. Congress eventually became the program's executioner. As Anthony Battista (the then House Armed Services Committee senior staff member) stated, "We were big believers a couple years ago, but now Aquila is an anachronism." Battista had two major criticisms for Aquila. The single battery of 13 aircraft requiring 300 tons of support equipment made it much too large and heavy for transport, and therefore it lost its utility. His second criticism was that the efforts to make it more survivable through the use of composites, jamproof data link, and other low observables was much too expensive. He viewed the small size of RPVs as inherently making them more survivable. The added "gold-plating" made the cost benefits unappealing.

Battista blamed 75 percent of Aquila's problems on the Army and attributed 25 percent to Lockheed. Robert Nettles (then Vice President for RPV Programs for Lockheed's Austin Division) stated that his program's problems started with the federal budget squeezes of 1980, '81, and '82, which caused growth and schedule delays. There was also a slippage of delivery of the government-furnished Harris data link, plus numerous changes by the Army which added to costs. Nettles stated, "Lockheed didn't get itself in this trouble by itself. It was partly Congress, partly Army, partly Harris."

In the operational test and evaluation phase during the summer of 1987, Aquila operators were only able to effectively spot one out of five moving targets and one-third of the standing targets. The overall vehicle, however, particularly in its ability to maintain a laser designator on target while jinking, performed exceedingly well. Operator rather than technical problems caused the Army to postpone the production contract. Many individuals, including the OSD Undersecretary of Defense for Tactical Warfare, Don Fredricksen, blamed the poor showing on the Army's unwillingness to furnish experienced spotters and reconnaissance pilots to serve as RPV operators for the testing. The Inspector General helped "seal the coffin" for Aquila's fate when he issued a report, quoted by Senator Roth in Congress, that Lockheed officials illegally tried to influence the testing by providing unsolicited comments and lobbying for less damaging scores.

With this, the "ball was then thrown back in Congress" and during the FY 1988 procurement budget all money for Aquila was zeroed out. The Army then canceled the program. Battista claimed that no one in the Army was willing to fight for Aquila in the budget because of its checkered history.

Lessons Learned from Aquila

1. Avoid the "gold-plating" tendency. The goal should be to field a system which is simplistic and less costly. Incremental enhancements can be made while the operators are gaining some operational experience.

2. Don't build an unmanned air vehicle and manage the program as if it were an unmanned spacecraft. Spacecraft designers are inherently more expensive and build in a degree of survivability and redundancy not required of aircraft. UAV program managers should include key personnel who have aircraft design experience.

3. Moving the program's management from one location to another causes severe personnel and technical problems and delays, as were incurred with Lockheed's removal of the Aquila program from Sunnyvale, California, to Austin, Texas.

4. The acceptance of unmanned air vehicles by the user community is dependent on meeting the following criteria:

   a. When lethality of the missions proposed for the system are so great that our cultural norms prohibit us from committing pilots/aviators to suicidal missions.

    b. When human resources need to be diverted to other priorities. UAVs can free essential manpower and associated resources to perform higher-priority missions by taking on less complex and redundant missions.

    c. When the overall effectiveness and efficiency of a task can be better accomplished through the use of the unmanned system.

Aquila failed to meet most of these criteria. The missions proposed for Aquila can be done with manned aircraft, and the pilots and military decision-makers are at this juncture in time still willing to accept the risks to an air crew. (The advent of high-energy weaponry and hypervelocity missiles may change this.) The large support complement required for Aquila took away an appearance of saving on manpower, resources, or related assets. The dramatic cost escalation of Aquila put it in the same price range as many manned spotter aircraft and therefore negated any cost benefits. Unable to clearly meet any of these criteria helped doom the program.

5. The cost escalation of a UAV can be inversely correlated to its marketability and acceptability by the user and Congress. It's the low cost in relation to manned aircraft that appeals to most decision-makers. Therefore it is this area which most readily sours and gets the most negative reaction when there are cost problems. The dramatic rise of Aquila from $100K to exceeding $800K per vehicle made it unpalatable to Congress.

6. The support and logistics operations of the system are just as important to the user as the performance capability of the vehicle. The vehicle can perform perfectly, but if the operational support is impractical, then the overall system will be criticized. The amount of support equipment should be held to a minimum.

7. While Lockheed's public relations department did a fine job at promoting Aquila in the military-related journals, it was lambasted in the general media. Whenever a program gets the main editorial in *The New York Times* to be highly critical of it (especially one which is relatively small when compared to other major weapon systems), it's in severe trouble. Lockheed was promoting itself in a constituency it had already won. It should

have paid more attention to the media influencing Congress and the general public.

8. Lockheed needed to do a better job of "issues management." Issues management involves taking control and shaping the issues impacting the program. The cost and operational comparisons of Aquila against competitor systems such as the Scout (which was fielded within several years of the program's initiation), juxtaposed to the Aquila's decade-and-a-half development time, made the Aquila look quite dismal. Lockheed did a poor job at making the case that Aquila was:

    a. Designed to survive a much more severe environment than was the Scout (Soviet jamming and ECM in Europe versus Arab forces in the Mideast) and therefore included a jamfree data link and low observable composites not utilized in Scout.

    b. Aquila had to fulfill a very difficult Army requirement to maintain the laser designator on a target while understanding aerobatic maneuvers. Lockheed let the criticism stick, "why buy a Cadillac when a Ford Escort would do," instead of converting it into, "a rough and dependable Jeep is needed, rather than a Ford Escort, to drive in the off-road environment."

Aquila Parallels with System X

Although the overall vehicle configuration of Aquila is very similar to that of System X, in general there are more differences between the two vehicles, both in design and development. Both have low delta wings, monoplane fuselage, with pusher propellers. Aquila is slightly larger and both have two-stroke engines. They have similar payload capacities. Aquila's low observable composites, antijam data link, and laser designator are features not included in System X, and they also account for the large price differential between the two systems ($800K per Aquila as compared to $60–80K per System X). The primary missions envisioned for each are also quite different, with Aquila's prime mission being that of target designator for the Copperhead round, while System X was originally meant for the suppression of enemy air defense (SEAD) role. The Aquila's secondary role of tactical reconnaissance would be very similar, however, to a System X configured for the close-range UAV role.

The two programs' developmental histories were also very dissimilar, with Aquila being bureaucratically inched along and being very visible and an easy target for many different constituents. While the System X airframe was largely brought about by _____ without governmental confines, the System X antiradar seeker version received a level of secrecy and protection similar to that of U.S. compartmentalized programs. Aquila can be viewed more as a system developed by the Army, which failed, while System X can be considered more as an off-the-shelf system/product available to the Army for purchase.

TACIT RAINBOW Developmental History

Although the "veil of secrecy" has been somewhat lifted on the TACIT RAINBOW (AGM-136A) program, much of its developmental history has not been officially released and still remains unclear. As early as the late 1970s, the U.S. Navy and Air Force issued requirements for a low-cost loitering missile system which was programmable before launch and capable of autonomously searching out and attacking enemy radar. The original formal requirements document asked for a low-cost, autonomous-after-launch UAV that could be operated beyond the forward line of own troops (FLOT) against a predetermined piece of enemy real estate, which was expected to be densely covered with air defense systems. The UAV would supplement existing or developing manned air defense suppression systems and precede manned strike forces, ideally to clear the way for their unimpeded passage.

Northrop Corporation's Ventura Division won the full-scale development contract to develop the TACIT RAINBOW in 1981. The program was managed under the Joint Tactical Autonomous Weapons Systems Program Office of the Aeronautical Systems Division of Wright Patterson AFB.

TACIT RAINBOW was one of seven "black" lethal drone developmental programs which the Air Force was undertaking by the spring of 1984. The success of the others to date is unknown, but being compartmentalized allowed TACIT RAINBOW's development to be done expeditiously. As the vehicle neared full-scale development completion and procurement initiation and was in the midst of many comprehensive tests, a decision was made by the Air Force to disclose information on the program to the public, as was done with the B-2. The program has experienced great difficulty in its transitioning from the "black" to "white" world, particularly in keeping the program within budget and schedule constraints. Its failures have received more publicity than its successful test flights.

More damaging than its test flight problems has been its large escalation in cost. Even in light of TACIT RAINBOW's slipping some 14 months behind schedule and having cost overruns of 600 percent, the Congress in 1988 provided full funding of the system. In 1989, Congress considered SEEK SPINNER "to be a duplicate of the more versatile and flexible TACIT RAINBOW."

In October 1989 the DoD budget accommodated a Navy decision to eliminate participation in TACIT RAINBOW by asking for no new Navy funding of the system. Serving as a harbinger of budgetary problems to come, the House Armed Services Committee also recommended zeroing out the AF TACIT RAINBOW program. The Senate Armed Services Committee (SASC) strongly disagreed, stating that the Joint Chiefs of Staff's Requirements Oversight Council continued to strongly support the weapon system. The SASC also recommended that the Navy reconsider the system. The conferees fully funded the system.

The October 1990 Electronic Industries Association (EIA) Ten-Year Forecast of Defense Needs stated that the ground-launched TACIT RAINBOW had a "good" chance of being deployed by the year 2000, and the air-launched version had a "fair" chance. (It considered System X as having a "poor" chance of being fielded.) Recent Congressional budgetary decisions, however, have given a major setback to the TACIT RAINBOW program and cast doubt about its future. The House Armed Services

Committee (HASC) in the National Defense Authorization Act for Fiscal Year 1991 originally included $202 million for the air- and ground-launched versions of TACIT RAINBOW. HASC recommended that the program be restructured and added $27 million to the $9.8 million requested by DoD for its R&D, and reduced the procurement request from $227.4 million to $59.5 million. HASC also recommended $59.5 million be used to establish the second source producer.

In October the Senate Appropriations Committee (SAC) DoD Appropriations Bill for Fiscal Year 1991 recommended $199 million for the air and ground versions of TACIT RAINBOW. SAC cut the TACIT RAINBOW budget because of continued technical problems identified in the flight test program. The report recommended delaying initial production by at least one to three years. SAC reduced the Air Force procurement line by $167.9 million from the $227.4 million requested. SAC increased the R&D budget by $27 million to a total of $36.8 million. SAC also decided to cut from the Army $2.6 million from the $105.3 million R&D budget for the ground-launched TACIT RAINBOW because the Army indicated that this was in excess of what was required. In November Congressional conferees decided to zero out Air Force procurement for TACIT RAINBOW and only fund $36.8 million for continued research and development. The conferees also stated that "in light of the continued development problems and the cloudy future of the TACIT RAINBOW program, they urged the Navy to proceed with the Tactical Air-Launched Decoy (TALD) and Improved (powered) TALD (ITALD) with all deliberate speed."

Systems Integration

Cost, being the primary design parameter, has kept the overall system somewhat simplistic. TACIT RAINBOW utilizes a relatively small air vehicle, conventionally configured folding surfaces, and lightweight alloy. To save on costs, many commercial off-the-shelf components were initially utilized. However, the air-launched requirement resulted in a specification that required MIL-SPEC parts. The subsystems integration included:

1. Airframe: A shoulder swing-wing monoplane. The fuselage is made from fiber-reinforced plastic. The wings fold for transport. Its wingspan is 5 ft. 5 inches, and the fuselage is 8 ft. 4 inches long.

2. On-board computers: Information is stored in its mission computer and on the operational flight program (OFP). The computer contains lists of target parameters, weather, and intelligence data provided by a mission planning system. The OFP contains the flight plan.

3. Navigation system: The fairly simple navigation system utilizes waypoint navigation. The TACIT RAINBOW flies a predetermined search area where it loiters while searching for a target that matches characteristics in its memory.

4. Passive home-on-emitter (HOE) sensor: For radar seeker.

5. Fused warhead: A 40 lb. warhead.

6. Jet engine: Williams International small turbojet engine.

Technology

The technology to perform the mission requirements for TACIT RAINBOW is readily available and not exceptionally demanding. The technology challenge, however, was to develop a low-cost system as a realization developed that a million dollar weapon to kill a $200,000 radar was a form of "competitive strategies" in reverse. The goal was to produce many such systems (that would not exceed $100K apiece) which can be fielded in the numbers to attack numerous emitters (the many-on-many concept). Therefore cost became the predominate design parameter. The dramatic escalation for development by 600 percent is, therefore, politically damaging to the system, although program management has been countering that it's the manufacturing cost where the technology will be proven successful, not in the developmental cost.

In order to save on factory labor, instead of using traditional aluminum airframes—which require many piece parts (stringers, bulkheads, and skins) to be fabricated and then assembled using rivets or other fasteners—TACIT RAINBOW's structure relies on stressed skins. Stressed skins are press molded from sheet molding compound, a composite material also used in the auto industry. This process reduces factory labor by an order of magnitude.

TACIT RAINBOW reflected a change in management philosophy, where the system and associated technology emphasis was focused on reducing manufacturing cost rather than to design the optimal system and employ the best technology (albeit most expensive) to do the mission and *then* find ways to save on the manufacturing.

The enormous escalation in developmental costs rather than procurement has led to funding cutbacks and currently threatens the program. Perhaps greater technology emphasis should have been in the program's development.

Scheduling

TACIT RAINBOW had fallen at least some 14 months behind schedule due to project setbacks, such as the June 1988 test when the engine failed to ignite after the drone was launched. TACIT RAINBOW was in the combined developmental/initial operational test and evaluation (DT&E/IOT&E) phase when the congressional cutbacks eliminating plans for 1991 procurement took effect. A revised schedule and management plan to accommodate the budget cuts have yet to be offered by the Air Force. Full-scale development was to be completed by the end of FY 1990. Some 25 government test launches of TACIT RAINBOW from B-52 and A-6 aircraft were planned. Launch from standard carriages on fighter aircraft and rotary launchers on manned bombers would have been verified. Starting in FY 1991, the Northrop production facility in Perry, Georgia, was supposed to have begun a small preproduction lot to provide test assets for the follow-on operational test and evaluation (FOT&E) in FY 1992. Low-rate initial production was to follow in three annual lots. Starting in FY 1995, Raytheon Corporation was to become qualified to compete with Northrop as the prime source on an annual basis. All of this, however, is now "up in the air" due to the November Congressional conferees elimination of procurement funding in 1991 for the air-launched version of TACIT RAINBOW.

Our analysis indicates Northrop will fall even further behind in TACIT RAINBOW development and production due to the closing of its Newbury Park plant in Ventura County, California. The loss of 800 skilled workers by the end of 1991 and the transfer of manufacturing to the Hawthorne and Pico Rivera, California, plants will cause Northrop unexpected delays in developing TACIT RAINBOW.

Costing

Due to the procurement budget cutbacks and the postponement of the initial test production runs for one to three years, it's impossible at this time to accurately estimate the current unit cost per vehicle. MICOM's current estimate is that the ground-launched multiple launch rocket system (MLRS) version of TACIT RAINBOW would cost approximately $125K per vehicle, with warhead. (Note: MICOM does not have a high degree of confidence in this latest figure but feels it is in the ballpark. MICOM officials believe that System X must come in significantly cheaper [under $60K] to adequately interest decision-makers there.)

Test and Evaluation

Four contractors' development tests (CDT) were conducted at the Naval Weapons Center at China Lake, California. On April 12, 1988, TACIT RAINBOW completed a successful test of its radar suppression function. Following air launch, the vehicle followed a preprogrammed path to a designated target. Once reaching the designated area, the system loitered until detecting a ground-based radar signal. The vehicle locked in on the signal, identified it, and then successfully engaged and destroyed the target. In June 1988, TACIT RAINBOW experienced a test failure when the Williams turbojet failed to ignite after the vehicle was launched from an A-6E.

In March 1989, TACIT RAINBOW entered the combined developmental/initial operational test and evaluation phase. The Air Force Flight Test Center at Edwards AFB had joined with the Air Force Operational Test and Evaluation Center (AFOTEC) to form a combined test force. A total of 25 launches supported by several captive carry missions was planned for the Naval Weapons Center, China Lake Test Range, 13 flown from a B-52 and 12 from the A-6 aircraft. Each test mission was designed to accomplish a subset of the overall objectives for the FSD test program. These include clearing the two aircraft carriage and separation envelopes, specification compliance for the UAV and the B-52 rotary launcher, and operational utility and supportability of the total weapons system. Each flight test mission is supported by the predictions of several simulations.

In May 1989, in the second operational test flight, the TACIT RAINBOW was successfully launched from a B-52 at China Lake. The vehicle flew a preprogrammed mission profile, including loiter and maneuvers before impacting the target successfully.

Political Factors and Key Decision-Makers Impacting TACIT RAINBOW

Being able to cloak the TACIT RAINBOW program in the "black" compartmentalized world certainly assisted its initial development by avoiding outside review. The poor Air Force and Northrop management of black programs in general has now tarnished the image of TACIT RAINBOW.

TACIT RAINBOW was more acceptable than other UAVs to the pilot/aviator community for two primary reasons, the first being that it was conceived by many as being more like a missile which could loiter a while rather than as a UAV which would be competitive to manned systems. Second, and more important, TACIT RAINBOW could be carried by the Air Force B-52 strategic bomber and Navy A-6E attack jet, allowing the aircraft to have greater stand-off distances without challenging the role of the manned aircraft. The Army's interest in launching TACIT RAINBOW from its platforms also gave the system added impetus, especially in light of Congressional requests for more joint service weapons programs.

TACIT RAINBOW has experienced a number of technical, cost, and scheduling problems, resulting in intense Congressional displeasure with the program's progress and in the Navy pulling out of the program. In light of Northrop's mismanagement of "black" programs, including TACIT

RAINBOW, some Congressional staffers were leaning toward canceling the program. The HASC ultimately recommended the restructuring of the Air Force TACIT RAINBOW program by two measures, the first being to shift more emphasis and dollars onto continued research and development, and second to reduce procurement funds by three-fourths. The Congressional conferees' decision to zero out production funding for FY 1991 will delay any initial procurement by one to three years. Congress has also requested that the Secretary of the Air Force report to HASC about total program quantities and the cost-effectiveness of having two producers, which is a way of penalizing Northrop.

Some of the Army support for TACIT RAINBOW has weakened. U.S. Army generals who witnessed System X tests in _____ came away impressed and are leaning toward System X to replace TACIT RAINBOW for the suppression of enemy air defense (SEAD) role. Nonetheless, the preponderance of Army decision-makers, including those at Ft. Sill and MICOM, are still committed to TACIT RAINBOW.

Lessons Learned from TACIT RAINBOW

1. Having a compartmentalized "black" program such as TACIT RAINBOW helps to protect the system from outside scrutiny early in the program's development and helps to guard and ensure a healthy budget. However, the current Congressional distrust for "black" programs due to their dramatic cost escalations and mismanagement is in fact making much greater "after the fact" critical review of the program and could lead to its cancellation at the time it becomes visible and ready for production.

2. Joint service participation is more readily received by Congress, but it also results in many management and political difficulties, which frequently result in design changes, scheduling slippage, and cost increases.

3. Air-launched variants of UAVs are least likely to be opposed by pilots and aviators and are viewed as adjuncts to manned aircraft rather than rivals.

4. Furnishing another competitor to an incumbent system for a given mission application has advantages as well as negative features. The advantages are that if the current system should falter, the competitor can then come in and fill the gap. Being perceived as the competitor to a system with an already established mission can, however, also backfire, as seen with Seek Spinner/Brave 200. Seek Spinner, a very differently configured vehicle than that of TACIT RAINBOW (although going after the same suppression of enemy air defense [SEAD] mission through antiradiation attack), was eventually viewed by Congress as being duplicative of TACIT RAINBOW. Congress thereby cut all appropriations for Seek Spinner. By diversifying System X's mission application so it is not just viewed as a SEAD system, it can also perform battalion targeting system (BTS) and close-range will help prevent it from a similar fate to that of Seek Spinner.

TACIT RAINBOW Parallels with System X

The TACIT RAINBOW parallels with System X are in complete contrast to that of Aquila. Unlike Aquila, TACIT RAINBOW and System X share the primary mission for suppression of enemy air defense (SEAD). However, whereas the System X configuration is similar to that of Aquila, TACIT RAINBOW is a very different type of vehicle than System X, being a jet-powered drone as compared to a monoplane with a pusher propeller.

While both TACIT RAINBOW and System X are going after the SEAD mission, how they approach it is very different. TACIT RAINBOW, being jet-powered, searches out and engages the target much quicker than System X, while System X has the ability to loiter for longer periods of time searching for targets. Each approach has its advantages.

The development of TACIT RAINBOW and System X both were done somewhat in the "black" world without much visibility, although TACIT RAINBOW was known to the Air Force "special access" community, while System X was largely unknown until recently to U.S. officials because it was an _____ program. System X has also progressed much further than TACIT RAINBOW and can be considered ready for acquisition, whereas TACIT RAINBOW requires further research and developmental time.

The primary driver for TACIT RAINBOW has been the Air Force and its ability to be launched from the B-52 and other aircraft. The ground-launched TACIT RAINBOW is important but of less significance to the success of the program. System X, however, is based on the ground-launched variant, without pilot/aviator involvement.

Recommendations

1. It is a good strategy for Company A to use System X to go after the Army BTS program as well as the close-range UAV program. Company A should also position System X so that if TACIT RAINBOW should falter (poor test results, price escalation, etc.), System X would be the logical choice to fill in the suppression of enemy air defenses (SEAD) role. Although there are certain Army decision-makers who would prefer System X, there are more who are committed at this point to TACIT RAINBOW. An aggressive approach to winning Army converts from TACIT RAINBOW to System X may backfire and cause animosity and difficulty in winning the other mission areas. Company A should pursue SEAD, but in a very subtle approach, and be there to pick up the pieces if TACIT RAINBOW falls apart. In addition to the other missions mentioned, Company A should be exploring other applications, including nondefense areas such as support of drug interdiction and environmental monitoring. The Drug Enforcement Administration is utilizing some Pioneer and Pointer UAVs in the former role. The FBI; Customs; Coast Guard; Immigration and Naturalization; Alcohol, Tobacco and Firearms; and other law enforcement agencies may be potential buyers of a recon/surveillance variant of System X. The Forest Service may be interested in a UAV which can get within the smoke areas and target through infrared/thermal sensors the sources of fires, without exposing their pilots to unnecessary risks. Senator Sam Nunn and other Senate Armed Services Committee members have

been advocating a stronger military involvement in combating environmental problems. They have made the case that "the same technology and sensors utilized to monitor the battlefield can also be used to monitor the environment. Unmanned air vehicles have been used in the past for environmental monitoring, and perhaps a System X environmental monitoring variant has merit."

2. Company A should set up an intelligence marketing effort to support the System X program. This should reside in the Company A program office rather than Company A business intelligence offices in _____ and _____, although both should furnish support to the program office. The purpose of the market intelligence effort is as follows:

  a. To develop an "issues management" plan to help shape and focus those issues impacting System X's acceptance among the user community. This could be accomplished in part through a "political accounting" analysis which identifies the key decision-makers in the BTS, close-range, and SEAD programs, their preference for and attitudes toward which systems, their salience (strength of conviction; i.e., can their attitudes be changed), and their influence on other decision-makers. This analysis then could help Company A target the right people to market or lobby, and who should be avoided. An issues management plan can also help target which publications would be the best not only to be furnished press releases and advertisements, but more usefully, to get "friendly" free-lance writers to furnish articles highlighting System X.

  b. To develop an ongoing business intelligence collection effort to keep Company A program managers aware in a timely manner of new competitor and customer developments. This process should include identification of intelligence requirements impacting System X in the various competitions, who would have the answers to the requirements (the targets of the intelligence gathering), and who are sources both within Company A and external (consultants, suppliers, industry analysts) that have access to the targets and could ask questions and obtain answers. Besides examining the lessons learned from Aquila and TACIT RAINBOW, Company A should also examine Seek Spinner and Pave Tiger. Company A should closely monitor the other potential close-range competitors and their systems.

3. A study on what is known or can be ascertained from the public realm about System X (and be performed by people without access to Company A internal documents about System X) would enable Company A to determine how their competitors or potential customers perceive System X, and what to change or take advantage of.

4. Work with key Congressional staffers and get them to understand and support System X.

5. Support _____ procurements for System X, even though immediate profit is little or none for Company A. If sufficient, System X enters the military system (U.S. and foreign). It may become a standard weapon system with eventual large procurements from which Company A can profit. General John W. Foss, Commanding General of U.S. Army Training and Doctrine Command (TRADOC) at Fort Monroe, Virginia, is recommending System X be procured and used in the current Persian Gulf crisis. Company A should support this TRADOC effort.

6. Transfer technology and related skills from the F-16 and YF-22 ATF programs to System X. This could make System X more competitive in price and performance and thus make believers out of the organizations that owe political allegiance to TACIT RAINBOW. A cohesive centralized intelligence program will help facilitate this and break the barriers between divisions.

This second report uses competitor intelligence in the initial white paper designed to attract investment dollars from a financial investor. The role of intelligence being exhibited here will ensure its place in the startup organization.

New Product Opportunity

Device Overview

We have developed a preliminary design for a blood pulse/heart rate monitor. This device is highly reliable, easy to wear, and can be produced at low cost. Competing heart rate monitors (HRM) have electrodes in a contoured transmitter band that is worn around the chest to capture electrical pulses from the heart. The pulses are sent to an oversized LCD wristwatch display or to a display on a bicycle, exercise equipment, or remote unit. Our device _____

_____.

Competitor Products

Our preliminary competitive intelligence is that there are seven companies that produce heart rate/blood pulse monitoring devices targeted for health and fitness. The two most popular are Polar Electro, Inc., and Cardiosport, Inc. Both companies produce a similar product line. Each product typically includes a chest band housing the sensors, which relay the heart rate to a "watch type" wristband. The low end of the family of monitors for both companies sells for around $90, and those devices with more features can cost over $300. Polar offers their own software-based, heart rate management and training system. Cardiosport has teamed with Online Digital Fitness Solutions Ltd., a UK company which offers a PC-based fitness training application. Sensor Dynamics offers a combination wristwatch and heart monitor for about $100, and a cheaper heart-monitor-only model for $64. Insta-Pulse markets a Pocket Heart Rate Monitor which requires the user to grip handles rather than wear a wrist device. It sells for $99. Casio markets the Casio Exercise Pulse Monitor Watch for $59.99. Its pulse measurement function features a measuring range of 30 to 199 per minute and displays pulse rate, measurement time, aerobic zone, and intensity level. In addition, it has the normal watch features of hour, minute, date, and alarm. Although a handy gadget, its accuracy is questionable, and it is not as popular among serious athletes as the Polar and Cardiosport devices. Casio also makes a better BP-100-1AV Blood Pressure Monitor which provides pulse and systolic and diastolic blood pressures. It sells for $120 to $170 but requires users to place their fingers onto sensors located below the display. A new entry is the Elexis pulse monitor wristwatch. It contains a sensor which fits over the fingertip and has an audiopulse indicator and a timed alarm. Its accuracy is similar to the low end Polar and Cardiosport models. It is being distributed via mail order and the Internet by Californian Best for approximately $60. Omron produces a number of medical blood pressure monitors, as well as a compact wrist blood pressure monitor. This device costs approximately $100 and is more sophisticated and accurate. The system contains a wrist cuff with sensor monitor and a display screen. It is designed to be used during rest periods, whereas the other systems are for use while exercising. It is focused more on the health than the fitness end of the market.

Market

The market niche the wrist-worn pulse monitor targets is the health and fitness segment. This segment includes consumers who are sports and exercise enthusiasts, as well as individuals who just desire to periodically monitor their vital signs for health concerns. Within the past decade the health and fitness market has become one of the most lucrative business areas. The following statistics demonstrate the strength of this market segment:

- In 1993, the last year for which gross receipts were reported, some $7.9 billion was spent on the personal consumption of goods and services provided by health clubs and fitness providers in the U.S. (source: The U.S. Dept. of Commerce's 1995 Statistical Abstract)

- 71 percent of people with annual incomes of $35,000 and up purchase fitness equipment. (source: The National Sporting Goods Association)

- Memberships in health clubs grew from 16.5 million in 1993 to 20 million in 1994. Much of this growth was generated by the over-35 crowd, who joined health clubs for the first time or rejoined after an absence. Health club memberships for people between the ages of 35 and 54 increased by 64 percent in 1995 and were up 75 percent for people older than 55. (source: American Sports Data Inc.)

- Baby boomers and seniors are an important and expanding market that will grow larger as baby boomers age and seek the health benefits of exercise (source: Fitness Products Council)

- In the U.S. people 35 and older comprise more than 56 percent of all frequent exercisers and 45 percent of all health club members. (source: Sporting Goods Manufacturers Assn.)

Given the superior performance and competitive price, this device should emerge as a leader in the market, as well as expand the customer base.

Technology

The design of this new monitoring device is superior to existing heart rate monitors. The most accurate of existing monitors employ ECG type electrodes on a belt worn about the chest. They are not easy or convenient to use. Other monitors use detectors which are worn on the wrist or finger, but they are simply not reliable. In this new monitor, a _____ is used. This is the same technology we have developed for the _____. This yields a wrist-type monitor which is very reliable, comfortable, easy to use, and inexpensive.

Startup Requirements: Phase 1

In order to capitalize on this opportunity for a wrist-worn pulse monitor, we suggest the following tasks be completed in the first phase:

- Incorporate the company.
- Develop a business plan addressing product and company vision; market and competitor assessments; product development, manufacturing, and distribution; marketing and strategic alliances; management; and personnel.
- Develop a detailed design of the device.
- Secure patent, name trademarks, and copyrights.

The business plan will provide a detailed assessment and "roadmap" for successfully taking this device to market, and it will detail the required investment and return on investment. We have assembled a highly qualified team to perform these tasks, which will take three months. Cost for phase 1 and estimates for costs to production are available.

All the elements of the competitive intelligence process are interrelated and synergistic. Enhancing one of the elements, be it collection, analysis, or dissemination, ultimately improves the quality of the others. Excellent reports will reflect that attention was given to all elements of the CI process. The two reports show that a concerted effort was made to collect intelligence on the competitors and the market. Analytical assessments were made leading to recommended actions.

5

The Quarterback Technique

Many different approaches have been used to set up intelligence organizations. Some have worked well and others have been dismal failures. The classical approach to organizational design involves analyzing the desired global behavior and then functionally decomposing the problem. In the competitive intelligence field most use a method that involves performing some sort of in-depth intelligence audit. We adopted such a method in our early trials. The methodology is something like the following:

1. Understanding how the company currently collects, analyzes, and processes important information.
2. Articulating the intelligence needs of the key decision-makers.
3. Determining the gap between what is needed and what is currently provided.
4. Designing a new intelligence organization.
5. Performing a trial test.
6. Working out the bugs.
7. Setting an ongoing organization in motion.

Teams of consultants would often spend several weeks interviewing key managers. They would ask questions such as how the managers currently obtain the information that supports their decisions. Examples would be collected of how intelligence had proved beneficial or inadequate. The information derived from the interviews would be integrated and analyzed. The consultants' findings were then briefed to the senior management. These typically included recommendations on how the new or enhanced intelligence organization should be structured. Some of the companies accepted these recommendations, acted upon them, and implemented the newly designed CI organization and processes. Some proved highly successful. In other initiatives, however, bureaucracies and turf battles, office politics and interpersonal squabbles, budget cuts and personnel downsizing overpowered the embryonic intelligence organizations. They wither and die or get distorted into something different than intended.

We at WarRoom have since canned this approach. We have moved away from this classical approach to one which enables organizations' natural ecosystems to evolve through our facilitation. The end organizational design is not predetermined but is arrived at as an outgrowth of an activity. We have learned that the most important element to setting up a successful intelligence organization or enhancing the effectiveness of a current CI group is to captivate the interest and spirit of the participants. The best way to do this is to set in motion an intelligence operation. In essence, the organization is built around the operation. In preparing for the operation, all the elements of the organization are naturally formed, people become skilled and committed, and critical intelligence is collected, analyzed, and disseminated. People are excited about being part of an operation, they rally behind the organizer, and key management becomes supportive.

A major American food company was worried that two large foreign companies with vast resources and a winning track record would decide to enter the particular niche they had dominated over the years. Patents had expired, and their current customers were open to alternatives. What new products they themselves sought to introduce, new marketing and pricing strategies, and other measures to shore up their customer base were all dependent on the perceived actions and plans of their potential competitors. The company had received quotes from some major consulting companies. The research and analysis required to perform an accurate assessment of the potential competitors intentions and plan of attack would cost several hundred thousands of dollars and would take up to four months to produce. The company couldn't wait! Important decisions had to be made now.

Instead, the company opted for a proactive approach to collecting intelligence at an international food conference. Carefully orchestrated meetings and dinners with competitor counterparts were arranged for some of the company's executives. The right questions, phrased in the right way, were planned and practiced. Formal presentations by competitor researchers were attended by the American company's participants. Again, the right questions were raised to the presenters. After each meeting or interaction, the individual who collected the information met with company analysts to review the facts. By the end of the three-day conference, the American company had ascertained with a high degree of confidence the intentions of their potential competitors. They were greatly relieved to learn that both major potential competitors were avoiding a head-to-head competition and instead were moving into some other product areas. The American company was able to focus on their market without unnecessary diversions or costly blunders.

Quarterback Overview

The operation we have developed and refined over time is called the Quarterback, and it provides a systematic and focused approach to collecting intelligence at a conference or convention. Conferences furnish the greatest potential for collecting the most useful intelligence in the shortest span of time for the least amount of money. This is true because there is a concentration of key individuals who impact your business environment. Competitors, customers, vendors, consultants, subcontractors, and journalists and analysts who follow your industry are all in attendance—at the same time and locale. Quarterback operations have produced dramatic results on a budget far smaller than a client would have spent without this new technique.[26]

Most people attend a conference to become more knowledgeable about their profession or industry and to "network" with their counterparts from other organizations. As a result of this interaction, information of value to corporate decision-makers may be obtained as a by-product or by sheer coincidence. Sometimes the valuable information is passed on in a timely fashion to the people within a corporation who can utilize it. More often, needed information never makes it to the corporate decision-makers, owing to the lack of any internal system able to readily disseminate the information.

Organizations and their representatives typically approach conferences in a "hit or miss" fashion, being *reactive* as to whom they see and what they hear. This ad hoc approach to obtaining competitive intelligence results in missing most of the "golden nuggets" of information needed by their corporations.

Many formal and informal activities take place at conferences that can furnish a plethora of collection opportunities. These activities range from presentations of technical papers in front of large audiences to private cocktail parties. Very few organizations approach these activities as collection opportunities, especially in a systematic, proactive way. Orchestrating a well-planned and well-conducted collection approach will result in an order of magnitude increase in timely and actionable intelligence, and the Quarterback technique provides the means to this end.

The same actions required to plan and implement a Quarterback operation in fact prove to be the most effective means to form a new, highly actionable intelligence organization, or to greatly enhance the abilities of an existing CI organization. Ongoing CI units have formed as an outgrowth of our Quarterback training and implementation at a conference.

The "quarterback" designation comes from the most essential player in football, who calls the signals and directs the offensive play of the team. In the CI world, the "quarterback" would be the person who oversees the systematic planning and execution of an intelligence collection effort at a professional conference. As is the case with football, unforeseen events occur, often calling for a change in tactics and plan of attack. So the better prepared one is at the onset and the better prepared one is to deal with the unexpected the better the payoff during the competition, be it in the world of sports or business. Such preparation is often derived through training, scenario planning, and lessons from past experiences.

Figure 5-1 illustrates the Quarterback technique. It depicts how the collection manager, the quarterback, works with a team of analysts and collectors to brief and debrief sources and to orchestrate interactions between the sources of intelligence and the targets.

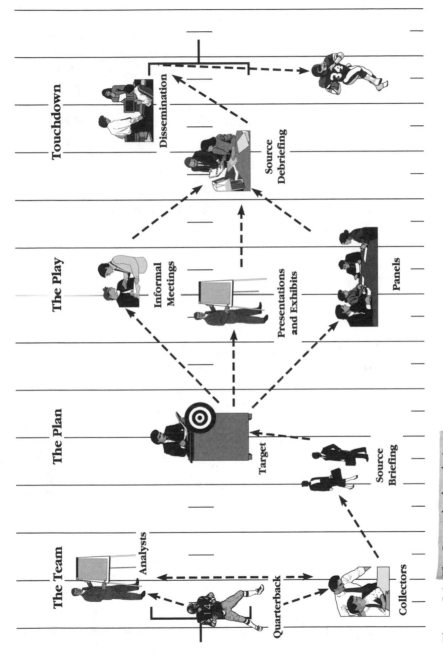

Figure 5-1. The Quarterback technique.

89

Key Players

Although individuals can obtain useful intelligence independently, their success will be eclipsed by the collective efforts of a well-orchestrated team. There are several key roles played by individuals who are members of a team that is instrumental in carrying out the Quarterback operation. Of primary importance is the actual quarterback. The quarterback is the seasoned CI professional who seeks and obtains senior-level backing and support from within his or her company for implementation of the Quarterback operation. It is also the person who plans and orchestrates the collection opportunities and activities during the conference. The quarterback is the overall general, chief architect, coordinator, and supervisor of the conference CI effort.

The *analysts* are the individuals who help generate collection requirements. Requirements generation is often done in cooperation with the quarterback and involves interviewing senior management to determine what is of importance to them, as well as what is of value in supporting ongoing CI and strategic planning efforts. Also, the analysts review and assess the raw intelligence gathered by the collectors at the conference.

Those individuals responsible for collecting intelligence at the conferences, primarily by briefing and debriefing sources, are the *collectors*. They function to facilitate interaction between sources and targets. Collectors also write reports upon debriefing the sources and provide the sources with follow-up requirements generated by the analysts.

The individuals with access to the targets are the *sources*. Internal sources are employees of the organization who work for various components (marketing, research, finance, etc.). External sources are individuals outside the company with whom the quarterback and collectors have a professional rapport and whom they trust. These can be vendors, subcontractors, consultants, media, and the like. Both the internal and external sources must have a professional reason for being at the conference and should have access or be able to gain access to the target. They may have worked with the target in the past or share some professional interest which provides a basis for an interaction. At the very least, they should be able to attend a presentation, understand the subject matter, and ask probing questions without revealing, or "flagging," the CI intent.

The *targets* are those individuals who have the knowledge to answer your requirements, but who might be unwilling to talk with known collectors and analysts of your corporation. The targets are the custodians of the information sought by the source.

Conference Selection and Preparation

There are numerous conferences that occur during the year that impact various professionals within the organization. These conferences include those that focus on particular corporate functions, for example, CEOs, strategic planners, finance, or research and development, as well as those that are geared toward specific industries or products. The quarterback must select those conferences which appear to offer the greatest potential for addressing the requirements and other concerns of senior management. Reviewing past proceedings, analyzing lists of attendees, and interviewing people in the company to determine what they think are the most worthwhile conferences are all factored into selecting conferences for Quarterback operations.

Effective intelligence collection does not start during the conference's opening plenary session, or even at preregistration. The most productive efforts begin during the initial planning of the conference by the sponsoring organization or association. The adept quarterback becomes active in the association and in the early conference planning, volunteering time to help shape the topics and the attendance of key people. In this way, the quarterback can influence the topics chosen for panel papers and discussions, as well as who will be invited to come talk about specific areas of interest.

Once the planning for the conference is set in motion, the quarterback closely monitors who will be attending and who will be speaking at the conference, including competitors, customers, and other knowledgeable observers of the business environment. Those the analysts believe are able to answer some of the requirements become the targets of intelligence. The quarterback then begins to assemble a team of individuals from within the company and trusted allies outside the company (internal and external sources). These people have a professional expertise that justifies their interest and purpose for attending the conference and can conceivably interact with a target to elicit some of the answers to their requirements. The quarterback must also determine who was planning to attend the conference anyway for reasons other than supporting the CI function. With these individuals, it becomes a matter of convincing them to assist in the Quarterback effort. The quarterback must also determine who would be useful to attend for CI purposes but had not planned to attend. The quarterback must try to interest potential sources in wanting to participate in this special operation and obtain the support of their superiors. In no way should individuals with serious reservations be pressured into participating. As is the case with many things in life, if one's heart is not in the effort, then success is less likely. Nor do you want to disrupt or create ill will with respect to other corporate functions.

At any conference there are numerous collection opportunities which occur during both formal and informal events. Formal activities include paper presentations, panel discussions, and exhibits. At these events, targets are already in the role of transferring information about their respective areas of expertise and are open to answering questions. Having the right sources in the audience to raise the proper questions or to visit exhibit booths is orchestrated by the quarterback and the collectors. Informal events include ad hoc meetings, talking at cocktail parties, going out to dinner, and any other interaction which was not a planned conference event. Again, it is part of the team's prior planning to anticipate these collection opportunities and to prepare for their implementation. Early on, the quarterback begins to link targets with specific requirements, determine which sources have potential access to specific targets, and decide which conference events and activities could help facilitate bringing together targets and sources.

It is important that the quarterback obtain a hotel room, or preferably a suite, which is near the conference event but not so apparent to potential targets that it jeopardizes the Quarterback operation. This room becomes the Quarterback "war room," where the quarterback and staff plan and implement activities during the conference. Reports are prepared and sent to headquarters from this locale, and this is where sources can be briefed and debriefed.

Conference Implementation

Elicitation

At the cocktail reception of the Distribution Resource Planning Conference, John spots his target. Slowly he maneuvers himself until he gets within close proximity of Robert. Robert, head of research for Hot Potato Software, Inc., appears to be getting bored with some minor chitchat with two other attendees. He begins to turn away and John positions himself in his path. John makes eye contact, smiles, and reaches out with a handshake. "Hi, I'm John Davies with Seer Research. Are you getting your money's worth from the presentations?" Robert implies he has found a few sessions interesting. John asks if he sat in on the Hardfolks panel discussion, and they exchange a few comments on what was said. John then brings up LogPlan's presentation on their agent technology. John remarks that it's doubtful anything will come of it since it can't handle large-sized operations. Robert disagrees and describes his own technology developments and how they have already proven their utility for major operations. John says it's okay in theory, but no major corporation would ever be willing to experiment with such a risky technology. Robert counters that, in fact, they are already in planning for a test bed project with Coca-Cola. John begins to shed some of his skepticism and states his admiration for Hot Potato's willingness to pursue such an innovative area. He wishes Robert the best of luck with his project. John tells Robert it was good meeting him and that he hopes they can talk some more over the next few days. They each head off in separate directions. Robert feels good that he has defended the integrity of Hot Potato's technical direction and that he is getting respect from others in his field for his bold research. John is happy that he has answered the intelligence requirements that were levied on him relating to Hot Potato's interest in agent technology and the state of their developments.

Elicitation is the technique of interaction that the source uses to extract intelligence from the target. The technique is built on the use of social and psychological tactics that disarm the target's natural defenses regarding sensitive information.[27] As seen in the interaction between John and Robert, John uses several techniques to make Robert accessible to questioning. First, they gain a common reference point from their comparison of some of the presentations. John starts off remarking on a talk that is unrelated to his real interest in agent technology. He then brings up another company's presentation related to agents and makes a misinformed statement about their application. This technique is much more effective than asking Robert directly about his own agent technology developments. It serves the same function, because Robert corrects John's false assumptions by using information that relates to his company's experience with agents. When John continues to voice some skepticism, Robert reinforces his views by describing Coca-Cola's willingness to test their technology.

Elicitation used by sources at a conference may bear some similarities to that used in the world of government espionage, but there are also many differences. First and foremost, sources are not highly trained intelligence agents. They are company employees or contacts who are at the conference for purposes other than just gathering intelligence. The goal is to prepare corporate individuals to be effective gatherers as an adjunct activity to their primary jobs. In most cases they are there to market, learn more about a particular technology or development, and network. Over time, they will become more proficient at gathering intelligence. If taken away from their primary responsibilities, you ultimately risk losing their involvement in and support of the overall CI program. Therefore, the idea is to provide them just the right amount of "trade craft" to make them effective for corporate CI purposes.

Government intelligence elicitation typically involves a long period of cultivation and interaction, frequently taking months, even years. The initial approach serves as an introduction that will allow for subsequent meetings and interactions. Conference CI elicitation is geared for a much quicker goal, obtaining useful intelligence during the conference. There may be subsequent interactions during the conference or at future professional gatherings. The goal of the quarterback is to gain useful intelligence during this first meeting or to set up a second meeting, lunch, or dinner appointment during the same conference in which to gain the intelligence.

The first step in elicitation is the *approach*. The approach is the most critical aspect to elicitation. It involves the first interaction and introduction between the source and the target. If things go well, the probability of gaining useful intelligence is high. If it backfires and the target is alerted to the intentions of the source and becomes guarded, then it is highly unlikely that worthwhile intelligence will be obtained.

Determining who should approach the target occurs prior to the conference, if possible, during the preconference planning. Many target opportunities, however, do not become apparent until conference registration or during some of the early sessions. Therefore, there should be flexibility in assigning sources to particular targets. What is most crucial is that the source have a logical reason for interacting with the target. They must have enough in common professionally that there is a natural reason for them to discuss business at the conference. John and Robert had a reason to talk together, and this was reinforced by their attendance at the same presentation and panel discussions. It is also important that the person who approaches the target comes from a similar position of importance or seniority. It is unlikely that a senior VP will dedicate much time or energy to a junior analyst. These and other factors should be taken into account when determining who approaches and when is the right time to "strike." It is worthwhile to plan for several different sources to approach a target. These, however, should include a mix of internal and external sources. They should not descend upon the target at the same time or use the same opening approach or lines. The last thing you want to do is to "flag" the target as to the true intent and purpose of the interaction. Multiple interactions from the same company asking the same sorts of things will certainly begin to *click* in the target's brain that something is up. A highly prized target should be approached by several sources at different times. The optimal mix, however, would include one person from within the company who is of a similar stature to that of the target (an internal source) and several external sources, such as a friendly journalist, an industry analyst, or a vendor who works with both companies.

Many CI rookies are intimidated by this initial approach to a target and by initiating a conversation. It is important for the quarterback and collectors to put the source at ease. She must adopt the attitude that although these interactions are important, they certainly are not a life-and-death situation. Sources can only try to do their best, and if it works out, super! If things don't happen as planned and the interaction doesn't lead to useful intelligence, then you try again with another source, and use the initial source on another target. The main thing is to try to reduce some of the pressure and tension on the source. Going in as a nervous wreck will certainly flag the target and make him defensive.

One method to use with rookies is the *buddy* approach. This is when two sources work together to psychologically reinforce each other in their interaction with a target. Prior to the approach, the two sources should practice their elicitation tactics and opening lines with the collector. They should also think and plan for some possible contingencies. For example, if a target says she has to excuse herself for a meeting or presentation, one of the sources might ask if they can meet again at a specific time during the conference to discuss an area of mutual interest. The two work in tandem and provide supportive statements with the target. While one person is talking, the other can be preparing to come from another angle. He can also be closely observing the target's body language.

Another method is the *tag team* approach. This is when one individual alone initiates a discussion with the target, gets as much as possible from the discussion, and then excuses himself or herself. The source then rendezvouses with another source in a locale not observed by the target. They discuss what was learned and come up with an angle for follow-up questions form the second source. To reduce the target's ability to surmise what's afoot, it is best that one of the sources be external to the company.

It is wise to avoid approaching two people who are in the middle of an intense conversation. It is easier to enter a group of three or more. Position yourself close to the group and start giving facial feedback to some of the comments being made. When you feel one of the others starts including you, you are free to join in the conversation.[28]

Elicitation calls for an indirect approach. Rarely does a source go directly to a target and ask what is on her mind. Initiating a conversation by saying something witty is beneficial, but one should not waste much thought and concern with struggling to come up with a great opening line. Rather, a simple opening like a casual comment on the event will suffice. It can be related to the conference facility, the food, key industry and association people in attendance, or the outside traffic. As a last resort, one can always remark on the weather. It is important not to come off as being too negative on any of the above. This just creates the impression of being a malcontent. Most first impressions are negative when the tenor is also negative. The upbeat, unusual observation usually works best to draw the target into a conversation.

After pleasantries have been exchanged, one can begin to move into the areas of interest. But it should be a careful move, sort of like a swirl moving slowly inward. One should start from a rather broad context and slowly move toward the more specific. It is useful sometimes to jump around a few different areas before homing in on the pay dirt. This keeps the target from sensing a very calculated effort on the part of the source. As seen in the John and Robert dialogue, feigning ignorance or displaying a misunderstanding of a situation often exploits a natural tendency for people to correct others. The use of flattery and appealing to the individual's expertise for important guidance can also elicit some valuable information. Once some important information is obtained, the source shouldn't break off abruptly to report to the collector. Rather, the source should slowly ease out of the conversation. It may be important to link up with the target at a later time for follow-up questions. One should end a conversation with something like, "I enjoyed talking with you, and I hope I can talk with you further before the end of the conference." John Nolan, who teaches seminars on elicitation techniques, states that according to clinical psychologists, people remember the beginning and the ending of conversations, but not the middle. Therefore it is best to elicit the most sensitive information midway through your discussion and finish up the discussion with harmless chatter about family, sports, or the weather. By doing so, the target will be less likely to become suspicious and may be more open for subsequent conversations.

Another indirect method is the *referral* approach. Rather than first going to the prime target of interest, seek out someone else in the target's organization. If the target is noted for some expertise or specific function, ask the individual who you should speak with who has that particular expertise. Of course, the individual will recommend the target. Now go approach the target. Tell the target you were speaking with one of his colleagues and the person recommended you talk to him. It makes a target feel important to be recognized and referred by colleagues. It is also reassuring the target that if you passed the referral's approval, then you are okay to talk to.

Reading Body Language

Some people are just more in tune to the nonverbal language coming from a target. Reading body language is an art form and not an exact science. It involves an interaction between spoken words and body positioning, including postures, gestures, and facial expressions. Significant differences exist among gender, national, cultural, and ethnic groups. People also exhibit great diversity in their idiosyncracies and mannerisms. Nonetheless, a great deal can be learned from the body language that the target exhibits, and sources will be able to use it to tactical advantage if they become sensitized to some of the subliminal signals.[29]

One of the most obvious signals is when people fold their arms. Like the boxer with arms raised to block a punch, the target is in a protective stance. This is not just a sudden arm-crossing, but rather a prolonged position. The person has not yet warmed to your presence, therefore, you need to slow down your approach. This is the *wrong* time to ask for anything sensitive. Instead, it is the time to be more casual and empathetic. Once the arms relax, the source can slowly move into intelligence-gathering mode.

Another defensive position is having the legs crossed at the ankles. This, however, can also indicate weariness. One way to determine that a person is weary rather than wary of you is that she will be shifting body weight from one foot to another. Again, it is wise to slow down the elicitation by moving to casual talk. When the ankles unlock, the source can again move toward the intelligence collection.

Obviously, clenched fists are a bad sign. Unless a source can say something to reduce the target's anger or tension, it might be better to retreat for the time being.

Signs that a person may not be telling the truth include a person's shoulders rising and falling a lot more than usual, which indicates an increase in breathing. Other signs of deception include covering the mouth with the hands, rubbing the side of the nose, and jerking the head quickly from side to side. Pulling hair, lip biting, gulping, and throat clearing may also indicate a hidden agenda.

A positive sign is palm rubbing. This means the target is eager to talk business. Touching the face indicates not only that the person is thinking seriously about what you said but that he is ready to respond with some information. This would be the wrong time to keep pressing with questions. At this point, it is better for the source to be quiet and let the target take the lead.

Not violating the target's personal space is important. Everyone is surrounded by an invisible bubble, which is about an arm's length (about 2 to 4 feet) away from the body. If someone allows you into this zone while you are talking, then they have accepted you and are likely to be very responsive. If the person backs up while you are moving in, then you better back off a bit. You won't burst their bubble, but they are likely to move away. Before moving into the target's personal zone, it is best to receive some positive signals. If the target touches the source's arm or leans toward the source, then she is allowing for a closer proximity and is more open to exchanging information.

Exhibit Booths

Most conferences include an exhibit area or accompanying trade show. The exhibits serve as an important vehicle to market products and advertise new developments and product releases. Exhibit booths also provide a lucrative arena for intelligence gathering.

For the conference organizer, the rental of booth space is an important income generator. There is a great deal of preconference preparation to sell exhibitor space and therefore plenty of advance knowledge as to what companies will have booths. It is important for the Quarterback team to gain advance lists of exhibitors. Periodically visiting the Web sites of the exhibiting companies and the management company or professional association sponsoring the trade show can help to determine who is exhibiting and what new products will be featured. Searching the Web sites and news media outlets for press releases a week or two before the show may also provide advance warning of what competitors will be highlighting. Getting an advance copy of the trade show issue of the sponsoring organization's journal will also assist in targeting booths and preparing an angle of attack or inquiry.

Once a floor layout and a listing of the exhibitors is available, it is worthwhile to start generating specific informational requirements that will be desired from each booth. It will be the collectors' function to coordinate which booths will be visited by which sources. The elicitation technique and approach should also be worked out in advance.

On the first day of the exhibit, or prior to the opening exhibit hours, if possible, while your own people are setting up their booth, it is beneficial to survey the floor and specific booths. A digital camera and a camcorder can be useful tools if their use doesn't flag competitors that they are being scrutinized. Often, there are myriad journalists doing likewise, so if done properly, it shouldn't signal your true purpose.[30]

The Quarterback War Room

At least one day prior to the conference, the quarterback and collectors should convert the suite or room into the war room. Butcher board paper, colored markers, easels, and removable tape are useful tools. A more sophisticated approach involves using laptop computers with good graphics software and printers. WarRoom Research is currently developing portable war rooms which can be quickly assembled and enable the electronic display of information. These automated war rooms incorporate state-of-the-art decision-making software tools and visualization displays. Regardless of whether one uses the simplistic or sophisticated approach, information connecting the requirements, targets, sources, events, and collector responsibilities must be laid out so that the quarterback and her or his team can best plan and monitor the status of collection activities.

There are some other tools advantageous to the team for carrying out the Quarterback operation. These include notebook computers, electronic organizers, digital cameras, and pocket tape recorders. None of these should be used in an evasive way on a target or in any illegal or unethical manner. The damage done to one's reputation through improper intelligence collection is far worse than any advantages gained from the intelligence collected. However, these tools, utilized in the proper way, can greatly enhance productivity.

For instance, a digital camera can take images of a competitor's exhibit booth which can be sent electronically through a computer modem to headquarters within minutes. Tape recordings of oral presentations are also proper and useful. Electronic organizers that feature a business card scanner are useful to track who various company representatives are interacting with, as well as to monitor the progress and mobility of "fast track" individuals.

During the conference, the quarterback and collectors facilitate meetings by making sure sources are where they should be, briefing them prior to the event, and debriefing them for intelligence gained as soon as possible after the interaction with the target. They also make sure the collection activities and approaches are legal and ethical, yet discrete and operationally secure. The team supports source interactions by furnishing expense money when required for dinner meetings or other out-of-pocket expenses which the source may be unable to fund. After the source is debriefed, a precise report is written and sent electronically back to corporate headquarters. CI staff analysts located either at the conference or at headquarters review the intelligence and provide any follow-up requirements that may be addressed through additional collection activities at the conference. Often, if the intelligence is of great importance, senior management is briefed immediately to alert them as to what was learned and to obtain their input on follow-up questioning.

There are several dos and don'ts which should be followed during a Quarterback operation. Never have more than one source at a time interact in an informal setting with a target. If a target is repeatedly asked similar questions from several people, he will soon recognize that he has been targeted. Conversely, unless the source is a highly skilled manager and can handle multiple targets, asking a source to interact with several targets could lead to undue psychological stress and an information breakdown. Sources need to have legitimate reasons to be at a given conference and have a plausible purpose for interacting with a target. There must be a professional or personal connection that the source can make with the target. It is the team's responsibility to safeguard and protect the source's professional reputation by keeping their activities discrete and proper. Finally, make it fun for the sources. Reduce the pressure on them. If intelligence isn't gained from one interaction, work on another. They need positive feedback and support.

After the conference, the team should reassemble for a "lessons learned" review. This includes both a look at the value of the analytical intelligence obtained as well as what occurred operationally. Improving future Quarterback operations also should be discussed. A nice touch at this review should be a congratulatory visit from the chief executive officer or a high-ranking substitute.

Quarterback Limitations

The Quarterback approach to collecting intelligence at conferences can be unexpectedly difficult. It appears so logical and systematic that to the inexperienced it may seem simple to orchestrate and implement. But be aware, when dealing with human beings, events and interactions rarely go exactly as planned, and things occasionally go awry. The seasoned veteran, however, has contingency plans and is prepared for the unexpected. One can often redirect or convert problem areas and difficulties into additional collection opportunities. Although a great deal can be learned in a classroom, such as from the Quarterback workshop conducted at SCIP '96, the best education is gained from participation in an actual Quarterback operation. It may prove beneficial for a company to bring in some consultant expertise to assist in the first few Quarterback efforts, the goal being to incrementally shift the burden and responsibilities more onto the client and away from the consultant. Each conference is different, poses new challenges, and offers additional learning experiences. The skills and capabilities of the CI professional will dramatically grow with involvement in each new Quarterback operation.

The Quarterback technique is an extremely powerful tool, but it is not meant to preempt or replace other intelligence collection, analysis, and dissemination mechanisms. Newly formed CI organizations or those in the process of being reengineered, reinvented, or simply enhanced will find that preparing for a Quarterback operation greatly improves the structure and functioning of their overall CI program. It helps to define or refine ongoing CI objectives and requirements. Plus, the visibility gained from a Quarterback initiative serves as a rallying point for the rest of the company to become supporters of CI. Interviews with senior management for

Quarterback-related requirements and the development of source networks should prove beneficial in ongoing CI efforts, well beyond the scope of the original Quarterback program.

Conclusion

The implementation of a well-orchestrated Quarterback operation at a conference (either in person or electronically), not only enhances the value of the information obtained by at least tenfold but also dramatically increases the productivity and benefit of the BI function to the corporation. It is difficult to put a monetary value on intelligence. A client recently engaged us to conduct a Quarterback operation focused on whether a competitor was going to enter a product line that would compete head-to-head against a new product of that corporation. If this happened, the consequences would have been disastrous for the client, since they were a manufacturer of a single food product. In a three-day Quarterback effort, intelligence was derived from some well-orchestrated dinners and presentation questions that the competitor would not be entering this specific market. It was estimated by the corporate CI staff that it would have taken a market research firm more than six months, at a cost of at least three-quarters of a million U.S. dollars, to produce information of similar value. Another Quarterback effort focused on whether a competitor was looking to acquire the same company the client was targeting. Not only was the answer obtained (in this case no) but the client also learned some of the criteria the competitor was using in its merger and acquisition research.

Mistakes were made in the conduct of both operations. In one situation a target was approached by several overeager sources asking similar questions. This should have flagged the intent of the questions. Fortunately, the target did not appear to become suspicious of what was going on and was probably caught up in being the center of attention. In another situation, an internal source freaked out about the prospects of eliciting intelligence from a target and failed to show up at an agreed-upon dinner. The target was later informed that the individual had become ill. Important lessons were learned from these mistakes concerning the selection and training of sources. Even so, these Quarterback operations were highly successful. In subsequent conferences, the quarterback and other CI professionals have greatly improved and refined their preparation, planning, and implementation skills. The advent of new technology and the participation of additional inventive minds will continue to enhance and evolve the Quarterback technique.

6

Cyber Collection

*It shouldn't be too much of a surprise
that the Internet has evolved into a
force strong enough to reflect the
greatest hopes and fears of those who
use it. After all, it was designed to
withstand nuclear war, not just the
punny huffs and puffs of politicians
and religious fanatics.*

DENISE CARUSO,
DIGITAL COMMERCE COLUMNIST,
The New York Times

Searching and Mining for the Gold Nuggets

A decade ago the first step for anyone gathering information on anything, from a grade school kid writing a report on dinosaurs to a market researcher examining an emerging industry, was to visit the library. Most libraries maintained the traditional card filing system to track books and various guides to periodic literature to locate magazine articles by subject. About five years ago many libraries began to provide on-line databases, as well as CD-ROMs to *The Wall Street Journal,* local newspapers, and certain magazines. Although these were useful tools, we found that it was often quicker to gather relevant books and publications by eyeballing the stacks and manually scouting out the books and publications.

The advent of the Internet has changed the way any serious researcher obtains information. The Internet is fundamental to basic as well as in-depth research. It provides the quickest means to gain information on about every subject. The scope and quality of the information is increasing geometrically, although it is also littered with "noise," misinformation, and utter nonsense. Key to its utility is knowing how to best search and comprehend its endless cyberspace of information.

The Internet is an outgrowth of the 1960s-vintage ArpaNet of the Defense Advanced Research Projects Agency (DARPA), a communications system developed to expedite information between DARPA and its university contractors. By the 1980s, the system was handling large volumes of traffic. By the 1990s, the formation of the World Wide Web provided the underlying technology to enable its use by the general public. A recent issue of *Science Magazine* estimated that the World Wide Web contained in excess of 320 million pages of information. It continues to grow at an exponential rate, more than doubling in size every four months.

In our first WarRoom contract, we were tasked with obtaining city and metropolitan demographic information for localities around the world. This research was being conducted to assist a major corporation in setting up logistics centers and distribution hubs. When we initiated the project, there were relatively few Internet sites that furnished worthwhile demographic data. Within a period of two months, however, the number of sites began to proliferate on the Internet. Most foreign sites provided countrywide rather than city data, although they also provided information on key researchers and contacts. This research demonstrated to us the real value of the Internet to CI. Occasionally, you may luck out and find the specific answers to requirements through your Internet searches. But in most cases, hard-to-find information, particularly that with intelligence value, will not provide the direct answers to your needs. It will, however, furnish significant leads on individuals and resources who may be able to directly address your specific requirements. Internet searches are the first element in conducting the environmental scan described in Chapter 4, and are even one of the first actions in planning for an intelligence operation directed against "live" targets.

In the old days (the 1980s), intelligence analysts were often stereotyped as computer geeks who would spend hours pouring through computer databases. Associating the collector with a computer was unusual, except for using it as a word processor to prepare a report. Today, the PC has become an integral part of the collector's methodology and mindset. As we described earlier, journalists go on-line to get their story ideas, and they use the Web for gathering images and other material. When researching a story, most reporters first try to reach a source, but their next fallback alternative is to "surf the net." Likewise, unless a CI collector has immediate access to a source who can furnish her with worthwhile intelligence, she should first surf the net looking for source leads and contacts.

Although providing an unlimited amount of information, the Internet suffers some inherent flaws. It lacks all of the tight bibliographic control standards that exist in the print world. There is no ISBN or Dewey Decimal system to identify, search, and retrieve a document. Many Web documents lack the name of the author and the date of publication.

Ross Tyler, a librarian from Okanagan University, characterizes the Internet as the world's largest library, where the books and journals are all stripped of their covers and title pages. They are shelved in no particular order and without reference to a central catalog. The ability to gather information on the Web depends on knowledge about the dozens of search engines that are offered by the Web. Each has its own database, command language, search capabilities, and method for displaying results. Rarely does one engine produce all the desired results. The intelligence professional needs to learn how to blend the various engines, search strategies, and cyber techniques in order to assemble the best recipe for gaining desired information. As Tyler again so aptly states, "The need is clear to familiarize yourself with a variety of search tools and to develop effective search techniques if you hope to take advantage of the resources offered by the Web without spending many fruitless hours flailing about, and eventually drowning, in a sea of irrelevant information."

There are two basic approaches to navigating through cyberspace. These are the use of *search engines* and *subject guides*. A search engine is a utility that will search the Internet, an intranet, a site, or a database for terms that you select. Search engines consist of three basic elements:

- A program that roams the area to be searched, collecting data and links to more data. There are different types of programs, and they are often called spiders, robots, worms, and crawlers.

- An index of the data collected to enable fast access to terms that you search for.

- A search interface, which is the form in which you enter your search terms and the software behind it that queries the index, retrieves matches, and ranks for relevance and organizes the data for follow-on searches.

Search engines differ in their approach to these three elements; therefore, there is an amazing contrast in the results from each. What is delivered from each engine depends on the size of the database, the frequency of updating, and the search capabilities. Search engines vary in speed, design of their search interface, the way they display their results, and the degree of help they offer.

Navigating through cyberspace is something akin to going at Star Trek's warp drive. It's hard to imagine that within a few seconds (depending on the speed of your modem or connection), you can travel through eons of cyberspace, bypassing galaxies of information. The search engine is analogous to going in hyperdrive. You set a destination and you are delivered there without seeing how you got there. Whether you get to where you really wanted to get depends on whether you have the proper coordinates.

The other Internet navigation approach is the use of subject guides. These are hierarchically organized indexes of subject categories that enable a researcher to browse the lists of Web sites by subject in search of relevant information. Using a subject guide is like jumping from star to star, and once you find an interesting solar system, you stop and explore the planets.

Whereas search engines are automated, subject guides are compiled and maintained by humans. There are pluses and minuses in using each. Since subject guides typically use a smaller database, their resulting lists tend to be smaller as well. Search engines index every page of a given Web site, whereas a subject guide is more likely to provide a link only to the site's home page. So although you may get less of a list, subject guides are less likely to provide sites that are really out of context. In general, search engines are best suited for locating a specific piece of information, whereas subject guides are best for information on a general subject.

Parallel and Meta Search Engines

The realization that there is a vast difference between the results of various search engines and that most comprehensive researches involve using several engines has resulted in the development of parallel or multiple search engines. These search engines enable the researcher to search several different databases simultaneously through a single interface. Parallel search engines do not allow the same level of control over the search interface and search logic as do individual search engines. Individual search engines and directories may have a special syntax or selectable search criteria that can only be taken advantage of by using the individual search engine. Parallel engines, however, are extremely fast and can be real time savers. In general, they seem to gather the most relevant information from the various other engines quite effectively. Most parallel engines sort results by site, by type of resource, by domain, and also have the ability to modify results.

There are two types of parallel search engines, *host-based* and *locally based*. Host-based parallel search engines sit on the Web and wait for you to type in the search word or phrase and hit the submit button. As soon as you do, they send a flood of queries to a number of single search engines on the Web. They then correlate the results and transform them into the Hypertext Markup Language (HTML) files for your browser for you to review. Locally based parallel engines let you use your own CPU to perform the correlation and HTML work.

Search Strategy

As in most endeavors, having the proper tools is only part of the equation for getting good results. How one uses these tools will ultimately determine your results. The competitive intelligence professional should never look at the use of the Internet in and of itself for any in-depth collection effort. The environmental scan, consisting of multisource collection from primary and secondary sources, is needed for real comprehensive CI purposes. The Internet search is therefore an integral first step to putting together a mosaic of collection activities.

Commercial on-line services, such as Dialog, Nexus/Lexus, and Dow Jones, use a pearl-building approach to finding one relevant citation in a controlled vocabulary index and then finding more based on its subject headings. This approach does not work well in Internet databases that lack a controlled vocabulary. Effective Internet searches involve techniques that enable you to go directly to the information source, guess at URLs, and strategize as to when to use the subject guides and search engines.

Following are the basic steps involved in conducting an effective Internet search:

1. Articulate your question or requirement.
2. Identify how such questions or requirements would be answered.
3. Identify search terms that state your question or could lead to the answers.
4. Consider synonyms and variations of those terms.
5. Be inventive, and deviate from the expected.

It is important that you get a handle on what you really want to know. Although searching by "free association" has some value and can at times be useful to increasing one's general knowledge, it rarely answers what you particularly need to know relating to an intelligence need. Trying to get smart on everything results in knowing very little about anything. Just as one cannot perform an effective job of intelligence gathering unless responding to very specific requirements, searching effectively on the Net requires a similar focus.

In developing a search strategy, it is also important to think in terms of how your question or requirement might be answered. Let's say my requirement is to learn what new products are under development by my competitor. One starting point is to search under the competitor's name and R&D (research and development). If I also suspect that they may be pursuing specific fields of research related to a potential new product, I may also search by the company name and by the suspect research area. So when we think of a search, it may be in terms of the question being asked and also in terms of possible answers. If nothing comes up in the expected research areas, perhaps they either are not pursuing it or have elected to keep it quiet.

Search results can vary greatly by the terms used, even if they mean the very same thing. It is beneficial to cast these questions and answers in several possible phrases or alternative descriptive wording. Although searching by free association is counterproductive, examining off-the-wall ideas or wording may prove fruitful. For example, we were trying to obtain information on a Cleveland law firm. None of the search engines produced anything. We then looked at some Ohio local issues and political Web sites that we thought the law firm would be active in. Some of these had their own newsletters and publications on-line and their own engines to search through previous issues. When we did this, we came up with a great deal of information on the law firm.

Going straight to the target is often the best first move in the quest for information. If your question or requirement concerns a competitor, go directly to their site. Most company sites include product information; public relations material, including press releases and favorable articles; staff directories; and mission statements. Some companies are actively looking for investment and include financial information and their market strategy. Some even include their annual report and links to the Security and Exchange Commission's *Edgar* site for their 10K report.

Jonathan L. Calof performed a case study that demonstrated the intelligence that could be gained by examining the home page of Advanced Information Technologies Corp. (AIT). A manufacturer of passport readers, AIT had controlled 90 percent of its primary market. For 16 years AIT had continuously increased sales and profits. In 1995 their earnings were up 34 percent from the previous year, and 1996 looked to be another banner year. Then the second quarter for 1996 came in and AIT took a nosedive. Its revenues were down 67 percent, and the company had a net loss of $2.5 million. AIT had sold one of its four divisions, a second was up for sale, and major attempts were being made to bolster a faltering new division. AIT's stock dropped soon after from $16 to $5.25. Calof found that there were plenty of indicators on AIT's home page months in advance that would have enabled a good CI analyst to predict their impending decline.

By examining press releases, executive biographies, and past annual reports, all on the AIT home page, Calof was able to witness a movement of the company away from reliance on one market, the production of government passport readers. In the 1994 annual report contained at their home page, the chairman talks about the company's success and their continued reliance on the passport-reader market. The New Products section of the home page only discusses products that exist within the existing lines. There are no indications of a change in direction. In February 1995, however, the Web site contains a press release that describes a letter of intent for AIT to acquire Walton Recording Devices. The acquisition is justified in that it will "provide AIT with an established presence in the commercial recorder products market." Another press release issued a few weeks later describes the acquisition as repositioning the company into three high-growth, high-margin businesses. The 1995 annual report indicated that the company expected that a large part of their growth would come from this new area.

Calof could deduce a shift in AIT's thinking. The acquisition was originally perceived as a tactical move. Now it became a strategic change. The implications of this change were quite profound for the company, and quite risky. In the government market, AIT's products were priced high, and the sales cycles were quite lengthy. In contrast, the commercial market had smaller dollar items, and the market was characterized by quick sales and fast changes.

By reviewing the help-wanted advertisements posted on their home page, Calof could not detect any effort to bring in the marketing and management skills required for AIT to make this shift. Looking at the biography of the marketing vice president revealed that although he had extensive government experience, he had no relevant time marketing in the commercial arena. All this indicated to Calof that the company was not positioned for this shift, and all of this was apparent well before the company's collapse.

After the acquisition of Walton, AIT acquired another company named Dedicated Technologies. What was interesting to Calof were the anomalies that existed when he compared the description of Dedicated Technologies on the AIT Web site to that maintained at

Dedicated Technologies own Web site, which was still on the Internet after the acquisition.

Shortly after both acquisitions, AIT's newly appointed chief operating officer announced on the Web site the sale of one of the company's divisions and the write-down on another. The COO's biography was contained at the Web site. He had an MBA from Wharton and specialized in finance. His past jobs were financial positions with high-technology companies. His initial management moves of cutting unprofitable divisions and downsizing rather than R&D or expansion were no surprise, and could have been predicted from the review of the Web site.

It is rare that you will find trade secrets, strategic plans, and proprietary information at the target's own Web site. But sometimes others, including consumer groups, investor discussion groups, and competitors, may maintain elements of the more sensitive information that you arc seeking. At the very least you should develop good source leads who may be able to answer your specific questions.

Often, time can be saved by going directly to the organization's Internet presence by finding its URL. For many Web sites, the unofficial standard of the www.company.com will take you directly to their home page. For example, Chrysler is www.chrysler.org, thc Symantec Corporation is www.symantec.com, and WarRoom Research is www.WarRoomResearch.com. Since Netscape Navigator and Microsoft's Internet Explorer automatically take a host address and add the common http:// at the beginning, you just have to begin with the www. The following is a list of the Web sites most often visited by CI professionals:[31]

1. Alta Vista (50 percent of respondents use). Internet address is: www.altavista.digital.com. This is a very fast, comprehensive search engine for Web sites and news groups.

2. Yahoo (25 percent of the respondents). Internet address is www.yahoo.com. It provides a subject guide to Web sites and also has keyword search facility.

3. Lycos (15 percent of respondents). Internet address is www.lycos.com. One of the oldest search engines for Web sites. Lycos is also sold as a program to allow Web servers to search internal and external Web databases.

4. Hoovers Corporate Directories (15 percent of respondents). Internet address is www.hoovers.com. This provides detailed profiles for 2480 companies and shorter listings for over 10,000 companies. It has a Web register of 2500+ corporate home pages. It can be searched by a variety of methods, some of which are free, and other more detailed information is fee-based.

5. SEC EDGAR (15 percent of the respondents). Internet address is www.sec.gov. This provides SEC reports on public companies which file electronically. It includes 10(k) and 10(Q) reports.

6. BUSLIB-L (15 percent of the respondents). Internet subscription e-mail address is listserv@idbsu.idbsu.edu. This is a business librarians listserv (Internet mailing list).

7. NewsPage (12.5 percent of the respondents). Internet address is www.newspage.com. This is a fee-based current awareness service that draws information from a variety of news feeds and databases.

8. Webcrawler (7.5 percent of the respondents). Internet address is www.webcrawler.com. Provides a search engine for searching multiple search engines with one command.

9. Switchboard (7.5 percent of the respondents). Internet address is www.switchboard.com. Provides addresses and phone numbers of over 10 million U.S. businesses and individuals.

10. CNN (7.5 percent of the respondents). Internet address is www.cnn.com. Provides up-to-the-minute news from the Cable News Network.

11. *The Wall Street Journal* (7.5 percent of the respondents). Internet address is www.wsj.com. It provides current updated news plus company snapshots, briefing books, customized news page, and a searchable archive.

12. Infoseek (5 percent of the respondents). Internet address is www.infoseek.com. Provides a keyword search of the Web, newsgroups, and some proprietary databases. Some of the services are free and others are fee-based.

13. Metacrawler (5 percent of the respondents). Internet address is www.metacrawler.com. This search engine searches and cross-

references results from multiple search engines. It sorts and removes duplicates.

14. SCIP (5 percent of the respondents). Internet address is www.scip.org; the Web site of the Society of Competitive Intelligence Professionals.

15. U.S. Census Bureau (5 percent of the respondents). Internet address is www.census.gov. Source for social, demographic, and economic information.

16. Thomas Register (5 percent of the respondents). Internet address is www.thomasregister.com. It is a buying guide that provides information about companies, their products, and services.

As we indicated, different search engines will yield different results, and a comprehensive search should involve the use of several engines. Most search engines use Boolean logic, logical operations that are used to combine search terms in many databases. Basic Boolean operation uses the words *and, or,* and *not.* When *and* is inserted between two words, it means it is looking for a Web site which has both words. *Or* implies having one or the other word. *Not* excludes sites which have the following word. Other engines use symbols such as + in front of the words it wants included in the search. Other sites use phrase searching, which requires the site to have all the terms in exactly the order you enter them. These usually include the phrase in double quotations (" "). Others signify the same thing by capitalizing the initial letters.

An effective approach to Internet searching is to start with the macro and then move to the micro. At WarRoom we do this by making four passes at the Web. The first pass uses the parallel or meta-search engines that give comprehensive coverage. This usually provides a quick compilation of most of the important Web sites that have a direct correlation with the search terms used. There are a number of parallel search engines that enable the search of many engines at once. These include:

Metacrawler: http://www.metacrawler.com/

Inference Find: http://www.inference.com/infind/

Dogpile: http://www.dogpile.com/

MetaFind: http://www.metafind.com/

All-in-One: http://www.albany.net/allinone/

Savvy Search: http://.cs.colostate.edu/ãdreiling/smartform.html

Isleuth: http://www.isleuth.com/

The second pass hones in like a laser and uses the search engines with the most power to focus the search. There are a number of major search engines. Five good ones are:

Alta Vista: http://altavista.digital.com

Excite: http://www.excite.com

HotBot: http://www.hotbot.com

Infoseek: http://www.infoseek.com

Northern Light: http://www.northernlight.com

The third pass looks at "webliographies," sites with lots of links on the subject in question. A fourth pass looks to see if there is a specialized search engine dedicated to our subject.

There are certain basic considerations one should factor in when using a search engine. These are as follows:

- *Factor in the search engine's limitations.* Some engines just include Web (http) documents, whereas others include Gopher, FTP, and Archie information. Some index document content, and others just index by document titles or URL text. This is why different search engines produce a variety of results. Understanding what is in the database enables you to devise more effective search terms. For example, if you know that a database contains URLs, typing in file extensions such as AU, JPG, and MPEG can lead to sounds, graphics, and other multimedia sources.

- *Factor in peak usage periods.* Search engines typically don't perform as well during peak usage hours, 12 noon to 3:00 p.m. Eastern time.

- *Word placement counts in search terms.* It's better to have a specific short list of search terms than to overload the engine. Some search engines giver greater weight to the first word used in a query.

- *Select best search options.* Some search engines let you search different parts of Web documents, such as titles, document content, or hypertlink text.

Jean L. Graef of the Montague Institute conducted a survey in 1996 on the use of the Internet for competitive intelligence.[32] He surveyed 40 individuals from different Fortune 1000 companies. Using the Internet for secondary research (finding published information) was considered its most important use by 55 percent of the respondents. Monitoring government information came in second. Also high on the list was its utility for collaborating with colleagues and the savings gained from using it over the services of commercial information brokers.

Surprisingly, Graef found that a large number of respondents (30 percent) stated that the Internet was extremely important in marketing their intelligence (CI) services internally. Other uses for the Internet which the CI professionals viewed as extremely important included:

- Locating experts (23 percent)
- Identifying new products and services for their department's consumption (23 percent)
- Improving the management of or access to internal information (23 percent)
- Saving money on fax or courier costs (23 percent)
- Publishing and disseminating their information products and services to internal customers (20 percent)
- Enhancing one's career, e.g., job hunting
- Marketing CI services and products to external clients (18 percent)
- Obtaining technical support and assistance related to hardware, software, or other problems (15 percent)
- Finding out what other people think about a product before deciding to purchase (15 percent)
- Marketing the corporation or operation division to customers or clients (13 percent)
- Taking training courses (13 percent)

- Obtaining and testing new software programs (13 percent)
- Obtaining help with management issues (10 percent)

Graef found that most of the CI professionals learned how to use the Internet through their own experimentation (70 percent). Forty-five percent indicated that tips from their colleagues were important to their use. Only 40 percent learned from trade periodicals, 33 percent from commercial or association seminars, 28 percent from books and manuals, 15 percent from internal training, and 5 percent from college or university courses. This is interesting when compared to the TFG Ostriches and Eagles study described in Chapter 2. Most intelligence collection today is still obtained from reading various publications and other open source and secondary research. Yet when it comes to developing one's own research skills, reading publications and open source research is largely ignored. The respondents, however, were frank in their acknowledgment that they needed greater information hunting and gathering skills (55 percent). Other needs identified included:

- Reviews and evaluations of Internet information resources (55 percent)
- How to protect confidential information on the Internet (45 percent)
- Hands-on instruction in the use of Internet tools and techniques (45 percent)
- Information on the impact of the Internet on the company's strategic objectives (33 percent)
- Webmasters skills (learning how to maintain an internal/external Web site (23 percent)

The Internet survey conducted by Graef also revealed that the CI researchers had several difficulties with their use of the Internet. It was difficult for them to determine the true qualifications of authors. It was also easy for someone to impersonate a well-known author or produce an ersatz version of a name-brand publication. There are no standards for citing or classifying publications by subject, author, or date. Price is no longer a guarantee of quality or authenticity. An increasing number of authors and publishers are providing their information via the Internet free of charge.

On the negative side, Graef found that a large number of the respondents (38 percent) found that their top management was indifferent or negative toward the use of the Internet. Only 7 percent indicated that their top management fully accepted its utility.

Graef's findings are surprising in that they seem to imply that competitive intelligence professionals are somewhat behind the times in their sophistication in the use of the Internet. To excel in the field, professionals need to be in the vanguard regarding the use of new technologies and developing innovative techniques and processes. Because of this, later in this chapter, you will find some Internet innovations that can profoundly impact intelligence collection.

Information Brokering

Information brokers are people who provide fee-based services for on-line database and public records searching. A recent comparison between what could be obtained via the Internet and what a major on-line subscription service could provide yielded some surprising results. In the past, only a fraction of what was provided from the on-line service could be obtained via the Internet. In the most recent comparison, however, perhaps 50 percent of the on-line service information was also available on the Internet. The remaining 50 percent, however, is quite important. And for competitive intelligence an organization should provide for the best research tools available, which includes on-line services as well as the Internet.

On-line services brokering information have existed for about 15 years. The dramatic growth of PC usage and particularly the use of the Internet altered how these companies conduct business. The customers of the information brokers now demand information within hours. What used to be the standard of a few years ago, overnight delivery of information, is no longer acceptable. Most consumers have e-mail accounts and expect files to be sent to them ASAP.

The growth in world commerce has also created a demand for international information. Information brokers have needed to obtain new data sources on foreign companies and industries.

Until recently, the expectation for information brokers was to run a search, print out the results, and ship it to the client. Competition with the Internet has forced information brokers to broaden their services. Now many also evaluate sources, detect and alert clients to discrepancies in the data, summarize the results, and make recommendations.

There has been a proliferation of specialized "boutique services" which provide more refined and focused data on particular niches. These services are more costly, but they differentiate themselves from other services, and from what customers can do from their own Internet searching.

NERAC is a prime example of an information broker that has evolved to be more competitive.[33] The organization began operating in 1966 as the New England Research Applications Center. It was an experimental collaboration between the University of Connecticut and the National Aeronautics & Space Administration. Over time, their focus broadened and they began to encompass the full spectrum of engineering, scientific, and business disciplines. In 1985 it separated from UCONN and incorporated under the name NERAC. It severed its ties with NASA in 1991 and today is a for-profit organization. NERAC relies on an in-house group of 75 industry-trained engineers and scientists to assist its clients in their informational researches. NERAC relies on a close customer-researcher interface. Research information is obtained within several hours and is either e-mailed or faxed to the client.

Using Web Sites to Collect Intelligence

Graef's survey described earlier had another interesting finding. A number of CI professionals were interested in learning how to set up and maintain their own Web sites. It can be argued that it would be more efficient for them to work closely with the company's Webmaster to develop Web sites and home pages beneficial to the CI activity.

A very effective way to gather information through survey research is to have the CI unit place the survey on the company Web site. E-mails can be sent to the targeted survey population, alerting them to the survey and inviting them to participate. At the bottom of the e-mail can be a hyperlink which takes the person who received the e-mail directly back to the Web site to answer the survey questions. For sensitive questionnaires or surveys, the Web sites of consultants or third parties can be used. Web sites also can be set up with no affiliation, simply serving to house the survey. In fact, a number of graduate students are conducting survey research in this fashion.

Profiling information can also be obtained from people visiting a Web site. Much can be learned from those who visit a site, including their searching habits, interests, geographical location, and more. Such technology shows great promise for advertising, where ads can be targeted specifically for the visitor. For example, a woman in her sixties making a virtual visit to the car dealer may get information on the safety features and fuel economy of their cars. The 25-year-old man may hear about the car's acceleration speed. More sophisticated profiling tools are being developed, and some of these will become increasing useful for intelligence purposes.

Intranets

An intranet uses the technologies of the Web, including HTML authoring, browsers, and TCP/IP connectivity, and builds a private web within an internal corporate information service. It enables the intranet users to have access to multimedia and large volumes of text at low cost, and to do so securely. Intranets have important CI applications. They can allow for virtual workgroups to form around intelligence topics and projects. They also make the dissemination and feedback of intelligence reports quite efficient.

Data Mining

Data mining has the connotation of digging for those "golden" nuggets of information. As in mining a mountain, data mining refers to sifting through large databases (often on mainframe computers) for valuable informational gems. For the mining machinery, data mining uses artificial intelligence to create competitive intelligence. This is where the two intelligences merge. Induction-based data mining tools use machine-learning algorithms to analyze records and trends in internal and customer databases. They are able to discover patterns, transactional relationships, and rules that can forecast trends and opportunities.

In the past data that was maintained in data warehouses required extensive trial-and-error queries or statistical segmenting, which took a lot of time and effort. Machine learning algorithms, however, are able to operate much quicker by identifying key intervals (range) and attributes (variables) in a database. They can compress a database so that only a few attributes are needed to derive predictive intelligence. A number of analysts predict that data-mining tools will have a major impact across a wide range of industries over the next 3 to 5 years. Advances in data capture, transmission, and storage will accelerate the utility of data mining. There are a number of automatic data-mining tools that can be utilized for the CI application. These range in cost from $2000 for smaller, stand-alone packages to higher-end products that can cost in excess of $50,000 and are specifically tailored for use in client-server environments.[34]

Robots, Spiders, and Intelligent Agents

New Internet technologies are being developed that will enable intelligent professionals to be the handlers of intelligent agents. These offer great opportunities for collection, but they also challenge legal and ethical considerations. To stay competitive, CI professionals need to be alert to what these new technologies entail and how they can use them. They also need to be aware of how they can be misused and abused, both by themselves and by competitors and adversaries.

Robots are programs that travel across the Web's hypertext structure and search and retrieve documents. They recursively retrieve all documents which are referenced. Web browsers are not robots, since they are operated by a human and don't automatically retrieve referenced documents. Robots are also referred to as *web wanderers, web crawlers,* or *spiders.* The software does not move between sites like a virus. The robot simply requests documents from the sites automatically.

Autonomous agents are programs that actually do travel between sites, deciding by themselves when to move and what to do. Intelligent agents are programs that help the user find things or make choices.

Inquisit is a company that has pioneered the use of agents for intelligence gathering. A company of about 35 employees, Inquisit's mission is "to provide professionals with the actionable business information they need to be successful." Their sole product is a subscription-based service, in which subscriptions are sold to individuals on a monthly basis or to corporations on an enterprise-wide basis. Subscriptions to the Inquisit service allow users to search a database of relevant business publications and have their search query results returned by e-mail, fax, pager, or cellular phone. Inquisit currently monitors and archives approximately 400 business and technical trade magazines and newspapers (a full list is available on-line). To perform searches, the user creates customized "agents" to monitor specific publications in the Inquisit database. When these "agents" find relevant information, they send an e-mail or other form of communication to the user. Users may specify that they would like e-mails only on a regularly scheduled basis or immediately when new information is found. The Inquisit system is a relatively closed system, and their agents may only be used to monitor the publications that have been selected by Inquisit. Their approach seems very useful and reasonable but does not compete with intelligent robot products such as Intelligent Automation's robot system.

Competitive Intelligence/Opposition Research Toolbox

With the explosion of content being placed on the Web, CI and political opposition researchers require advanced tools to support their requirements for information collection. Not only are tools needed for the standard types of seek-and-find operations, but tools are also needed to continually monitor prespecified areas of the Web, maintain references, and to mine large amounts of information. Some domain-specific tools are available today that are useful, but none are truly customizable and general-purpose for the Web. Intelligent Automation, Inc. (IAI), is a Rockville, Maryland, Internet and Web R&D company that is developing a customizable suite of tools that can assist in Web-based CI and opposition research.

The novelty and relative ease of Web publishing has drawn a large number of inexperienced users who are not familiar with the issues of information security. Information is often mistakenly made available to the general public that would never have been let out the door in general printed materials. In the hands of the competition, this information could tip the scales in their favor.

The IAI toolbox will contain automated information seekers, such as robots (or spiders), that can monitor prespecified areas of the Web for relevant information. IAI's information seekers can be scheduled to continually monitor certain Web sites for new information or changes to old information. When the competition places new resources on the Web, these robots can find and catalog the resources as well as mine the resources for relevant information. In certain cases, specialized algorithms will be required to mine domain-specific information from the Web resources. The IAI toolbox will contain a plug-'n-play interface so that user-supplied algorithms can be integrated with the already-existing tools.

The results of the information-gathering and data-mining efforts will be stored in an archived database. The database can be used to generate reports on the information that was found, including graphs and projections, as well as to store relevant contact and location information about the data-gathering efforts.

E-mail Elicitation

The U.S. Government has recognized that "foreign entities," including intelligence and security services, and corporate competitors are increasingly using unsolicited electronic correspondence via the Internet to elicit information for U.S. companies.[35] It shouldn't be surprising that a new form of communication would be exploited, particularly one which is the chosen form of information conveyance by scientists and "hi-tech" business people. Knowing how to elicit information using e-mail is an art form that is evolving and becoming more sophisticated.

We all know business people who avoid answering their telephones but are very quick at responding to their e-mail. E-mail makes it a lot easier for certain people to communicate. Some individuals are uncomfortable with direct interactions, even when they are not in person. It is easier for many to express themselves and convey information when the personal interaction and intimacy is removed. A hesitancy to speak may in fact be a vulnerability that can be exploited. A person may be more than accommodating via e-mail, if by doing so they don't have to talk with you on the phone.

If you come across a potential source that avoids the telephone exchanges, you can use it to advantage by giving that person an out. Leaving a phone message or e-mail indicating that you won't be a bother since all you need is some information which can be e-mailed to you may result in increased cooperation.

E-Quarterbacking

Technologies such as the Internet, electronic mail (e-mail), and groupware have enabled large groups of people to communicate and collaborate with each other over long distances and from distributed locations. Internet providers and on-line services such as America Online and CompuServe furnish electronic forums, "chat" discussion rooms, and other teleconferencing adaptations. Many of the same techniques utilized for Quarterback operations (described in detail in Chapter 7), with a little improvisation and innovation, can be adapted to electronic and virtual conferences. The quarterback can orchestrate formation of a forum or group "chat" session, including getting a source to volunteer as chat host or facilitator, and thus orchestrate collection opportunities. External sources can be used to discretely question competitors and elicit information. There are obvious differences between the in-person human interactions required of the quarterback and the electronic exchanges of the E-Quarterback. The optimal collector of intelligence in each milieu may possess a different set of skills and personality traits. Yet the basic process and approach is much the same.

State-of-the-Art Web Site for Intelligence Collection, Dissemination, and Issues Management

Intelligent Automation, Inc. (IAI) has developed a prototype Internet-based advanced media management tool and Web site to demonstrate its application to advocacy campaigns and for intelligence gathering. A hypothetical antitobacco advocacy campaign and litigation effort was used to demonstrate this technology and approach. This demonstration site used the most sophisticated intelligence collection and dissemination techniques ever devised for the Internet. This approach can be applied to numerous other applications utilizing CI. WarRoom Research was also involved in developing information security system safeguards for the Internet tool.

The Internet is emerging as the single most powerful communications tool of the decade—and it may join the ranks of the mass media during the first decade of the new millennium. Its potential impact on business and politics is a revolution in the making. Already, using on-line technology, American citizens are accessing information on the diverse issues that affect them, on the products they buy, and in communicating and sharing opinions with people and organizations worldwide.

While the Web has been used to disseminate information on advocacy campaigns and associated issues, it has not been used strategically as a tool with which to influence these issues. Many advocacy campaigns have adopted a Web site to show that they can address the future and that they are in touch with technology. But outside of window dressing, the real political and business value of campaign Web sites offered by ordinary developers is today somewhat minimal. Although Internet usage among the general populace continues to grow dramatically, the average citizen, businessperson, legislator, or decision-maker neither gleans their information nor is influenced surfing the net. The mass media of television and radio is and will continue to be for the near term the primary media in which to convey messages and sway decisions.

IAI's approach was to transform the current static design and approach of advocacy campaign Web sites to a very interactive and dynamic design that can help shape on an ongoing basis the issues and media impacting a promotional or advocacy campaign or issue. IAI developed a new advocacy campaign Web site paradigm in which the Web site and associated Internet technology is used as a device for intelligence collection and dissemination and issues management. In addition to the standard features geared toward the special interest, general populace, and the cyber brigade of activists, a primary focus of the site is to influence the media and their coverage and portrayal of events, day by day. Never before has such an array of strategic and tactical information weaponry been at the disposal of a campaign to manage and influence events and issues. Several efforts are now under way using the same technology and approach for other advocacy, political, and advertising campaigns.

The initial demonstration of the Web site (using a fictional advocacy campaign) featured a section of the Web site that was exclusively for members of the advocacy campaign. Access was password protected, and this section included sensitive information related to:

- Issues management: Recommended actions members could take to help influence the media
- Strategy planning: How to capture and map the legislative process, determine the optimal paths within this process, and actions members can take both to help it occur and forestall the progress of the opposition
- Intelligence/opposition research: Key alerts and updates of activities of the opposition, as well as analysis of their intent and actions
- Schedule and events important to the advocacy campaign
- E-mail listing of advocacy campaign members

There was another section of the Web site that was open to visitors who were not members of the association but were interested in antitobacco litigation and education. This included information related to:

- Terms of the settlements of prior litigation
- Lessons learned during trials and litigation
- Information about current and upcoming suits
- A forum for questions and answers
- A network of lawyers involved in litigation
- Connections to other tobacco educational Web sites which were linked by the user profile (level of education, smoking history, etc.)

The advocacy campaign also contained unique proprietary tools for the campaign staff to maintain information and to orchestrate targeted messages and information to the media. These are indicative of the types of features and capabilities that can be provided to an actual advocacy campaign or other business and competitive intelligence application. The actual design and makeup of the advocacy campaign Web site is derived from the client's desires and expectations, coupled with the expert advice and recommendations of the Web developers.

7

Visualization Intelligence
Techniques

There are a gazillion different competitive intelligence analytical techniques and approaches which are specific to certain industries and corporations. The intent here is not to run the gamut of such approaches but to discuss some fundamentals that should be addressed by any decent CI analytical activity. This chapter also focuses on some tools and techniques that are not industry-specific and can enhance the basic skills and capabilities of the analyst.

In his book *Competitive Intelligence* Larry Kahaner states that good analysts usually are born, not made. He maintains further that intelligence agencies such as the CIA look to hire people capable of thinking linearly and in patterns. They don't have to think sequentially in order to leap ahead with a deduction. By thinking in patterns, analysts are able to discern the underlying nature of their competitor's intentions, plans, and actions.

Corporate success increasingly depends on a timely awareness on the part of key executives of rapidly changing events outside their organization. Yet most organizations are trapped in a "catch 22." To raise their intelligence about opportunities and possible threats, they become so involved with gathering information they become swamped by mountains of data. They have a hard time winnowing the important from the trivial.

The ability to quickly disseminate and comprehend intelligence is an essential asset to operating in today's time-sensitive, highly competitive environment. Although narrative information can be prepared in concise intelligence formats, the written word is still limited in its ability to portray the dimensionality and density of information. The notion that one picture can represent a thousand words is probably an understatement when considering the latest data visualization techniques pioneered by Edward Tufte and other leading "visualization linguists." These individuals have advanced both the art and science of utilizing graphics to visually display large quantities of information by the combined use of points, lines, a coordinate system, numbers, symbols, words, shadow, and color.

Visualization has been underutilized in the business and intelligence analytical arenas, yet it offers in-depth comprehension that often far exceeds narration. Visualization is also a fundamental component to the use of war rooms. It facilitates team-based understanding and decision-support.

Competitive intelligence has some unique requirements in the processing of information. Accurate information must be collected and disseminated in a timely fashion to enable decision-makers to respond and make an impact. Intelligence reporting must therefore happen quickly and be presented in a way that is readily understood. The advent of team-based decision-making also requires the preparation of intelligence that can be utilized in group settings. Visualization techniques can greatly enhance the processing and comprehension of intelligence.

A useful technique that WarRoom applies to CI analysis is a derivation of mind-mapping, developed by Tony Buzan. Buzan's basic premise is that creative thought does not parallel the way speech and the printed word are presented. Rather than operating in linear fashion, the mind reacts to ideas and generates new thoughts in a nonlinear way. In taking in ideas the mind focuses on key words and concepts and then processes them in a way that helps to retain them. The mind associates these words and ideas with one another, with past experiences, and with "sparks" of new, creative thoughts. The mind works associatively as well as linearly. It is comparing, integrating, and synthesizing as it goes. Often the mind develops innovative thought in an instant. It is only when we try to communicate these thoughts using standard narration that we have to describe the parts of the idea in a linear sequence.

Buzan initially developed mind-mapping as a technique for developing or capturing complex ideas. For example, the essence of an entire lecture or book can be caught on single sheet of paper. It is similar to Evelyn Wood's speed-reading technique that enables readers to capture and remember the essence of what they read.

As we have already indicated, the analytical mind thinks in patterns and in a nonlinear fashion. Forcing techniques on the analyst which depend on linear narrative forms actually hamstrings thinking and stifles comprehension. A way to overcome this is to use visualization techniques such as Buzan's, which are not bounded by grammatical structure.

Mind maps use images, color, and spatial relationships to convey ideas, elements of whatever is under consideration, and relationships between them. Mind maps can be used to convey several different competitive intelligence processes.

- To examine the possible options to explain why a competitor did what they did.

- To examine possible competitor scenarios and the range of actions the client can take under each scenario.

- As a mechanism to plan CI collection operations.

- Once a group of intelligence consumers becomes acquainted with the technique, mind-mapping can be a useful tool for disseminating intelligence, often conveying in minutes what might otherwise take several hours of in-depth reading.

- Projecting mind-mapping on a display in a war room setting is also an excellent facilitation tool for group "brainstorming."

Some competitive intelligence analysis involves the assessment of external factors impacting competitiveness. It can involve applying a numerical quantitative rating scheme to qualitative judgments. One visualization tool for analyzing external factors is "quality function deployment" (QFD) software. QFD was first introduced in Japan by Yoji Akao in 1966. The approach did not get to the United States until 1994. It was initially used as a method to develop design quality aimed at satisfying the consumer's demand by using design targets and major quality assurance points throughout manufacturing. It has since been applied to various other areas. QFD contains a "house of quality" matrix in which the key external factors going down the vertical axis are compared to the client's criteria along the horizontal axis. Different symbols represent the "degree" of synergy or conflict among the criteria and key factors. For example, a filled in circle = 9, a strong relationship; an empty circle = 3, showing a moderate relationship; a triangle = 1, which signifies a weak relationship. The results of this analysis are useful in evaluating and prioritizing the key external factors. The ability to quantitatively and visually compare and contrast the key external factors is in itself beneficial, enabling an efficient "net assessment" that can be made by quickly "eye-balling" the QFD graphic. But perhaps the greatest value is derived from the process of thinking about and discussing the key external factors, which takes place during their assessment.

Perhaps the leading authority on visualization techniques is Edward Tufte of Yale University. Tufte is the author of three self-published, yet highly successful books (some 460,000 copies in print) on the subject of visualization. Tufte self-published because the established publishing houses were unwilling to depart from conventional book formats. His books are beautifully illustrated and use fine quality paper. Besides the content, what truly sets them apart is the layout of information and the creative use of paper foldouts and insets. Tufte places his footnotes (called sidenotes) alongside the narrative, where they are easily referred to, rather than at the bottom of the page or at the end of the chapter.

In *Visual Explanations* Tufte dramatically demonstrates how analysis, if represented by the right visualizations can lead to increased and more efficient understanding, and ultimately to right decisions. He describes the London cholera epidemic of 1854 and how John Snow, the physician to Queen Victoria was able to perform some excellent medical detective work with the use of a proper visualization. By recasting the original data from their one-dimensional, temporal ordering into a two-dimensional spatial comparison, Snow was able to deduce a connection between the deaths and the proximity of an infected water pump. Basically, he plotted the location of incidents of disease on a top-down map of London. He determined that there was a high correlation of cholera in the proximity of the Broad Street water pump. The role that water played as a carrier of cholera was understood for the first time. Action was taken: The water pump was removed and sanitary guidelines related to the use of other water pumps were given to the populace. From this example, Tufte outlines a clear sequence for the development and utility of visualizations:

- Data to information

- Information to evidence
- Evidence to action

In a very compelling depiction of the Challenger disaster, Tufte takes us through various memos, documents, and official charts and tables that were examined by the rocket manufacturer Thiokol and NASA engineers during the last 12 hours preceding the decision to go on with the launch. He demonstrates that if the analysts from both NASA and Thiokol examined the same narrative and numerical data within the proper visualization context, they could have avoided the tragic explosion. Tufte reveals how one simple graph using data readily at hand could have alerted them to the danger of the O-rings failing at various temperatures.[36]

Much of Tufte's focus is on two fundamental issues: (1) how to present multivariate data in two-dimensional space and (2) that progress and goodness is represented by increased resolution in time and space. In Tufte's words, possibly "the best statistical graphic ever drawn," the map of Napoleon's Russian campaign of 1812, drawn by the French engineer Charles Joseph Minard in 1869, effectively demonstrates these principles. The map (Figure 7-1) displays the relationship between information density and comprehension by capturing six different dimensions of information.

1. It shows the geographical features from France on through into Russia.

2. The French Army's movement is displayed by a band on the map.

3. The width of the band indicates the attrition rate. The size of the army starts with 422,000 men in June 1912 at the Russia-Poland border. In September the band has extended to Moscow. The French retreat begins and the band has narrowed to 100,000 men. By the time the men return to France, the band is a very thin line representing the 10,000 survivors.

4. Along the map is a calendar showing the time corresponding to the movement.

5. Also shown are temperatures of the coldest days during the campaign.

6. Finally, the locations and dates of key battles and actions are high-lighted.

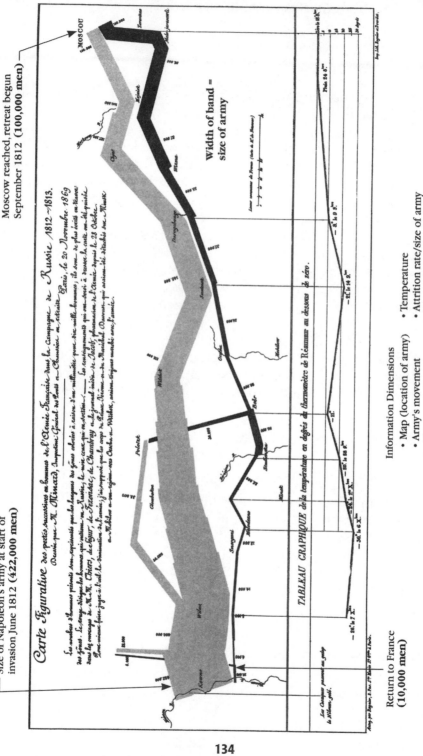

Figure 7-1. Weather defeated Napoleon; Napoleon's invasion of Russia (as mapped by Charles Joseph Minard, 1869).

134

The chart reveals that the greatest attrition rates of the French troops came as a result of extremely frigid weather rather than losses suffered in battle. In other words, Minard's chart shows that it was the weather that defeated Napoleon.

The case studies that follow are meant to acquaint you with the emerging CI field of visualization intelligence (VISINT) and the general principles and consequences concerning the design, editing, analysis, and critique of CI representations. These case studies include the use of visualizations in both a collection program and in several analytical efforts. They also demonstrate computer-generated visualization and the capture and control of the flow of intelligence by incorporating visualization into a war room facility.

Visualization Case Study 1: The Quarterback Technique

The graphics represent the use of visualizations to assist in the planning and implementation of a competitive intelligence collection operation. The first graphic (Figure 5-1 in Chapter 5) illustrates the Quarterback Technique, which enables the systematic and focused collection of intelligence at a conference. It depicts how the collection manager, the quarterback, works with a team of analysts and collectors to brief and debrief sources. Interactions are orchestrated between the sources of intelligence and the targets (those who can answer/address intelligence requirements).

Visualization Case Study 2: Historical Trends Analysis

A client was interested in examining how key industry events and internal company and departmental developments were impacting the company's advertising campaigns. The graphic enabled key industry, corporate, and departmental events, as well as the major advertising campaigns and an assessment of their success, to be juxtaposed with each other within a timeline.

Visualization Case Study 3: Robotics Technology Forecast

A manufacturer desired to invest in robotics technology that would help speed their introduction on the factory floor, but it was difficult to determine which investment would have the greatest impact. Figure 7-2 demonstrates how the robotic system was broken down into its key subsystems, components, and technologies. Each of these

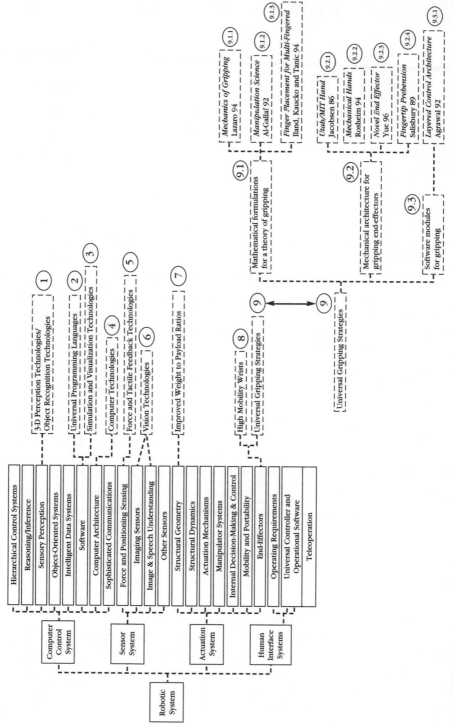

Figure 7-2. Visual representation of a robotics system, broken down into subsystems, components, and technologies.

technologies was further delineated by competitive technologies and their developers. A "delphic" estimate utilizing a group of robotics experts was made on each technology to determine when the specific robotics technology would be introduced without any additional concerted effort, and when it would be possible to speed up its introduction with a focused effort and additional funding. The robotics timeline graphic (Figure 7-3) was designed to enable the manufacturer to see where their investments would have the "biggest bang for the buck." It displays on the top those technologies where significant developmental time (up to 7 years) can be reduced with the manufacturer's assistance. The bottom depicts the technologies where funding would have minimal impact. The chart also shows how early (by what year) the technology can be introduced.

Visualization Case Study 4: Acquisition War Room

The graphic of the Acquisition war room (Figure 7-4) visually depicts the information flow and logic that would be used to assist a team of merger and acquisition specialists and intelligence professionals in selecting and examining prospective companies as acquisition targets. The lower tier captures and maps the acquisition process. The next two tiers above represent the type of intelligence needed to plan the acquisition. WarRoom has incorporated the MoneySoft Lightning Deal Reviewer (hyperlink: www.moneysoft.com) as an excellent software tool to structure and collect essential acquisition information. This serves as the foundation of information for planning and implementing the acquisition intelligence gathering. The next step is to perform in-depth collection from key individuals—as represented by the Quarterback technique—(see Case Study 1). WarRoom has adapted a criminal investigation visualization linking tool named Watson, developed by Harlequin Incorporated (hyper link: www.harlequin.com), to competitive intelligence collection. It enables the graphic linkage between targets and sources, the Quarterback, analysts and collectors, and key events and activities. More in-depth intelligence on the target acquisition is collected and input back into Lightning Deal Reviewer in order to compare the openly available information with the in-depth intelligence. These can be compared and contrasted visually using another software package developed by Jasca Corporation called

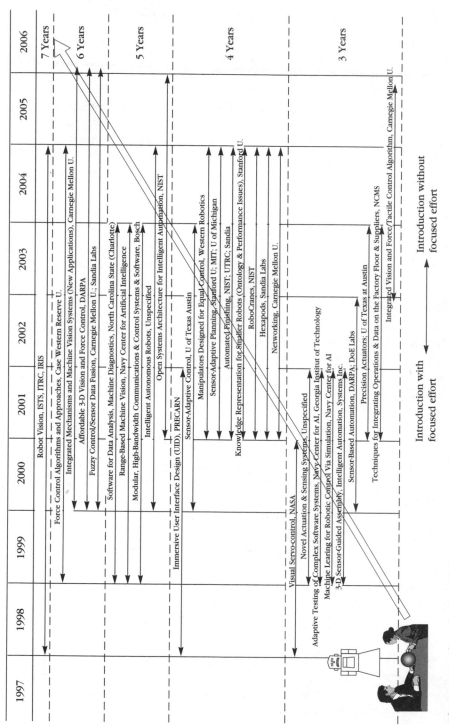

Figure 7-3. The robotics timeline shows graphically where an investment would gain optimal results.

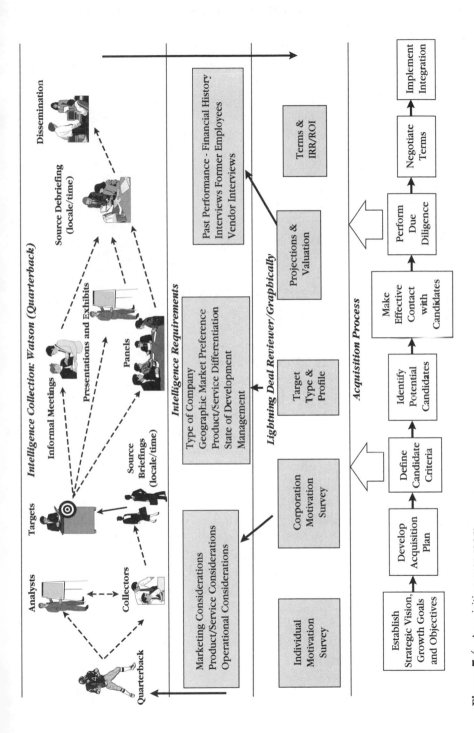

Figure 7-4. Acquisition war room.

139

Graphically!! (hyperlink www.jasca.com). Graphically is optimized to convert business financial data such as that produced by Lightning Deal Reviewer and transform it into vivid visualizations enabling more effective decision-making. Although each tool and activity is useful itself, the synergy derived from their coordination and integration within a war room setting makes them especially valuable as an executive decision-support system.

The second graphic (Figure 7-5) illustrates WarRoom's approach to planning and designing a war room. It demonstrates the multidimensionality of effective graphics by incorporating the logic flow represented by tasking and product output and the timeline for the development of each phase of the effort.

Example of Visualizations Used in Intelligence Analytical Products

Visualizations are effective briefing tools. They also should be integrated within the body of intelligence analysis and reporting. They can create greater interest in the reader, and often can convey information more effectively. In some cases the reader may skim the verbiage but still understand the material quite well because of the accompanying visualization. Following is an example of a report that combines market intelligence and visualizations. It was prepared to support a proposal to a government research funding organization. It had become increasingly important for the government that research it supports find its way into the commercial market. Company B had received an award for a second level of funding for its noise cancellation research. Before the money could be transferred, however, the government officials requested a transition plan showing how the technology would evolve from their funded research and make its way into the market. The report shows the effective use of visualizations to support the narrative used in a market research report, utilizing collected and analyzed intelligence. Blanks have been inserted to sanitize information which may be advantageous to a competitor.

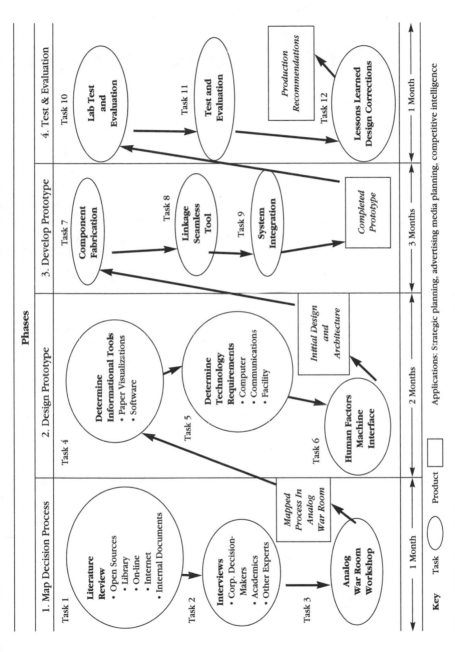

Figure 7-5. Strategic Planning war room—prototype research design.

Phases

| 1. Map Decision Process | 2. Design Prototype | 3. Develop Prototype | 4. Test & Evaluation |

Task 1 — **Literature Review** • Open Sources • Library • On-line • Internet • Internal Documents

Task 2 — **Interviews** • Corp. Decision-Makers • Academics • Other Experts

Task 3 — **Analog War Room Workshop**

Mapped Process In Analog War Room

Task 4 — **Determine Informational Tools** • Paper Visualizations • Software

Task 5 — **Determine Technology Requirements** • Computer • Communications • Facility

Task 6 — **Human Factors Machine Interface**

Initial Design and Architecture

Task 7 — **Component Fabrication**

Task 8 — **Linkage Seamless Tool**

Task 9 — **System Integration**

Completed Prototype

Task 10 — **Lab Test and Evaluation**

Task 11 — **Test and Evaluation**

Task 12 — **Lessons Learned Design Corrections**

Production Recommendations

1 Month — 2 Months — 3 Months — 1 Month

Key ◯ Task ▢ Product

Applications: Strategic planning, advertising media planning, competitive intelligence

141

New Materials and Techniques for Reduction of Noise for Commercialization

1. Summary

Several innovative noise control technologies are derived from this project. These technologies include material for vibration damping, ear-cup design, and electronic noise filtering. Each offers significant near-term and longer-range opportunities. Company B's commercialization strategy for these technologies involves partnering with established companies that are leaders in their respective industries. These companies have the necessary infrastructures and distribution mechanisms to bring new products incorporating the new technology to the market. Initial planning for new product developments that would incorporate the technology developed is under way between Company B and several companies. Company B is aggressively targeting other key applications and potential partners.

2. First Product

Our effort will yield the following potential products by the end of the project:

Improved material with application to soundproofing and vibration damping. _____ and _____ have both committed funds to exploit this new material for their current and future products. NASA has expressed strong interest and immediate need for our material, which can yield improved damping without significant weight increase. Several large ongoing NASA projects have been identified and targeted for use of improved vibration damping means. Beyond these applications, better soundproofing in cars, aircraft, office partitions, etc., would be valuable products.

Improved ear-cup seals which are more comfortable and have superior performance over the state of the art. _____ has already tested our improved ear-cup seal and intends to update some if not all their muffs based on the results of our refinement. They have committed funds for that purpose and have already expended $_____ to upgrade their product line.

Improved electronic noise-filtering module for direct use in Navy aircraft, but also for use in commercial applications such as filtering of road noise picked up by hands-free car phones. The Navy has indicated that they have an immediate Navy application for our work. This technology can significantly enhance their development of a waterproof head-mounted bone-conduction microphone. The microphone works well in picking up speech, but for many applications, the noise picked up by the microphone precludes its use. When combined with our electronic noise filtering, the application domain of the microphone is significantly expanded. The Navy is also working to apply their new waterproof microphone in communication systems for fire fighters. _____, a manufacturer of communications equipment for fire fighters, airline personnel, and other high-noise industrial environments, is also committed to adapting this technology to their product line.

3. Commercialization Strategy

Company B has developed a systematic and rigorous six-step analytical approach to commercialization. This method is depicted in Figure 7-6. First, we perform a _technology assessment_ to determine the feasibility of the technology for specific commercial applications. This incorporates a technology benchmark analysis in which we compare our technology against other competing technologies. We extrapolate the near-, mid-, and long-term benefits of this technology for the particular application. We obtain a collective "Delphi" assessment from technologists within Company B as well as by interviewing leading experts outside the company. When possible, we conduct simulations to determine the

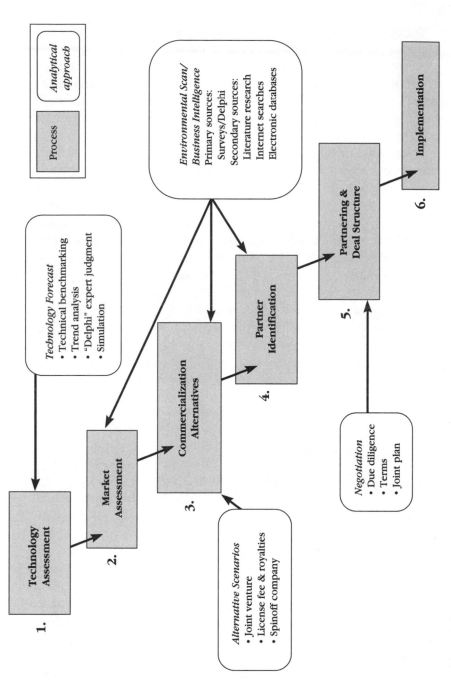

Figure 7-6. The six-step analytical approach to commercialization.

performance capability of the technology for the specific proposed commercial application.

If the technology is determined to be feasible and attractive for commercialization, we then perform a *market assessment*. We employ an environmental scan and business intelligence collection methodology. The *environmental scan* provides a systematic data collection methodology utilizing *primary source* (interviews and surveys) and *secondary source* (literature search, electronic database and Internet data mining) *intelligence gathering* approaches, as well as incorporating some innovative "third wave" techniques. We use a combination of gathering techniques in order to obtain inputs from varied sources. The market assessment determines whether there is an existing market or whether one needs to be created for this technology and application. It evaluates the overall size, competitors, and various market penetration tactics.

If the overall market appears worthwhile, Company B then examines the best commercialization approach for this market and for meeting the overall goals of the company. Options include setting up a joint venture with a partner which is already positioned in the market; obtaining investment to spin off a new company or subsidiary and develop a new infrastructure for product introduction; or licensing the technology for a fee and royalty payments. When the commercialization approach is chosen, Company B performs a systematic search for either the right partner or investor. Once these organizations have been targeted, Company B develops a partnering strategy and initiates discussions, followed by negotiations relating to the deal structure. A joint business, product introduction, and implementation plan is developed between the partners.

Our basic commercialization strategy for this project is based on teaming with partners who have existing products, marketing capability, and a reputation as producer of related products. This approach has worked well for Company B in the past and has resulted in our very successful commercialization of several products. Our environmental scan of leading noise control companies (i.e., Noise Cancellation Technologies, Andrea Electronics, and the French firm TechnoFirst S.A.) has revealed their real profitability has been derived from partnering with companies which wield a lot of weight in their industries. Although each of these companies has introduced a product line on the retail market, their greatest revenue and product innovations came from the partnering arrangements. This approach especially makes sense for competing in the colossal, competitive markets for audio and telecommunications. Therefore, our approach as outlined in this document is to strategically align ourselves with well-established companies which can more effectively take our technology to market.

4. The Noise Control Market

For many people, noise from aircraft, automobiles, construction, machinery, and a variety of other sources is a constant source of torment. The U.S. Congress passed the Quiet Communities Act of 1997 (H.R. 536), which stated that nearly 20,000,000 Americans are exposed to noise levels that can lead to psychological and physiological damage, and another 40,000,000 people are exposed to noise levels that cause sleep or work disruption. Noise pollution can be extremely harmful to business productivity, causing breakdowns in computer audio applications such as speech dictation, video conferencing, Internet telephony, and computer telephony integration. The ability to control vibration and noise will become even more important as speech processing becomes an increasing part of our lives. Nicholas Negroponte, founder and director of the Massachusetts Institute of Technology's Media Laboratory, senior columnist at *Wired* magazine, and author of *Being Digital,* views the business of noise cancellation as one of the big growth areas.

The *Yahoo* search engine listing of noise control companies contains 27 substantial companies which feature a major product focus or orientation around passive or active noise reduction. In addition to these companies, a number of major corporations have divisions or units which specialize in noise control technologies. Noise and vibration control consists of a very large range and diverse group of products, needs, and opportunities. Products derived from the noise and vibration technologies being developed in the Phase 2 effort can penetrate several distinct market niches, including (1) material for vibration damping, (2) ear-cup design, and (3) electronic noise filtering.

The promoters of the SpeechTEK '98 conference, Comtek International, have estimated the value of the 1997 speech recognition market at $500 million. Rob Enderle, senior analyst at Giga Information Group in Cambridge, MA, has estimated this market to be about $1 billion in 2000. Another estimate is that approximately 10 percent (or $50 million for 1997, $100 million for 2000) of the speech recognition market is focused on noise cancellation. This market, however, is rapidly growing with the overall expansion in hands-free communications and voice-actuated systems. From speech on the Internet and in call centers to voice-activated stock transactions and automatic transcription of complex medical and legal reports, speech technology is become fully integrated with common business transactions. Speech-to-text dictation systems are now available in computer retail outlets for as little as $90. The ability to process spoken input by interactive voice response telephone systems is becoming commonplace, and organizations like Chase Manhattan Bank, UPS, and United Airlines are finding new, creative, and cost-effective uses for speech recognition, speaker verification, and speech synthesis. *BusinessWeek* stated that this market beyond 2000 could be astronomic.[37]

The global market for hearing protection is $560 million, of which $241 million per year is for protective ear muffs. The U.S. market is $200 million for hearing protection, of which $37 million goes for muffs. This is a market in which our strategic partner, _____, already has a significant market share and presence. _____ is an operating unit of the _____. _____ has annual sales of approximately $____ million.

5. Company B Strategy and Tactics for Penetrating the Noise Control Market

Company B has developed an initial strategy to guide the commercialization actions needed to successfully transition the noise control technologies from the government funding to penetration in the marketplace. This transition process is displayed in the visualization shown in Figure 7-7. Naval aviation will be the primary initial customer for the Phase 2 technology, which will be customized to meet Navy aircraft. The visualization shows that the technology developed for the Naval Aviation ear cups at the end of this project would be transferred into three near-term products.

Improved Ear-Cup Seals

The most immediate transfer would be to take the ear-cup design developed for Naval Aviation and apply it to the commercial ear-cup market. _____ has already spent $100,000 and has committed to expending $200,000 during this phase to participate in and to evaluate the results of our work, and then incorporate these into their product line. _____ already has a significant share of the world market in hearing protection earmuffs, so they are an ideal partner to commercialize the new design. Ear cups utilizing some of our design features can be in the marketplace within one year of the start of this phase.

Improved Material

The new material used for the Naval Aviation ear cups is also of significant interest to _____: They have already spent $_____ evaluating and using the new material. They have committed funds as enumerated below for evaluation and use of the results of the subject work. It could be a very smooth transfer of material technology for their commercial ear cups, enabling the new material to be in the product line within two to three years of the start of this phase.

The material is of significant interest to _____ for vibration control in their precision instruments. They have already committed funds for use of the new material as enumerated earlier. Initial precision instruments utilizing the new material could be on the market within two to four years from the onset of this phase. Subject to good test results, _____ has also expressed interest in helping us apply

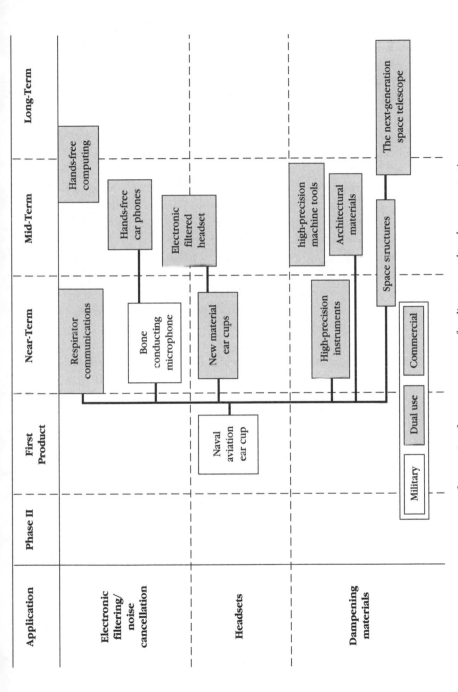

Figure 7-7. A transition process for moving from government funding to marketplace penetration.

the new material to applications beyond their own current product line of precision instruments.

Several large projects of NASA have immediate need for improved damping and sound absorption materials as detailed in the enclosed letter from NASA. These are long developmental programs, such as the Next Generation Space Telescope, which is projected for deployment in 2007. Initial material prototype testing would occur almost immediately.

For the mid to long range (near term is 1 to 3 years; mid is 4 to 7 years; long range is 8+ years) there are a number of other attractive applications for the new material. This includes use in building materials and architectural designs for office and plant noise control, use by automobile and aircraft manufacturers for vehicle quieting, and use in the next generation of precision machine tools and lithography machines. Company B is in the process now of identifying and networking with companies operating in these arenas, to pursue possible partnerships. An example is our preliminary discussions with _____, which is interested in the application of the material to control vibrations for their next generation of precision machine tools.

Electronic Noise Filtering

The initial near-term electronic noise filtering opportunities relate to their incorporation in respirator communication systems developed by _____ for fire fighters, airline personnel, and other industrial areas associated with noise. _____ has already furnished Company B with fire-fighting self-contained breathing apparatus (SCBA) to facilitate initial testing. It is possible that their next generation of SCBA respirator communications equipment can feature our electronic noise filtering technology within two to four years.

The other near-term application for our electronic noise filtering is to support the Navy by using our electronic filtering hardware in conjunction with their waterproof microphone. This technology may be retrofitted with existing systems. We are also exploring partnering for the next systems being developed for fire fighters.

A near- to mid-term opportunity exists in the penetration of the speech/voice recognition market described earlier. Maintenance systems are now using voice-understanding technology to allow technicians to control test equipment and record test results using audio alone, with direct computer transcription. These systems, however, do not work well in noisy environments. When combined with our work, we can achieve good speech understanding even in noisy environments. We have already done preliminary tests of this application. _____ has committed $_____ to commercialization of our electronic noise filtering, which would be directed at this application. The longer-range extension of this market niche is for hands-free computing. This involves verbal commands for all common computer functions. In order to facilitate this opportunity, Company B is pursuing discussions with some major information technology corporations.

By far the largest commercial market for our noise reduction algorithms is for improved hands-free systems for car phones. Although the technology can be available for near-term opportunities, we realize that it is very difficult and may take several years to position and partner ourselves in this very competitive, difficult market.

6. Competitors and Advantages

Although there are numerous players engaged in the diverse areas of noise control, our environmental scan has identified three primary competitors. These include Noise Cancellation Technologies, Inc. (NCT), of Stanford, CT; Andrea Electronics Corp. of Long Island City, NY; and TechnoFirst S.A. of Marseille, France.

NCT designs electronic systems that reduce noise and vibration. The company's systems are designed for integration into a wide range of products in the transportation, manufacturing, consumer products, and medical equipment industries. NCT is currently marketing seven products, including the NoiseBuster consumer headset, an aviation headset for pilots, an industrial muffler for use with large vacuums and blowers, headsets for patient use in MRI systems, and headsets to reduce siren noise in emergency vehicles. NCT had sales of $5.7 million in 1997 and a one-year sales growth of 78.1 percent.

NCT is in transition from a firm which focused primarily on research and development to one concentrating on commercializing its technologies. The company has experienced financial difficulties, but starting in 1995 it got back on track with a change in partnering and internal management. NCT took four product partnerships off its balance sheet, transferring ownership of the joint ventures to its partners and agreeing to take only royalties on sales involving its technology. NCT's latest partnership is with Automotive Systems Group of Johnson Controls in Milwaukee to develop an alternative speaker system for car audio. NCT signed an agreement in March 1998 to have Lewis N. Clark, a leading travel accessories supplier, distribute its NoiseBuster Extreme! headphones. Airline passengers are a major market for this product.

Andrea Electronics Corporation had revenue of $26 million in 1997. Their Active Noise Cancellation Division accounted for about $5 million. This division, formed in 1993, manufactures active noise cancellation, microphone systems, and headsets. Sales are expected to increase dramatically as a result of their recent partnering. Andrea recently signed sales agreements for its two retail headset packages with two leading U.S. computer supply retail superstores, Computer City and Micro Center. Also recently, Andrea announced that its PC headsets would be bundled and sold with IBM's *World Book 1998* Deluxe Speech Edition. This is an interactive encyclopedia that allows users to look up information by speaking and listening to their computers. Other Andrea OEM and software partners include Microsoft, IBM, Lernout & Hauspie Speech Products, Dragon Systems, NEC, Mpath, Multitude, IDT, HyperGraphics, and ILINC.

The French company TechnoFirst has significant potential in penetrating the U.S. and world markets. The company was founded in 1990 as a spinoff from the *Laboratorie de Mecanique et d'Acoustique,* CNRS in Marseille. TechnoFirst has a product line of headsets with active noise cancellation. Revenues in 1996 exceeded $20 million. TechnoFirst has a partnership with

Dassault Electronique for the ANCAS active seat for noise reduction in airplanes. The have partnered with Aldes Aeraulique for the active muffler for ventilation and air-conditioning network; with Saint Gobain Vitrage for active double-glazing window; with E.D.F.-G.D.F for gas leakage localization in noisy environments; with Sagem for an industrial active headset; with Intertechnique for the active headset used in the Rafale fighter; with GIAT Industries for the active headset used on the Leclerc tank; and with D.C.N. to supply active headsets for the French Navy.

These and other companies provide for a very competitive environment. We believe that we offer superior technology. The new material will be lighter and have improved noise attenuation properties over the current material used by our competitors. Our ear-cup seals will perform better and be more comfortable than other designs. Our electronic noise filtering will have superior performance to other approaches, especially in increasing intelligibility.

Better technology and products do not guarantee commercial success. Ultimately, forming key partnerships with the right companies will lead to successful product introduction and endurance for the long term. One validation of the potential value of our work for hearing protection is that _____, which is a world leader in hearing protection, has already spent $_____ on the new material and has committed funds both during and after this phase to participate with Company B and _____, and then to help market the results. As a metric on the focus of _____, they sell an amazing 100 million sets of passive hearing protection plugs per year, plus many other related products, such as hearing protection earmuffs.

7. Money Requirements

Company B will not need any additional money to bring the product to market. The results of this work will be optimized for Naval aviation but will otherwise be near a commercial product. The commitment from _____ to provide $_____ to evaluate the new material and to apply the material to their product line will provide the funds to develop products in the vibration damping application arena. _____ has also expressed interest in "supplying additional resources" to work with Company B to apply the material and technology to new products in the vibration damping area. _____ will market our results for hearing-related products and has already committed to provide $_____ during this phase and $_____ after this phase to do the required product tuning and then marketing of the new products. NASA will provide the funds necessary to use the new material in their programs once the new material can be reduced in weight and fully tested for its vibration damping capability.

8. Marketing Expertise

Company B does not envision directly marketing the products developed from the subject work. We have been very successful in commercializing the results of government contracts, and in each case we have teamed with a company which already has products and a marketing and service force in the particular area. This is the same approach we are taking with our development of improved passive hearing protection systems in our collaboration with _____ and with _____ to exploit the new material for vibration damping.

Summary

Visualization has become an essential tool for scientists seeking to understand and convey complex dynamics and processes. This emerging discipline, combining both science and art, is just beginning to make its mark in the business world. As this chapter demonstrates, "VISINT" can be an important asset to the intelligence analyst in understanding and disseminating intelligence. The proper visualization techniques can also aid the collector in planning and managing his operations. The noise cancellation case study demonstrates that visualizations can effectively augment and enhance what is provided in a written report.

In some situations, a visualization by itself may be the most effective way to disseminate intelligence, without the need to include accompanying narrative. As a weather forecaster may rely on a weather map to detect trends without the need for excess verbiage, so may an intelligence professional or decision-maker, who is familiar with reviewing a specific type of visualization, best be served by only reviewing the visualization. This may be particularly true in some very time-sensitive situations. The narrative can be provided as background information, when the time is available to review it. We believe as intelligence becomes more systematic, focused, and utilized, visualizations will proliferate within the organization.

8

War Room Design

As stated earlier, maximizing the flow and control of information is key to competitiveness, whether it be on the battlefield, on the campaign trail, or in the marketplace. An innovative tool and approach to planning and managing information and intelligence in these very intense, time-sensitive environments is the war room.

A war room is a very focused, intense effort to organize complex programs, to develop program and strategic plans, and to visualize and assimilate data and linkages between information that impact multidimensional plans. The war room enables a collaborative team to break down complex programs and information processes into comprehensible parts, to promote structured dialogue and brainstorming, to comprehend program intricacies, and to establish program concepts quickly. WarRoom Research has developed war rooms for a number of business applications, including strategic planning, competitive intelligence, mergers and acquisitions, new product development, and media campaigns.

War rooms can vary from glitzy hi-tech rooms in which computer generated information is conveyed through high-resolution displays to a low-tech approach utilizing foam boards or magnetic white boards. Regardless of the level of technology used, there are several key attributes that transform a conference room into a highly effective war room optimized to support team-based decision-making. All war rooms should incorporate the following capabilities or features:

- To capture and map process logic flow
- A high degree of information density

- A lot of dimensionality
- To facilitate team-based thinking and decision-making
- Utility as an advocacy tool
- To track, monitor and anticipate events
- To proactively delineate courses of action
- To assign responsibility and accountability
- Effective security safeguards

War room location and dimensions are very important, since they impact accessibility by the decision-making team, upper management, and others within the company whose interest and participation is sought. This impacts the overall utility of the war room. Ideally, it should be collocated with the CI or planning group that is overseeing the specific application of the war room. It should be large enough to support the number of planning sessions and participants anticipated. It needs to be of useful size not only for planning but also for monitoring the status of the program and related efforts. It also serves as an advocacy tool for selling the program to upper management. A conference table should be located in the room. The table is needed in the room for staging the information intended to go on the walls. Sufficient space must be provided to enable the manager or team members of the effort to walk other managers around the room, explain certain facets, and gather their input. Locating the room on an inside wall has the advantage of not wasting display space to windows and also reduces the security threat that your planning will be compromised to competitors.

The war room can be located within a fixed, dedicated site in which the structure can be altered and modified. There is, however, great value in being able to quickly put up and disassemble the war room. Making it portable, with modular components which are easy to move, allows the information to be presented in other locales and to groups that cannot get to the fixed site. For example, the war room could be quickly relocated to the CEO's boardroom for a special briefing. Making it modular also enables multiple war rooms to be in use, and affords the capability to take down one within minutes and replace it with another. For example, the marketing war room can be in use and then replaced with a mergers and acquisitions war room to accommodate the intelligence and planning needs for the M&A group within the corporation.

There are several approaches to developing a low cost *analog* war room framework. In all of them the war room walls are organized into sections and panels. In a fixed site, bulletin boards for affixing paper information or magnetic boards for attaching magnetic-backed information can be used. The preferred approach for both fixed and mobile analog war rooms is the use of foam boards. The panels consist of very light foam boards which are available from many office supply mail-order companies. The foam boards can be attached to the walls using Velcro snaps or attached from the ceiling with paperclips.

The first and most important step in developing a war room is to capture and then map information flow, the process through which the functions and activities are to be carried out, and the specific tasks that will need to be performed. This is accomplished by displaying this information flow within a war room framework.

Typically, a core team develops the first "straw man" logic flow for the war room. They may have used input from a combination of primary and secondary sources, including a literature review, an Internet search, and surveys and interviews with corporate officials and outside experts.

After this initial process is mapped out on the walls of the room, other knowledgeable people and experts are invited and "walked" through the room. Their advice on correcting specific logic train flaws and enhancing the process can be easily captured and then displayed in the room. After obtaining the input from many knowledgeable sources, the end result is a very robust war room, reflecting a clear and logical information process. This in essence becomes the analog war room, and it in itself can suffice for many applications and uses.

The next phase of the development involves the infusion of information technology into the war room facility. This involves the selection of specific tools, hardware, and software which transforms the information flow captured on paper and displayed on the walls of the analog war room into digital format, thus creating the *digital* war room. The basic approach is to use off-the-shelf software tools that are then integrated together using an open-architecture approach. This allows the user to choose the specific tools that are needed as well as to upgrade or change these tools as the "state of the art" advances. The tools selected will perform such tasks as automated text retrieval, data mining, decision modeling, data visualization, and data storage and linking. The best war rooms are in fact hybrids, integrating the use of some static boards with some computer-generated information. The war room developmental process is depicted in Figure 7-5.

The war room provides a format for individuals within the team to follow the whole process and logic train. It enables the linking of myriad data sets depicting a complex program or process. Senior executives and middle management often find it difficult to easily articulate plans and generate support from upper management and colleagues in other departments. The war room provides a solution to this information glut and visualization problem. It can help break down complex strategic planning, competitive intelligence, and other business processes, approaches, and planning into comprehensible parts. It can promote structured dialoguing and brainstorming. The most significant benefit of the war room is that the entire thought process of a major program or project can be put in context.

The war room enables the professional to "walk" other senior managers through the war room, and this process, facilitating their comprehension of the program's "web" of intricacies, helps to quickly establish program concepts. It also enables the staff to monitor and track activity on a real-time basis and to determine measures of performance.

Multimedia rooms permit glittery presentations, but they neglect to incorporate a process to facilitate effective decision-making. Traditional command and control rooms focus on communications but also fail to incorporate an overall decision-making process or provide decision-support tools. Preferable to traditional boardrooms and conference rooms are highly effective decision-making war rooms.

The following case studies provide a description of the design and application of various types of war rooms developed for a number of different situations. They incorporate a cross section of war rooms representing a diverse array of companies, industries, and applications. The war rooms either were used to facilitate the development and implementation of a CI program or activity or were involved in other key management activities in which CI played a very important role or was an essential component. Since these examples come from real life, to safeguard the sensitivity of the information and the anonymity of our clients, the information is kept general. In some cases it has been slightly altered to prevent association with any actual person or organization.

War Room Case Study 1: Competitive Intelligence Program War Room

Only a few years old, a software company had established itself as a major niche player. Their success, however, was being emulated by several other start-ups. A couple of very large software companies were also threatening to enter their niche. The CEO wanted to establish a formalized program to monitor the competition. A competitive intelligence professional was recruited to develop a CI program. He, in turn, chose a war room framework as the structure and model on which to build their program.

WarRoom worked with a team of five individuals over a two-day period to set up the war room architecture. In addition to the CI director, the team consisted of a market researcher, librarian, and two marketing representatives. There was no fully assigned CI staff, but it was assumed that these individuals would devote part of their work to performing CI functions until they or someone else was officially assigned to the CI director.

A small conference room was selected which was in close proximity (on the same floor and wing) to the CI director's office. It was also one floor below the CEO, the VP for strategic planning, and other key management. It was a room of about 20 by 20 feet, and it had a rectangular table in the middle that would seat ten. The room was windowless, which was fine for security purposes. A cipher lock had been installed to limit access into the room. Approximately a dozen foam boards (each about 6 by 4 feet) were laid out leaning against the walls of the room, encircling the table and the team. A PC and color printer was set up on the table. Also on the table in front of each chair was a notebook computer. These were linked to the PC via a groupware program. Glue sticks, various colors of tape, and other graphics materials were placed on the table. A removable type of glue stick was chosen so that information could be easily added or removed without damaging the foam boards. An Ibid electronic whiteboard was placed near the end of the table. This allowed what was written on the board, using various colors, to be saved on the computer and then printed out.

Two WarRoom staff assisted the CI director and the team in facilitating development of the war room. The intent was to use the war room to define and describe the initial structure of the CI program, to lay out plans, and to monitor activity. It was also to be used as an advocacy tool within the company to educate other company officials as to the purpose of the CI program and to gain their support and involvement.

The first step for each participant was to type a paragraph on their vision for the CI organization, which served the same purpose as a mission statement. The team reviewed the various inputs and then consolidated them into one statement which the group was comfortable with. The vision statement read:

> The CI department will provide senior corporate decision-makers with intelligence on the actions and behavior, capabilities and intentions of the company's competitors. It will also provide knowledge on other factors in the environment which can significantly impact business. Intelligence will be disseminated in an ongoing, systematic fashion to facilitate effective and proactive decision-making. CI department, personnel and consultants will abide by all legal and corporate ethical standards.

This statement was printed out and placed on the foam board with the glue stick. It was located at the top of one of the foam boards with the heading VISION. Underneath the vision/mission statement was glued the heading GOALS. Each member selected five major goals for the CI group. Using the groupware, these goals were combined and synthesized, and redundant goals were eliminated. The team then prioritized the goals, and those selected were placed under the heading. Several of the goals selected were:

- Create an organization that responds to both the strategic and tactical intelligence needs of corporate decision-makers.

- Foster involvement from individuals throughout the corporation, including support for both the provision as well as the consuming of intelligence.

- Establish a highly efficient mechanism in which to collect, analyze, and disseminate intelligence.

- Coordinate activity with corporate security so that sensitive intelligence is safeguarded and competitor CI efforts are monitored and minimized.

Each goal had a different colored dot placed in front of the narrative. On the top of a second foam board was the heading OBJECTIVES. Underneath this was a listing of actions and activities that were required to achieve the goals. Objectives were linked to specific goals by matching the color used for the goal. Several objectives were linked to more than one goal, so they had several colored dots. Examples of objectives included:

- Interview key decision-makers to determine their intelligence needs.

- Develop an extensive internal and external source network in which to gather intelligence.

- Develop an "open source" intelligence program in which to review periodicals, Internet Web sites, and various on-line databases.

- Develop an intranet CI function.

Finally, at the bottom of the second board were listed PERFORMANCE MEASUREMENTS. These were milestones or quantitative ways to evaluate the progress being made in accomplishing the objectives. They also were linked by colored dots. Examples of performance measurements included:

- Interview all company officers, vice presidents, and directors by a certain date (within first month of operations).

- Establish a list of ten prioritized intelligence requirements, which will be updated as requirements are answered and new needs are identified.

- Incorporate the CI function within the executive information system (EIS) on the corporate intranet within the first month of operation.

- Develop a mechanism to produce intelligence alerts on a daily basis and periodic analytical studies on a monthly basis, or timed to support major decisions.

■ Recruit and hire two analysts and two collectors by a specified date to work full-time for the CI director. Identify CI part-time support staff from other key organizations, including strategic planning, marketing, R&D, public relations, and security.

The boards containing the formalized articulation of vision, goals, objectives, and performance measures were placed on the wall (actually hung from the ceiling right next to the wall using paper clips). It was the first information a person would see upon entering the room. This served to describe the purpose and function of both the room and the CI program.

The next step of the group was to capture and lay out the CI process. Using groupware as well as the Ibid board, each team member developed what she or he thought was a logical intelligence process and flow of information. Each person's layout was discussed and then integrated. A final process and logic flow for the intelligence program was selected. The process was:

■ *Requirements:* Identification of the specific intelligence needs of the company's senior management to support important decision-making.

■ *Targets:* Those individuals or organizations which can address or answer the requirements.

■ *Collection opportunities:* The tactics used to gain access to these targets.

■ *Sources:* Those individuals within the company (internal) or outside the company (external) who can gain access to the targets.

■ *Intelligence reporting:* The written reports describing intelligence gained from the interaction between the source and target.

■ *Analysis:* A method or approach to further refine the collected intelligence to make it more meaningful in responding to a requirement.

■ *Dissemination:* To whom and how the intelligence was to be disseminated, to ensure that the individuals who needed it obtained it in a timely fashion to support their decision-making.

■ *Feedback:* The additional questions raised as a result of this intelligence. Good intelligence always leads to additional questions and requirements. This is feedback into the requirements section.

Each of these was placed as a heading on a separate foam board. (Figure 8-1 displays the logic flow and process for the CI program war room.)

The information needed to flesh out these boards required a number of interviews and meetings. Using the groupware, an initial "straw man" listing for many of these categories was developed by the team (see Figure 8-2). The lists were printed out, affixed to the boards using the glue stick, and the boards hung around the walls in proper sequence. The narratives also used color-coded dots so they could be linked back to requirements, objectives, and goals. The CI director described his understanding of some of the key issues, concerns, and requirements that he had derived from the CEO and other key officers. The team members added a few other requirements, and an initial "straw man" list was generated. These included:

- Competitor plans for new software products, including technology, schedule, and marketing strategy.
- Alliances and joint ventures with computer hardware manufacturers and other software vendors.
- Distribution arrangements with major retailers.
- Plans for foreign distribution and special modifications and features to customize the product for foreign markets.

After the requirements were generated, the team began to identify which individuals could possibly address or answer these requirements. In most cases these were key managers in the competitor's company. Using the groupware, specific names were listed, when possible, or at least the appropriate positions or titles. The team was only able to identify two targets for one of the requirements. The other requirements had from five to ten targets. After listing the targets, the team brainstormed creative ways to gain access to the targets. Postulated approaches ranged from placing a direct call to the target on the phone to using a journalist to ask certain questions and getting a vendor or retailer to act as a source. Other options included using a consultant to send a survey and running a Quarterback at a conference. Specific events and activities were recorded when possible. These included selecting an upcoming conference and naming a friend who was a writer for a trade journal.

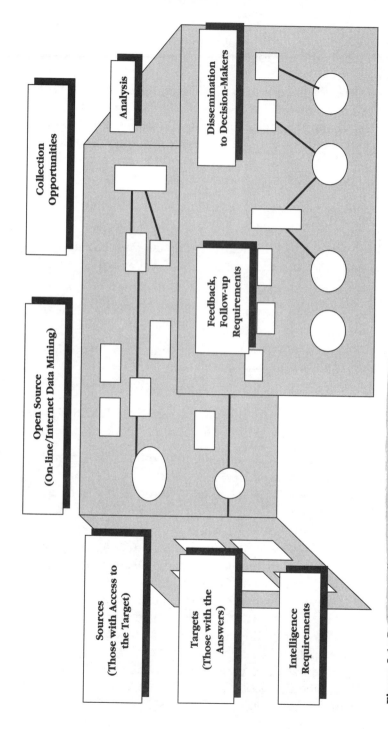

Figure 8-1. Business intelligence war room—the process and logic flow.

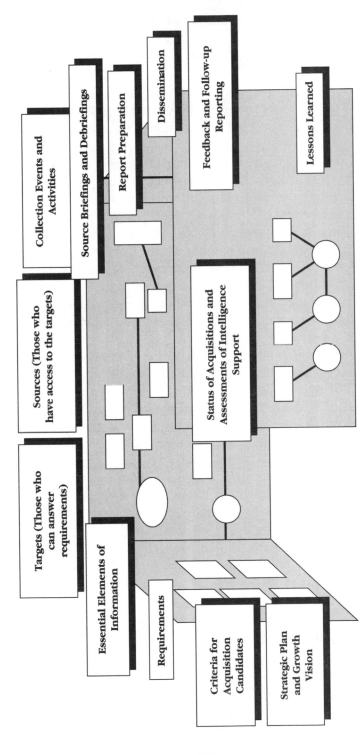

Figure 8-2. Acquisition intelligence war room—a "straw man," or generic, process and logic flow.

The team began to identify possible sources within the company who might have direct access to a target or had a friend or contact who possibly could gain access to a target. Individuals nominated as sources included those involved in professional organizations in which the competitors were also active. Other candidates included a person who was an alumni of the same university as the target. It was understood that these were only suggestions and that no one individual would be pressured to be a source who was not really interested.

Since no actual reporting had occurred during this initial war room design phase, the rest of the boards remained blank except for their headings. They were, however, placed hanging from the ceiling in their proper locations. It was midway through the second day, and the CEO and several key managers where brought in one at a time to look at the war room. The CEO was quite happy with the progress, and had a number of recommendations for requirements, targets, and sources. He also included names of individuals who should receive the intelligence reports. After each recommendation was made, a yellow self-stick removable note was placed on the appropriate location on the foam board. Later, new verbiage would be printed out and placed on the board. After the CEO came the VP for strategic planning. She too had some important inputs, as did the other senior managers who were "walked through the war room." All of these inputs were integrated into the narrative and framework of the war room.

The CI director was quite pleased with the process and the war room. He had put in place an actionable plan in which he and his team could pace their activities and monitor their progress. He also had an effective tool with which to win support and involvement among other managers in the company.

Since the development of the initial war room layout, some computerized tools have been integrated into the framework of the room. The room has also been refined and enhanced, and utilizes better graphics and visualizations. It remains the hub of all CI activity.

War Room Case Study 2: Quarterback Operation War Room

A pharmaceutical firm that offered the only drug treatment for a particular ailment was concerned that a competitor was working on an alternative drug targeted against the same malady. A decision was made that a Quarterback operation should be mounted to obtain information on the competitor's plans and intentions. A conference was selected that offered numerous opportunities for interaction with the competitor's managers, as well as with doctors, government officials, journalists, and industry observers, many of whom could serve as sources. Three months before the conference, a war room was set up to plan the Quarterback operation. A quarterback was selected by the CI manager. The quarterback had significant analytical and collection experience and was an effective manager. Those responsible for planning and implementing the Quarterback operation included the quarterback, one analyst, two collectors, and two WarRoom consultants. WarRoom was engaged throughout the Quarterback operation. It was the expectation that being on hand to help facilitate the first Quarterback would enable the firm to implement subsequent Quarterback operations on their own.

The Quarterback team assembled to construct a portable war room. Portability was essential since the same configuration being set up to plan the Quarterback would be used in a hotel suite at the site of the conference. There it would be used to implement actions and monitor developments.

Foam boards approximately 5 by 4 feet were placed on six wooden easels. The logic flow was similar to that of the CI project war room. Foam board headings included:

- *Requirements:* The specific intelligence needs desired from the conference.
- *Targets:* Those individuals at the conference who could address or answer the requirements.
- *Sources:* Those individuals which the Quarterback team would use to approach and elicit information from the targets.
- *Collection events/interactions:* The particular informal or formal activity in which the source can interact with the target.
- *Briefing/debriefing:* The collector would brief the source about the requirements, approach, and elicitation techniques prior to the target interaction and debrief them afterwards as to intelligence obtained and how the approach and elicitation technique went.

- *Dissemination:* Getting intelligence to the analysts and decision-makers at the conference or relaying it back to corporate head-quarters.

- *Feedback:* Obtaining follow-up questions and other intelligence needs to enable the sources to interact again with a target during the conference.

The team was able to interview the strategic planner, head of R&D, and VP for new product development. Through these interviews, the team was able to develop essential elements of information (EEIs). The EEIs amplified on the overall requirement regarding the competitor's plans and intentions on introducing the new drug. The EEIs served as the conference requirements. These included finding out the status, testing, and evaluation by the FDA; reviews by foreign government drug regulators; schedule and quantities projected; and pricing strategy.

Since this was a really focused collection effort, the team had little difficulty in identifying the targets of opportunity who could address the requirements and EEIs. Since several of the company's executives were active in the association putting on the conference, they were able to get last year's conference proceedings, as well as a list of planned speakers and those attendees who signed up in advance to obtain a reduced admission rate. The likely targets were placed on the TARGETS foam board. One of the conference sessions provided an ideal setting to raise some of the questions from people in the audience. The team orchestrated the removal of a colleague, with his consent, who was scheduled to give a talk. He, in turn, recommended to the conference planners that they invite a leading scientist who just happened to be with the competitor and was working on the suspect drug.

The team questioned those who had attended last year's conference to see if they were going this year. They also asked those individuals if they knew of anyone else going to the conference from the company and if they had any good friends or colleagues from outside the company who were planning to attend. Those who were going to the conference were queried about their willingness to serve as sources. They were also interviewed to find out if they had access to the targets and what possible connections and common interests they may have with the target that would help them gain access.

Approximately ten sources within the company were identified as strong and willing sources. These individuals were placed on the SOURCE board. Color tags linked the sources to the targets and the targets to the requirements/EEIs. A list of external sources was identified, consultants and individuals outside the company, in whose involvement the company sources and Quarterback team were confident. These were also placed on the SOURCE board.

The Quarterback team reviewed the formal and informal activities that were planned for the conference. There were four different talks and two panel sessions in which targets were participating. The team assigned internal and external sources to attend these talks. The phrasing of certain questions that could be asked by a session attendee without drawing too much attention to their true purpose was developed and practiced. Which sources would be best to ask a particular question was also worked out. Cocktail parties, exhibits, and parties hosted by companies were also considered, and likely targets and sources were identified and tactics developed and practiced for those opportunities. The appropriate event and tactic was placed on the COLLECTIONS EVENT/INTERACTION board. These were also color-coded, tied to the appropriate source, and could be linked all the way back to a specific EEI.

Starting several weeks before the conference, internal sources were briefed as to their requirements/EEIs and trained in elicitation skills. An elicitation approach was developed and practiced for each planned interaction between the source and target. A similar although lesser degree of preparation was performed with each external source. The status of their briefing preparation was maintained on the BRIEFING/DEBRIEFING board.

Two days prior to the conference, the Quarterback team arrived at the conference location and set up operations in a hotel located across the street. Care was taken to ensure that their suite was not next to the competitor's or to another active participant in the conference. The boards had been shipped a few days ahead of time and were awaiting the Quarterback team when they arrived. Easels were rented from the hotel for use in the suite. The boards were arranged in logical sequence on the easels. When a maid or pizza delivery person came to the room, the boards were quickly turned around. On the back side were architectural drawings to avoid arousing any suspicion. The team also brought notebook computers (with e-mail and Internet connection), a portable printer, digital cameras, tape recorders, and palm pilots.

The day before the conference, the team got the lay of the land, exploring the various hotel conference venues and the locations of nearby restaurants, bars, and coffee houses. They also had last-minute briefings with selected sources. The quarterback also used the war room suite as his hotel room. Other team members got rooms in the same hotel. There was at least one person in the war room at all times.

As the conference commenced the war room served as a command and control room, with the quarterback orchestrating the various interactions and intelligence-gathering activities. Sources were briefed prior to their target's talk or interaction. A few briefings took place within the war room, but most, including all external source briefings, took place at other locations. Many were in the open, but in environments where they could not easily be heard without the listener being noticed. The collectors and the war room staff had cellular phones. They communicated and coordinated schedules of interactions and conference activities with the quarterback. The analyst assisted the quarterback in managing some of the information, debriefing some of the sources, providing some follow-up questions, and preparing the reports that were e-mailed to headquarters.

After the event or interaction, the source met with a collector. The source was debriefed, in some cases using a micro tape recorder. In a few situations, the source and collector communicated the results by cell phone back to the war room. Several times, they actually met back at the war room. On most occasions the collector took notes about what was learned and then went back to the war room to give his report. Digital snapshots were taken of exhibit booths, viewgraph presentations, and speakers that related to the EEIs. These were transmitted to one of the notebook computers and then e-mailed back to headquarters.

Fewer than half of the interactions produced any useful intelligence, but those that did were extremely valuable. Intelligence that answered some of the requirements/EEIs was glue-sticked onto the boards. Some of these were converted into reports that were e-mailed back to headquarters to be reviewed by other analysts and managers. Follow-up questions were raised. Through the boards, the quarterback was able to monitor and track upcoming events and the locations of targets and sources. He was able to orchestrate opportunities where the source could run into the target again or for an approach to be made by another source. A very hectic pace was maintained throughout the conference. Sources were briefed and debriefed during the day's formal activities, as well as during the evening dinner, receptions, and parties. Reports were written and disseminated at all hours.

The conference came to a close, and the following day the Quarterback team held an "after-action" and "lessons learned" meeting in the war room. They determined that about 75 percent of their requirements/EEIs were answered. They knew when the competitor was expecting FDA approval, the dimensions and equipment in the drug production facility, expected quantity, how the drug was being marketed overseas, and they had a good sense of what the pricing strategy would be. This information was essential in developing their own marketing strategy to counter the competitor's moves. There were plenty of mistakes made during the conference and plenty of room for improvement. These were recorded and used in the training and preparation for the next Quarterback. Figure 8-3 displays the portable Quarterback war room layout.

War Room Case Study 3: Strategy Planning War Room

A defense contractor that had depended solely on the Navy to provide contracts for its undersea warfare-related technology found the end of the Cold War to be very bad for business. The defense budget was being cut drastically, and the particular area hit hardest was undersea warfare. The Russian submarine threat was nothing like it had been under the Soviets. The "new world order" left little room for undersea threats or responses. The company realized that they had to break into a new customer base and provide some innovative products and services. Such new offerings, however, had to be an outgrowth of their capabilities and competencies. They realized that they needed to develop a strategic plan to guide the transition. The company's management selected a war room approach to "jump start" their planning and transitioning.

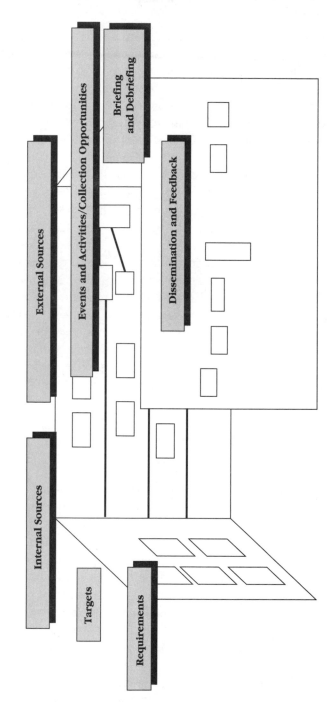

Figure 8-3. Portable Quarterback war room layout.

In a three-day workshop, WarRoom facilitated a war room strategic planning session. The group consisted of 12 company officials, including the VP for strategic planning, senior program managers, and a number of senior researchers. The session was held in a room typically used by engineering design teams. It already had two-thirds of the walls covered by magnetic white boards. On the floor were numerous boxes of magnetic strips and shapes of various colors that could be attached to the white board. The strips also could be written on with erasable markers. There was also a computer, a projector, and a pull-down screen. Although groupware was not used, effective brainstorming occurred with the use of Inspiration, a software tool that uses some of the principles of Tony Buzan's Mindmapping, as well as other visual techniques. It uses outline and diagram visualizations to generate ideas, stimulate group thinking, and develop plans. It was also a tool that the group was familiar with.

Prior to the workshop, WarRoom submitted a "straw man" information flow for the team to use in the strategic planning workshop. A few changes were requested, but this served as the initial framework for the workshop. The information flow consisted of:

- *Current status:* Where the company stood today in terms of revenues and profitability, personnel, competitive win rates, and expectations.
- *Core competencies:* Expertise and skills inherent in people and infrastructure, not necessarily what was being funded.
- *Corporate vision:* Where the leadership and visionaries within the company wanted to go, what they wanted to become.
- *Goals and objectives:* What steps they had to take to achieve their vision, and how big, or measured, these steps should be.
- *Measures of performance:* How to evaluate the progress in achieving the goals and objectives.
- *Products and services:* The current and new products and services offered to achieve the G&Os, and which ones responded to the company's core strengths.
- *Customer base:* Customers in addition to the Navy, including other government agencies, foreign countries, and commercial clients, that might have a need for these products and services.

- *Market opportunities:* Identification of formal solicitations and informal networking opportunities to identify business prospects.

- *Competitors:* Other companies that are positioned or likely to go after the same market opportunities, and their strengths and weaknesses.

- *Alliances:* Companies that would make good partners to pursue these opportunities.

- *Marketing:* Steps that need to be taken to initiative pursuit of the market opportunities, and a mechanism to monitor these marketing activities.

- *Proposal status:* The steps required for writing the proposal and monitoring the status of its progress.

- *Monitoring and evaluation:* An overall status board displaying the progress and results of all the different marketing pursuits and how that progress relates to overall companies revenues, profitability, and growth.

The information flow is displayed in Figure 8-4.

Magnetic strips with these headings were placed on the boards circling two-thirds of the room. Using the Inspiration software package, comments were obtained from the group characterizing the current status of the organization.

Much of the company was in a state of shock. Several Navy programs that had been the "breadbasket" for the company were coming to a close. There were few Navy programs in their area of focus on the horizon. Although the company's financials had been healthy, the out years were looking dim.

Using Inspiration, a list of core competencies was created and projected on the screen. The list included areas of technological expertise derived from past company contracts. It also contained the skills and capabilities of their employees. Many of these were obtained from their work prior to or outside of their involvement with the company, and the company had either ignored or was too busy to take advantage of these attributes in the past. These core competencies were taken from the screen and placed on the magnetic board with marker.

The company took its standing mission statement and broadened it to address a revised vision. What had been a Navy and national

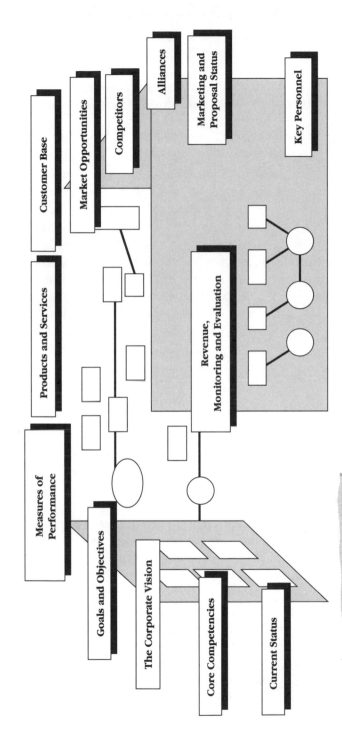

Figure 8-4. Strategic planning war room.

177

defense orientation was revised to include providing technological solutions to important technological and economic needs of the country. This implied a willingness to consider other governmental agencies, state and local opportunities, and even some commercial endeavors.

Using Inspiration, the company officials began to describe some goals and objectives. The goals were the more general desires and the objectives quantified them. These captured the desire to shift some of the focus, for example, goals that included obtaining Navy contracts in other than antisubmarine warfare. Their information technology capabilities were pretty strong, and although in the past they had largely been focused on acoustics and signal processing for underwater applications, they also could pertain to communications. The company described some other defense areas outside the Navy they had neglected in the past and would examine more closely. This soon led to a discussion of similar nondefense technological needs that other government organizations might have, including the Coast Guard; the National Oceanographic and Atmospheric Agency; the intelligence community; federal, state, and local law enforcement; and some foreign Navy possibilities. There was even one idea generated concerning a tourist submarine application. These desires were translated into goals and objectives. It was found that during this search process for G&Os, the associated discussion and input was relevant to many other areas within the war room, including products and services, customer base, and in some cases a particular marketing opportunity. In fact, there were several opportunities that some of the workshop participants had been alert to, but they had not seriously considered pursuing them because in the past, they would not have received corporate backing. Now they were being challenged to pursue them and were actually getting pumped up about the prospect of helping their company diversify.

In fact, the G&O section served as a catalyst to provide meaningful input throughout the war room, and the facilitators and corporate management decided to run with it. On the third day, much of the war room was in pretty good shape. The team had a good sense of where they could pursue new work and in general, the types of opportunities they should be pursuing. A few specific opportunities were identified. During the evening after the second day, one of the participants reviewed his CD-ROM version of *Commerce Business*

Daily and found a number of government solicitations that would have been ignored in the past, but which fit into the new goals, competencies, and strategy. These were added to the board.

Although the group knew of a few possible competitors, there were actually too many government contractors to focus on. Rather, it became more important to closely examine possible alliances with players who could get them into some of these new areas. They thought of a number of companies that were strong with certain customers, yet did not have the technological capability that this company had. The prospect of teaming with them to pursue a new request for proposal (RFP) from one of the other company's established customers looked worth pursuing.

The workshop ended with the company management becoming confident that they had a new strategy and direction. Marketing-related action items were placed on the magnetic boards regarding which companies they would be approaching to discuss possible teaming and what new prospective clients they would be trying to cultivate. The war room was now to be used to track and monitor progress at breaking into these new customer bases and niches. Our understanding is that the company has been successful in maintaining and securing what they could in their core Navy business area, and this continues to be the main revenue base. But they also have been successful in branching into new market areas. They view their growth in terms of continuing as a government contractor, while pursuing a much more diversified customer base.

War Room Case Study 4: Capture Plan War Room

An aerospace company decided to mount a major effort to win a very important NASA contract. A number of other companies had teamed with the aerospace company and would serve as subcontractors if they won the proposal. Orchestrating the input, activity, and interactions of many different players participating in the proposal was a monumental effort. The "capture team" manager decided to use a war room framework to help manage the effort. They had a lead time of five months until the proposal was due. They contracted with WarRoom to provide the initial war room design, although outside of a few select tasks, we were not involved in the operation of the actual war room during the proposal effort. The aerospace company had a number of specially designated proposal rooms, one of which was dedicated to this effort. It consisted of numerous whiteboards on the walls encircling the conference table. With the capture plan manager's guidance, a framework was to be devised in which to develop the capture plan and the proposal, and a mechanism provided to monitor the proposal team members' activity and contributions, in order to hold them accountable.

The first step was to map out the capture plan process. Our information flow for the capture plan war room was as follows:

- *Program overview:*   What was known about the program and where it was headed, including funding.

- *Customer:*   The leadership and politics of NASA, particularly the importance of the program to the organization and their strategic plan and vision.

- *Requirements and criteria for source selection:*   The official requirements and criteria enumerated in the RFP and the reasoning for why they were included.

- *Program issues:*   Some of the technical, economic, and political issues related to the program.

- *Market intelligence plan:*   What intelligence is needed on the customer, external actors, i.e., Congress, White House, etc., who could impact the program, and competitors.

- *Win strategy:*   What it will take to win the contract and how to get there.

- *Issues management:*   Influencing and shaping the perceptions of the key decision-makers involved in or influencing proposal selection.

- *Contact plan:*   What people should be contacted and how, whether directly or through a third party.

- *Communications plan:*   How to influence the media, which in turn influences the key decision-makers.

- *Action items by key people:*   Specific actions that should be undertaken by capture team members.

- *Proposal development:* Storyboarding the proposal and assigning sections to team members for authorship.

- *Red teaming:* Having a group outside the capture plan and proposal team critique the proposal.

- *Monitoring and status tracking:* Monitoring the progress of the effort, flagging weak areas or gaps in information and schedule delays.

This configuration is illustrated in Figure 8-5.

With a few slight modifications, the capture team manager approved of this configuration. We recommended that one of the team members be assigned responsibility for each section, and his or her name was written underneath the heading on the whiteboard as the section manager. This person was responsible for the productivity, timeliness, and completion of the section. The capture team manager was responsible for overseeing the efforts of all the section managers. In some cases the section manager assigned specific tasks to other team members or to staff from their own company. These tasks and the person responsible for their completion were identified in the appropriate area. We set up a status board system that used colored circles to identify where each section was in its development. A green circle implied everything was on go and on track. The yellow circle indicated caution and that there were areas of concern. The red circle indicated there were major problems. The capture team manager and some of his assistants maintained the status of the boards. This provided an immediate "eyeball" status of the effort. It also alerted all the team members to how everyone was doing. This served as a group psychological lever to keep people focused and on target.

The capture team manager felt confident that his team would be able to further develop and refine the various sections of the war room. We were asked, however, to provide inputs into the war room structure for the Market Intelligence Plan, Issues Management, and Contact sections. Our approach was to develop an information flow for the following subsections:

- *Market intelligence requirements:* The specific intelligence requirements relating to the customer (NASA), external actors, and competitors.

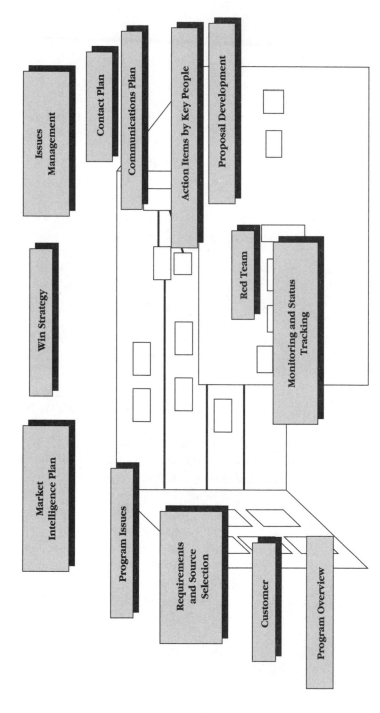

Figure 8-5. Capture plan process.

- *Intelligence collection plan:* The strategy and tactics on how this intelligence is to be obtained.

- *Market intelligence analysis:* Any refinement of the intelligence within some analytical framework in order to answer the requirements.

- *Issues management:* The proactive use of intelligence to assist in shaping the perceptions of the decision-makers impacting the procurement.

The market intelligence requirements were delineated by whomever they were targeted against:

- The customer—NASA
- The competitors—other aerospace companies and teams vying for the contract
- The competitor's subcontractors/vendors and external actors influencing the competition

Intelligence was sought as to NASA's perception of the aerospace company's team and of competitors. This included what NASA thought of the technology and approach, past performance, and management and business practices. Of even greater importance was intelligence relating to NASA's source selection priorities, those beyond what was listed in the RFP solicitation. Intelligence was also desired on the future requirements and growth desires of the NASA program managers.

Requirements directed against the competitors included:

- Finding out about their capture plan, if any
- Pricing strategy
- Perceptions of the customer and of our team

Requirements targeted against the competitor's subcontractors/vendors included their design and pricing information. The external actors who could possibly influence the competition included Congress, lobbyists, and the media. Requirements for them centered on their perceptions and actions.

The intelligence collection plan was similar to that described earlier in the case study on the CI program process. The information flow consisted of:

- *Identification of the targets:* Those who could address or answer the requirements.

- *Source development:* Those who could gain access to the targets: Internal, the team's employees and consultants; and external, sub-contractors, vendors, competitor subs and vendors, journalists, financial analysts, and industry association staff.

- *Collection opportunities:* Orchestrating the interactions between sources and targets, i.e., source interviews, Quarterback.

- *Specialized analytical needs:* Further refinement of the intelligence to assist in answering the requirements. Those conducted included benchmarking/benchtrending,[38] strengths versus weaknesses, and political issues/accounting.

- *Intelligence reporting mechanism:* Dissemination and follow-up.

WarRoom developed a marketing intelligence analytical technique for the team to use within their capture plan war room setting. This was called Competition Scenarios. A chart displayed a heading for each area of competition: technical performance, schedule, management, and price. Each contractor could win that area (+), tie (=), or lose (−). Since there were four criteria, the range of possible outcomes would be 4+ for the best possible scenario for the team to 4− for the worst possible scenario.

This chart was the backdrop to a war room strategy session in which the team was asked to explore the likelihood or probability of all possible outcomes. Once this was done, they examined possible measures and actions required to alter the undesirable outcomes. These could include measures taken to improve performance, influence the weighting factors, and proposing innovative alternatives that would overcome the undesirable outcomes. The team found this session to be very beneficial, and it led to some new tactics and actions that were also highlighted on the walls.

The Issues Management section of the war room included another analytical technique refined by WarRoom called the Political Accounting Analysis. This approach was originally developed by William Coplin and Michael O'Leary in their book *Every Man's Prince* to understand and influence political decision-making. The adapted technique involved identifying key decision-makers influencing procurement; determining their perceptions on the technology, schedule, and management; and identifying their position, influence, and salience (how important it is to them). Intelligence derived from the Market Intelligence Requirements section of the war room also fed into this analysis.

Once the perceptions and beliefs of the decision-maker were clear, the next phase involved developing the Contact Strategy. The Contract Strategy consisted of:

- Correlating specific issues and interests with the decision-makers.

- Determining who, when, and how these individuals should be contacted. This included what persuasive information would be used to enhance their perception of the client and degrade that of the competitors. It also involved deciding whether it was preferable for the client or team to contact the decision-maker directly, or indirectly through a consultant or lobbyist.

The next step of the Issues Management campaign dealt with issues exposure. Here, the issues and related areas sought for maximum exposure were determined, as were those which were best minimized. The issues for which greater exposure was desired were fed into a Communications Strategy. This was all exhibited and linked in the war room. The Communications Strategy targeted and prioritized what media would be best to convey the information and message that would ultimately bring about the areas in which the team wanted greater exposure. These included authoring articles for publication, submitting conference papers, and providing selected press releases and interviews to journalists and free-lance writers. By facilitating favorable articles, the team, in essence, was able to gain free advertising.

The aerospace company eventually won the NASA contract. This mechanism was instituted for the development of future capture plans targeted against major procurements.

War Room Case Study 5: Research and Development Investment Planning War Room

A sporting goods and fitness company which had a strong technology-driven orientation for new product development decided to use a war room for their research and development investment planning. The company's management believed that rather than simply responding to market demand, they wanted to create and influence the demand. They strongly felt that a technology-push orientation was warranted for their market. Research and technology development, however, was not done in a void. It was guided by their vision and market strategy. To best develop this strategy, the company decided to conduct a facilitated strategic planning workshop.

After interviewing some of the company's key managers and visionaries, WarRoom developed a foam board framework with a "straw man" information flow which consisted of:

- *Sports and recreation trends:* Projections of technological innovations, sporting and exercise enthusiasts' interests, and demographics.

- *Forecasted equipment needs:* What is needed to take advantage of sporting participants' desires and of technological opportunities.

- *Innovation opportunities:* New approaches and concepts to address the forecasted equipment needs. This section also has a subset of off-the-wall ideas.

- *Equipment design concepts:* Specific design features needed to respond to opportunities.

- *Technology required for concepts:* Specific technologies needed in design concepts.

- *Where technology resides:* Where one has to go to obtain the technology; whether it is in house or located at a university, competitor, or other company.

- *Estimated costs for developing technology and product:* The estimated costs using in-house technologies, if possible, versus leveraging technologies from elsewhere.

- *Prioritizing the technologies:* Determining which technologies are most essential for developing the most important products.

- *Selecting an investment strategy:* Which technologies should be obtained, for how much investment, and in what timeframe.

These headings were put on boards and placed around the company's main conference room. Prior to the workshop, WarRoom conducted an environmental scan looking at the future of sports and recreation. Thirty-two key *trends* where discerned. One of these was that the growth in the Internet would lead to virtual on-line competitions. This and the other trends were placed on the boards prior to the workshop. During the workshop the company had a facilitated brainstorming session to provide input into the various section headings which responded to the initial trends derived from the environmental scan. Using colored dots, each of these inputs was linked to a category in the preceding section.

Several of the *forecasted equipment needs* responded to the virtual on-line competition trend. One was extending the electronics used in controlling and monitoring most exercise equipment for speed, time, and calories to link it via a computer onto the Internet to facilitate professional feedback and virtual competition.

Innovation opportunities were then linked to the forecasted equipment needs. One of these was providing virtual training via the Web site and e-mails to the sport clubs or home gym purchasers of the company's equipment. Several different *design concepts* were developed to enable the use of Internet instruction and the monitoring of exercise systems. One of the design concepts involved the use of a profiling system to determine the optimal exercise regimen for a particular individual. The next step was to examine which technologies would go into these design concepts. The workshop participants came up with a number of relevant technologies. At this point the workshop ended so some of the corporate researchers could examine the particular technologies in greater depth. Many of these technologies addressed numerous design concepts, and through the color-coded system, one could eyeball the importance of a particular technology in terms of its utility to potential new products and innovations. Over the next month data was collected on the various technologies, particularly where the expertise resided, and how much was inherent within the company or could be developed in-house. Technologies which were located outside the company and for which in-house development did not seem feasible were examined as to acquisition or transfer possibilities. Perhaps the technology could be as purchased or licensed, a joint venture or partnership orchestrated, or the particular company could be acquired. The company performed some intelligence gathering on these technologies and on the organizations pursuing their development. They also examined which of their major competitors were after some of these same technologies. The researchers then came up with "guesstimates" of to how much the acquisition of these technologies would cost and in what timeframes they could obtain them.

The workshop participants reconvened after all this new data was presented on the war room boards. The group could eyeball the relative importance of a particular technology by tracing through the color linkages the design concepts it responded to, the innovations it related to, and the trends and opportunities it was derived from. The group could also see the technology's cost relative to other technologies and which of their competitors were working on similar technologies. With this common frame of reference, the group was able to rank and prioritize, debate and argue, and then rank and prioritize again the various technologies. The company's technology investments and part of their research and development budget were then based on these figures.

War Room Case Study 6: Media Planning War Room

An advertising agency was invited to compete for a large contract from an automotive manufacturer. The advertising company had, in fact, a long history of referring to rooms in which they brainstormed and storyboarded ad concepts and pitches as war rooms. It was standard industry practice for large companies to invite several prospective firms to pitch their proposed advertising campaigns. So it was with the automotive manufacturer. WarRoom was brought in to design a portable war room approach which would allow the advertising company to easily bring their war room across the continent to their prospective client. The desire was to be able to walk the client through the logic behind their advertising campaign. In these settings, advertising firms often use skits, multimedia presentations, and other ways to demonstrate their creativity. The advertising agency wanted to convey to the automotive manufacturer an understanding of the sound media strategy that they would be employing. They also wanted to demonstrate their creativity.

Using an exhibit display system that features a pop-up frame, WarRoom was able to assemble a portable war room in which to display the media campaign information flow. Working with the ad agency, we were able to capture and display the logic flow of this campaign. This, in turn, served as a backdrop to the various skits and multimedia which the ad agency used in the pitch. Being a very artistic organization, they took our basic war room design and enhanced the graphics and visualizations used in its presentation.

During the pitch, the ad agency was able to creatively demonstrate a particular point and show where it fit into their overall game plan. Unfortunately, the ad agency did not win the contract, but they were informed that their presentation was by far the most effective. Other factors influenced their loss to a competitor. The ad agency has continued to use a war room approach as background for their media pitches. Figure 8-6 shows a generic approach to a media planning war room.

War Room Case Study 7: Advocacy Campaign War Room

Advocacy campaigns often involve a concerted and coordinated effort of companies from an industry or those representing a similar interest to influence legislation or change elements within a market or the societal structure. Intelligence is often shared among what are typically competitors, as well as with law firms and lobbyists, to effect change for the common good of that interest group. Well-orchestrated advocacy campaigns (as with military or political campaigns) involve a calculated series of operations designed to bring about a particular result. Successful campaigning requires esprit de corps, a clear understanding of what it takes to win, goals and objectives, strategies and tactics to achieve the G&Os, and effective marshaling and management of resources, people, and equipment. Intelligence is a very important foundation to all of these facets of a campaign.

In large part due to the evolution of information and media-related technologies, the nature of advocacy campaigns has drastically changed in recent years. This in turn has changed the way advocacy campaigns are managed. Harnessing the "flow and control of information," i.e., the secure collection, analysis, and dissemination of intelligence, is key to having an effective campaign that is both productive and timely.

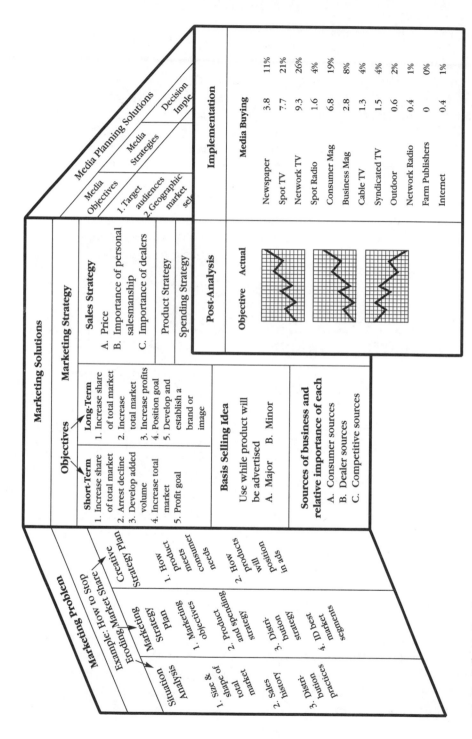

Figure 8-6. Media planning war room.

190

A major utilities company was in the fight of its life. For years the company had been guaranteed a captive market with no real competitors. They were able to build a very expensive nuclear infrastructure. But environmental concerns and the desire for more consumer options had dramatically altered the business environment. The utility had become a beached whale, and a number of sharks were circling, ready to take over. The company knew it could not prevent the move toward deregulation, but believed that if it could slow down the pace by perhaps two years, this would provide enough time to refocus and compete in the new marketplace. The CEO needed a strategy war room where he could plan and implement a program to forestall deregulation. It would also be a room to monitor and track competitors.

WarRoom was contacted by a third party that was assisting the individual charged with developing this war room. We soon were engaged in developing a design for the utility company to assist in this major advocacy campaign.

In a three-day strategy session, WarRoom personnel met with the utility company's manager overseeing the project and a key consultant of theirs involved in strategy development. Because of the importance placed on the war room by the CEO, a major conference facility was already dedicated to the effort. It was in a secured facility that had white boards and bulletin boards wrapped around the walls. The strategy session, however, was held far away from the utility company in a conference room halfway across the country. Our role was to devise the process and design of the war room, but not to be involved in filling in the information specifics. Therefore, outside of broad generalities, we were not kept apprised of the specifics of the effort's intelligence.

The utility company manager had tried to assemble some informational boards that looked at their competitors and their strengths and weaknesses. We found a basic weakness in his approach. His data was a snapshot in time, not tied to the actions and scheduled needs of the advocacy campaign.

We came up with a new approach and war room design that served as a role model for subsequent efforts. To be placed in the center of the war room, clearly visible when someone first entered, was a process board that captured the legislative process through which deregulation laws would be enacted. On the top was the state process, and on the bottom was the federal process. WarRoom just provided a preliminary sketch of the process, since the utility manager could later work with his lobbyists and advocacy campaign team experts to fully capture and present the state and federal processes. The display mechanism actually used in the war room was a bulletin board, so the information was eventually printed out using various graphics and pinned to the boards.

The process showed how the legislation was initially introduced, what outside groups would be interacting with various legislators, and what committees it would have to proceed to and from. It eventually wound its way to the chief executive for his signature (i.e., either the governor or the President). Included were various blocks (all of one color), each with information printed on it describing a step of the legislative process. We then identified the best possible scenario to forestall or delay the legislation from working its way through the process to enactment. Using dotted lines, we designed certain pathways that displayed how this scenario would unfold. In some cases there were alternative routes to delaying the legislation and therefore alternative scenarios. We also described a worst-case scenario in which the legislation would be pushed through in record time. This came to represent what would be the optimal scenario for their competitor energy company and its allies. Several different scenarios were postulated, including optimal, worse-case, and mixed results.

Another board on the side of the war room was used to describe the various scenarios and to lay out supporting data. Back at the middle process boards, critical junctures were identified along each scenario's dotted line. These were the critical points where a decision or action had to be made for the scenario to ensue. Another side board was used to describe what strategy and tactics could be used to influence decision-makers at these critical junctures. These were examined from both the utility's and its allies' perception, as well as from the standpoint of their competitor and its partner. Another board described the intelligence needed to support the decisions and actions needed for these strategies and tactics. An intelligence collection plan was built around these actions. Finally, we developed a tactics action board to track and monitor each development as it occurred during the legislative process.

The key attributes of the advocacy campaign war room are as follows:

- An advocacy campaign decision-making process, utilizing decision-making mapping.

- The alternative scenarios or pathways the organization and its competitors can take to navigate through this process.

- A display of the critical junctures during the process at which key decisions have to be made.

- A competitive intelligence/environmental scan of information requirements and key indicators needed to support effective decision-making during the critical junctures, plus a collection plan for obtaining this intelligence.

- An executive action/issues management status board which displays the progress of tasking by key individual.

We were quite pleased with the approach used, since we had captured eight different dimensions of essential information (recommended by Tufte). These included process steps, sequence, timing and schedule, alternative scenarios, critical junctures, strategies and tactics, intelligence needs, and implementation status. The CEO was extremely proud of his war room. He had an actionable war room that not only laid out a plan and approach but also provided an efficient mechanism to track the progress of their deregulation advocacy campaign. Figure 8-7 shows the information flow used in an advocacy campaign war room.

War Room Case Study 8: Merger & Acquisition War Room

A manufacturing company was aggressively pursuing growth through acquisitions. It asked us to sketch out a war room approach that it could use in its pursuit of new acquisitions and to determine where intelligence could assist in their acquisition process. We first captured and mapped out the acquisition process. This included:

- *Establishing strategic vision, growth goals, and objectives:* Make sure that any acquisition fits into the overall direction and strategy of the company.

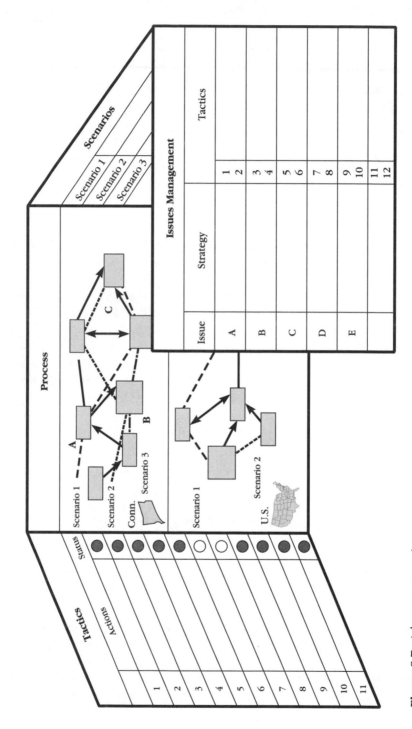

Figure 8-7. Advocacy campaign war room.

- *Developing an acquisition plan:* Develop the approach and boundaries in which the company pursues an acquisition candidate.

- *Defining candidate criteria:* Define the attributes, financials, technology, product base, market, and management style that the company is looking for.

- *Identifying potential candidates:* The process of the company search and targeting.

- *Making effective contact with candidates:* The best tactic for approaching the company and owners.

- *Performing due diligence:* Using CI to make sure that what has been reported is accurate and that all relevant information is brought out.

- *Negotiating terms:* The negotiation strategy, posturing, and process.

- *Implementing integration:* The plan and implementation of its integration once the company is bought.

Visualization Case Study 4 described and displayed in Chapter 7 (Figure 7-4) shows how this war room was laid out. It depicts the information flow and logic that the manufacturing company's team of acquisition specialists and intelligence professionals used in selecting and examining prospective companies as acquisition targets. We were asked to integrate the war room logic flow with a software used by the company, this being MoneySoft Lightning Deal Reviewer.[39] This software provided a tool for structuring and collecting essential acquisition information. We found that in our process there where two important steps where intelligence played a major role: the Define Candidate Criteria and the Perform Due Diligence steps of the acquisition process. The Lightning Deal Reviewer software, in turn, helped to identify intelligence requirements that would assist in the acquisition decision-making.

The manufacturing company assembled a war room where they laid out the process we had captured and linked the information to the acquisition software. They further described the intelligence requirements highlighted in the inputs for the Lightning Deal Reviewer software. Various open sources were mined to provide some of the intelligence inputs. WarRoom also recommended that some in-depth collection effort be directed at key individuals who either worked for or with the targeted acquisition. A Quarterback operation seemed to be appropriate since an upcoming conference was being held where intelligence targets would be in attendance.

Since the company wanted a means by which they could rapidly evaluate different collection activities, we proposed a criminal investigation visualization linking tool, called Watson and developed by Harlequin Incorporated,[40] be used to assist them in their Quarterback. Watson enables a graphic linkage between targets and sources, the quarterback, analysts and collectors, and key events and activities.

With the Quarterback, the manufacturing company was able to obtain more in-depth intelligence input and insert it back into Lightning Deal Reviewer in order to compare the openly available information with the in-depth intelligence. The manufacturing company used this war room approach to guide them through the successful acquisition of the targeted company, and they have used a similar process in subsequent acquisitions.

Lessons Learned from These Case Studies

It should be clear from the review of these case studies that a war room is not just the facility or tools and technology that exist within its confines. People, their interactions, and the total process also help form its character and attributes. War room design is an art and science. We learn more with each development.

Truly effective war rooms should contain several basic components in their design. The war room should enable the decision-making support team and other key executives impacting the program to become quickly immersed in a structured and disciplined approach to decision-making. They must gain an appreciation for the need to capture and map the decision-making process and logic flow. They must become familiar with team-based thinking and decision-making. The importance of information density and dimensionality in relation to its visualization needs also to be realized. Team members should learn how the war room is used to track, monitor, and anticipate events; how it delineates courses of action; and how it can be used as an advocacy tool within the organization to promote certain tactics and actions. Safeguarding the decision-making thought process and associated intelligence are also key components demonstrated within the war room.

There were some important lessons learned from these case studies relating to the attributes of an effective war room.

- The foundation on which all else is based is the capturing and mapping of the decision-making process and logic flow. If you have not graphically captured and laid out this process in your facility, you do not have a war room.

- Effective war rooms should incorporate a high degree of information density and lots of dimensionality, as described in our discussion on visualization. If not, you are not getting the most out of your war room.

- The war room is not a one-person tool or operation. Its real utility is as a facility to enable team-based thinking and decision-making. This is because much of its benefit is as a means for others to quickly gain comprehension and develop a common frame of reference. It is also an effective tool for team brainstorming.

- The war room is an effective advocacy tool by which to gain support from senior management within the company, and from others whose involvement you want. This includes cultivating sources. Walking someone through the war room is perhaps the most effective tool to brief that person and gain his or her participation and interest.

- The war room is not just a planning device. Once a plan is prepared, the war room should be used as the mechanism to implement the program and track and monitor events and activities.

- The war room should be used as a mechanism for proactive involvement, a means to delineate courses of action.

- Once the courses of actions are determined, the war room should be used as a device for assigning responsibility and accountability. The war room will not, in itself, produce success. It is only a tool for the gathering of intelligence that people can use and act on.

- The war room should incorporate effective security safeguards. If it is so important and essential to decision-making, access to it by competitors or adversaries could be quite a blow to your functioning.

How to Protect Your Company

9

Safeguarding the Keys to the Kingdom

Protecting Your Intellectual Assets

During the first few years of consulting to corporations setting up their own competitive intelligence organizations, a newly appointed CI manager instituted an aggressive approach to collecting intelligence. From within his company he had set up a network of sources. They had targeted prospective individuals who could provide much-sought-after intelligence. There was a problem though. Many of his sources had difficulty remembering the specific intelligence questions and requirements that his company's senior management had posed. He solved this dilemma by having the requirements printed up in very small print on cards resembling business cards. He disseminated these to all of his sources and had them take the cards to a conference where they were attempting to collect intelligence.

One of these cards ended up inadvertently being swapped while introductions and business card trading was occurring. Unfortunately, the card ended up in the hands of a competitor. The competitor learned some very important information. The requirements revealed far more about the company that had issued the cards than about the competitor. It revealed what was of most importance to the company and its leadership and gave forewarning of its plans and intended actions.

In the process of learning and implementing the collection of intelligence, the company neglected instituting a complementary security safeguards program. An organization's competitiveness will in large part be determined by how well it collects, analyzes, disseminates, and safeguards information. An organization's security is ultimately based on how well it safeguards information and knowledge assets. One cannot be done well without performing the other effectively.

According to the American Society of Industrial Security (ASIS), there were more than 1100 documented incidents of illegal economic espionage in 1997. Major U.S. corporations reported 550 suspected incidents. ASIS estimated the losses from this foreign and domestic espionage targeted against U.S. intellectual property at $300 billion.[41]

Competitive intelligence and effective security safeguards are like yin and yang, different yet complementary, opposites yet essential in defining each other. In most organizations, however, there is little communication or understanding between those who are tasked with protecting information and those who seek out that of their competitors.

Just as you are able to gain a great deal of intelligence to assist in your strategic planning and tactical marketing decisions, so can your competitors gain insight into your plans and intentions through an orchestrated intelligence effort, including corporate espionage directed against your company. Although effective at guarding physical property and personnel, traditional security practices are not capable of safeguarding a company's intellectual assets. The two approaches of OPSEC and counterintelligence are essential components to protecting your organization's most prized possessions.

Operations Security

Immediately upon leaving the world of national intelligence and still in the process of transitioning to the embryonic competitive intelligence realm, coauthor Shaker worked for a company hired to develop an OPSEC program for one of the nation's most guarded weapon systems. Even after being hired, he was not briefed as to what the program was. He was asked to guess what he was to be working on. His colleagues working on this black program consisted of a team of crack former CIA and military operational and security personnel.

Never before had such a group been assembled. The size and the scope of the effort could mean only two things. Either this was one of the major black programs that everyone already knew a great deal about or the government is in fact really good at hiding some programs so that no one without a "need to know" has an inkling of their existence. Shaker opted for the former and guessed that it was the Stealth bomber.

After being informed that in fact it was the B-2 program, Shaker was told that he was not to be given any classified data about the aircraft for the next three months. Instead, he was asked to prepare an analysis of whatever he could postulate about the bomber from open sources. This was before the Internet and the widespread use of on-line databases, so a great deal of time was spent at various libraries. He researched the possible technologies related to Stealth. He examined the technical papers and probed into the authors' backgrounds. He could detect trends by examining where the authors worked, as they moved from company to company, project to project. Sometimes the gaps in information were more telling than what was said in the publications. If a researcher had published extensively about a radar absorbing structure and was working for an aircraft company, and then suddenly his publications stopped, then it was an indicator that his research was being taken seriously.

Over time, Shaker was able to put together a pretty good composite of the B-2, including its likely configuration, materials, subsystems, and operational tactics. This study was furnished to the Air Force program sponsors, who determined that approximately 75 percent of the information postulated about the B-2 was correct, although much of it did not have in-depth detail. If this is what one person could glean within three months, what could the thousands of Soviet KGB and military professionals have learned over the years?

There was a realization in the Air Force that the costs of managing black programs had become prohibitive. Cost overruns had led to the cancellation of other major programs. So what good was security if it made the overall costs so high that the program was eliminated. There was a more important realization, however. Trying to protect everything in a massive program was ineffective. Selecting specific safeguards for the most important and sensitive aspects of the program would be a better approach. This, factored with some other intelligence, led to a decision to move the B-2 from the black world to gray. The most sensitive, important facets of the program would continue to be protected, but those areas which had already been disclosed or generally accepted were either downgraded in classification, or in some cases declassified.

The security lessons learned from the governmental arena have begun to seep into the commercial world. Just as individuals trained in national intelligence have helped to enhance the competitiveness of corporate America, so have persons schooled in operations security been able to elevate the ways in which companies protect themselves.

Intelligence has been described as putting the small pieces of a puzzle together to create an overall understanding of the total picture. Finding the right piece to a puzzle comes natural to humans, although the actual process is somewhat complex. The person needs to perceive something about the shape, texture, or color of a piece that is related to another piece's shape, texture, or color. There is a signature or identifying characteristic that creates an awareness to the person that this is what they are looking for.

The day-to-day actions of organizations and personnel create numerous signatures and indicators. It is the job of intelligence to recognize these and the job of operations security to reduce the ability to observe or recognize them. The goal of OPSEC is to deny the competition the pieces of the intelligence puzzle.

The more security conscious of us practice OPSEC even in our personal lives. Before going on a vacation, we ask the post office and newspaper publisher to stop delivery, or we have a neighbor pick up the mail and paper. We connect porch and inside lights to a timer so that they will be preset to come on periodically to make it appear as if someone is at home. A radio may be left on and a car parked in the driveway. We do this because an overly stuffed mailbox, several papers in the driveway, and a darkened porch signify that no one is home. Adopting this same awareness and applying it to the organization is a fundamental component of OPSEC.

Closely behind espionage and prostitution, vying for the title of oldest profession, is security. There is no doubt that elements of OPSEC have been around since antiquity. Its development as a formalized methodology and recognized discipline, however, did not occur until the Vietnam War. A small team of individuals was assembled to try to determine how the North Vietnamese and Viet Cong were obtaining advance information on certain U.S. combat operations in Southeast Asia. The team, code named Purple Dragon, found that the traditional security and intelligence countermeasures were insufficient in denying critical information to the enemy. Obvious indicators and signatures were passing through the filters. What was particularly alarming was that these dealt with intentions and capabilities, perhaps the most important information in defeating an adversary. The Purple Dragon team developed an analytical approach to examine U.S. operations from the adversary's perspective, to *red team* how the information would be obtained. This approach led to some corrective actions and early successes. The term *operations security* and its acronym *OPSEC* replaced physical security as the focus of effective safeguards. OPSEC became an essential linchpin between the worlds of intelligence and security.[42]

Over the years since the war in Vietnam, the governmental use of OPSEC has grown, and its approach has become more refined and sophisticated. A sister organization to SCIP, the OPSEC Professionals Society, was founded in 1990. Although the preponderance of its members are still government and defense security personnel, a number of them have become more involved in the commercial arena. The concern with protecting our nation's military secrets began to spread to safeguarding the information of contractors, and then to trade secrets and other proprietary information located in all commercial companies. Today, the OPSEC Professionals Society sponsors seminars and workshops and distributes literature and videos designed to foster and promote OPSEC principles, tools, and techniques.[43]

The Department of Energy has developed three "laws of OPSEC" that can be applied to government and business alike.[44] They are:

- The First Law: If you don't know the threat, how do you know what to protect?

- The Second Law: If you don't know what to protect, how do you know you are protecting it?

- The Third Law: If you are not protecting it, the adversary wins!

OPSEC is really a systematic process that:

- Understands the threat
- Identifies the information that needs to be protected
- Protects that information from exploitation

Understanding the competition and other adversaries is essential to providing effective safeguards.[45] If you don't know what parts of your information would benefit a competitor, then you have to try to protect everything, and you end up not safeguarding anything very well. Employees must be made aware as to what would likely be of interest to competitors. Prior to this, however, there needs to be a dialog between the CI and security staff. Security management must be apprised of what their own company desires to learn about the competition and their methods and sources used to obtain this intelligence. Security management must also be sensitized to the fact that the true "keys to the kingdom" come in other forms than just physical property or paper or electronic currency.

These keys are the intellectual assets of the company. In some cases it may be a trade secret or proprietary information. In other situations it may be some unclassified, unappreciated piece of minutiae, but when combined with other information, it could comprise an important piece of the puzzle. A number of years ago, a foreign intelligence agent disclosed that they always knew when the U.S. was in a high state of alert by the number of pizza delivery vehicles going to the Pentagon. Similarly, a list of travel plans of key company officials could indicate an impending merger or acquisition. Security must enlarge their scope to reduce and mitigate those signatures that give their company's competitors a competitive advantage. They in turn need to work with and educate the employees as to the real and postulated threats.

If you don't know what to protect, you won't know if you are protecting it. So part of the OPSEC approach is to identify what we need to protect.

In order to safeguard your company's proprietary information, intellectual assets, technology, plans, and intentions, a rigorous and systematic OPSEC process should be instituted. OPSEC furnishes an analytical framework to determine:

- Profiles of selected competitors or adversaries
- Information or intelligence that is of greatest value to the competition

- The likely targets of intelligence or corporate espionage directed against the company
- The possible and probable mechanisms that can be utilized to collect intelligence against the company
- The company's vulnerabilities
- Safeguard mechanisms that can be instituted to limit or minimize these vulnerabilities

Identifying your own critical information or knowing who your adversary is and what they want to know, is a little like the chicken and the egg. Which comes first? As long as you examine both, it really doesn't matter. Knowing who your competitors and your other adversaries are and what they need to know about your company to give them a competitive edge is the first basic step to the OPSEC process. The CI group should work closely with the security organization to identify who competitors and adversaries are. And they should not just be considered those who have been historically viewed as competitors. Companies grow and evolve over time, and their product focus changes. Former partners may become adversaries. New technologies and start-up companies may move in on your turf. Therefore, current and potential threats should be examined closely. Many times, two companies view each other differently. One will see the other as a competitor, and the other will not. Knowing who your adversary is will help you to determine what information would be of value to them. It is more likely that you have more than one competitor or adversary, and each may be interested in a different type of information. Each may also have a different capability and approach to collecting, processing, analyzing, and disseminating intelligence. Some companies may abide by very strict ethical standards. Some foreign companies, for example, may not honor all the legal restrictions that apply at home.

Once you know what they are looking for, it is important to determine what is vital information to your own organization. It may be that the competitor wants something that has become dated or is no longer an issue or priority with your company. Spending time and resources to protect it would perhaps not be worth the effort, unless denial to the competitor in itself makes it worthwhile. Again, realize that trying to protect everything results in not protecting anything really well. Your resources and focus become too dispersed. Determining what constitutes your "trade secrets" and the other golden nuggets of information that are central to your organization's success are necessary for good OPSEC.

Good OPSEC also involves knowing the possible mechanisms that can be utilized to collect intelligence against your vital information. These include the open source collection techniques, elicitation approaches, trade craft, and cyber techniques that the competitor or adversary would be using. It is necessary to analyze your vulnerabilities and which of these techniques would most likely work against your personnel and infrastructure. By matching the threats against the vulnerabilities you can begin to assess where the greatest risks lie and what should be considered the highest priorities.

Safeguard mechanisms and various countermeasures need to be developed to eliminate the vulnerabilities and threats and to minimize the utility of the intelligence to the competitor.

To walk organizations through these steps, those in charge of implementing OPSEC typically conduct *vulnerability assessments,* often referred to as OAs, for OPSEC assessments. These are typically performed from the viewpoint of the adversary, meaning that a critical analysis is performed from the perspective of a competitor trying to obtain this sensitive information. Members assigned to the team role play as if they were actually the competitor, proceeding step by step through this analytical framework. The team conducting the OPSEC assessment should be interdepartmental, with both security and CI staff as essential participants. Another key participant should be an intelligence analysis specialist who has researched the "ins and outs" of the company. Also included on the team should be information technology specialists who perform information systems security. Other important contributors should be a representative from the legal department, particularly an individual who is familiar with and can oversee intellectual property matters.

The team should be focused on identifying essential elements of friendly intelligence (EEFI). These are very similar to the EEIs described in Chapter 4, but refer specifically to those signatures or identifying characteristics that are exploitable by an adversary. Once these concerns or vulnerabilities have been identified, various countermeasures specifically targeted against these EEIs must be developed and implemented to safeguard this essential information.

Red Team

If the best way to develop an effective intelligence program is design it around the implementation of an operation, such as the Quarterback, the same is true with effective security. Augmenting OPSEC should be some realistic tests of the security apparatus and employee alertness. Attempts should be made to obtain information using the techniques and trade craft the competitor probably would use, as identified in the OPSEC analysis. Your company can hire a team of professionals to test your security safeguards.[46]

Ira Winkler, former Director of Technology at the National Computer Security Association, asserts how, with the approval of a company's security officialdom, he was able to steal an estimated $1 billion worth of sensitive business information. He supposedly achieved this through an attack methodology utilizing a combination of open source research, misrepresentation, abuse of access, insider hacking, and internal coordination of external accomplices.

As the story goes, Winkler first tried to determine what was worth stealing. Through open source on-line research, he ascertained the company's top developmental effort, a project that was valued at being worth billions of dollars.* He was able to obtain information about specific executives associated with the project, the financial status, and assorted problems related to its development. He gained a sense of the company's culture and philosophy. By scanning Internet newsgroups, Winkler was able to get employee postings and learn more about the individuals as well as the company's hardware and software. The technical postings enabled him to ascertain some technical vulnerabilities. The personal newsgroups and other Internet resources such as four11.com, provided personal interests and aided in his "social engineering" attacks.[47]

By entering a "host" command against their domain name, Winkler was able to obtain a listing of all the computer systems within the defined domain, operating system information, the company's TCP/IP addresses, and the number and types of computers in use throughout the company.

Since Winkler was in league with the security professionals of the company he was penetrating, they made it quite easy for him. They

---

*How the firm determined and assigned value to this program is unknown.

gave him access and cover as a temporary employee and provided him with company information, including a telephone directory, press releases, and company newsletters. From the telephone directory he was able to learn who the information security manager was, as well as other key points of contact. The newsletter described the company's top six developmental efforts and the names of the employees working on them.

Winkler conducted his social engineering in the guise of an "information security supervisor." He had business cards with this title and the company's logo printed up at a local printer. Upon filling out some personal forms with false information on his social security number, address, and telephone numbers, he was given an access badge.

Winkler initiated his attack by phoning a researcher on the top developmental program. He indicated that he was a recent hire who was charged with protecting some of the company's top secrets. He therefore had to learn more about what he was protecting and where it was located. Through this person Winkler was able to introduce himself to others, including the team leader. The team leader was very accommodating, furnishing him with copies of project meeting minutes and a distribution list of the people who received them. Winkler was also added to the distribution list. Through the team leader, Winkler was introduced to the Government Affairs Office representative and a project business manager, both of whom furnished additional sensitive information to Winkler. Winkler inquired about obtaining external access to the company's internal network. After forging the security manager's signature on a form for obtaining the smart card used in obtaining internal access from outside, he was issued one. He also forged the authorizing signature enabling him to obtain a pager used for security purposes.

Winkler is frank in acknowledging that the security personnel in on the vulnerability test often accompanied him or were in eyesight of his activities. This gave much of what he did legitimacy and may have served to reduce suspicion and challenges regarding who he was.

From the Government Affairs representative, Winkler obtained a number of documents, including the manufacturing process associated with the developmental product. This was considered the most important sensitive information related to the product. The Government Affairs representative also provided Winkler with information on other sensitive items being given to the government along with the password for accessing the document. Upon finding this, Winkler discovered that there were similar documents from additional high-priority development efforts located in the same directory. What was originally access to just one sensitive project now became information on two other high-priority programs.

After gathering the goods on the highest-level development project (which somehow Winkler estimated was worth $1 billion), he went about attacking the second highest developmental project. He used his newly made contacts to leverage his access and introduction to the business manager of the company's second-highest-priority projects. He learned from the business manager his process for accessing his files and the nature of the various reports maintained in his files. Winkler was unable to watch the manager type in his password, but back at his office Winkler used several common password combinations and succeeded in guessing the password. Again, he obtained extremely sensitive information of untold value.

This was all accomplished on Winkler's first day of red teaming the company. That evening after dinner, Winkler, accompanied by his security representative, went through various unlocked offices and file cabinets. By simply giving the nonverbal cues that what he was doing was proper, none of the cleaning personnel questioned what he was doing. He obtained information on licensing scenarios and the strengths and weaknesses of each potential licensee. He also found information relating to pending lawsuits, manufacturing details, and marketing data.

In one office Winkler found a monitor that was still on. The person was still logged into his mail account. Winkler went through the various e-mail messages and obtained development schedule information and other sensitive documents.

From the host command described earlier, Winkler had learned that the company had a number of Sun and PC-compatible computers. Winkler had obtained some complex scanning equipment available to computer security experts.[48] He loaded his portable computer with various hacker tools and unplugged his office's PC from the ethernet connection and plugged in the portable computer. Using the scanner Winkler was able to locate several exported file systems that were known to contain sensitive information and had certain vulnerabilities. His equipment was also to perform password guessing based upon a scan of identified user accounts. Three of them were immediately compromised. Using various hacker techniques and an account compromised by the scanner, Winkler was able to log into a remote computer. Again he obtained hundreds of megabytes of sensitive data.

With the smart card described earlier, Winkler was able to work with a team of accomplices. He express mailed them the smart card and necessary software. Winkler also provided them with information on user IDs and passwords. The accomplices were able to capture the password file. Using the Crack program against it, they obtained 10 percent of the passwords. They faxed Winkler a list of the compromised accounts, and correlating this with an on-line list of employees, Winkler was able to identify the departments in which they worked. He sent back a prioritized list of accounts along with some specific keywords that indicated sensitive information. The accomplices were able to obtain additional highly valued information.

Within a couple of days, Winkler was able to obtain an incredible amount of information that would put the company at an extreme disadvantage to its adversaries. To be fair, it is questionable how far Winkler would have gotten without the inside help of the very people (i.e., security folks) who were meant to guard against him. However, it also raises the question of what damage a true professional intelligence operative skilled in human intelligence and elicitation techniques would have accomplished teamed up with some highly capable cyber criminals. The weaknesses and vulnerabilities exposed in Winkler's exploits should be scrutinized and fed into a process to develop effective countermeasures. More important, recognize that Winkler's techniques are ethically questionable and, unless appropriate and legal arrangements are cleared within the organization, may be in violation of the Economic Espionage Act of 1996. The rights of employees and consultants are often violated by social engineering, despite prior contractual arrangements to conduct a thorough security assessment.

Competitive Counterintelligence, Deception, and Misinformation

> In wartime, truth is so precious that she should always be attended by a bodyguard of lies.   Winston Churchill

It is often possible—by adopting all kinds of measures of deception—to drive the enemy into the plight of making erroneous judgments and taking erroneous actions, thus depriving him of his superiority and initiative. Mao Tse-tung

Competitive counterintelligence goes one step beyond OPSEC by taking measures to neutralize the competitor's or adversary's intelligence operations. This may include specialized training of corporate employees and executives to mitigate the actions of the competitor, and it may include a deception program targeted against the competitor's CI program.

Arion N. Pattakos, one of the original founders of the OPSEC Professionals Society, a former military intelligence and security professional, and currently Director of Programs Integration of Beta Analytics International, has taken OPSEC one step further into the realm of competitive counterintelligence. He has developed a program that incorporates an OPSEC analytical approach similar to the one described earlier and develops a formalized program for controlling information.[49] Pattakos' steps for this program are as follows:

1. *Obtain a policy statement from the CEO.* For employees to seriously safeguard essential information, they must get the message from the top as to its importance.

2. *Establish an information protection policy committee.* This group serves to establish corporate information security policies and their implementation. Special subcommittees may be set up to address specific issues, such as secrecy agreements and public releases that may reveal some sensitive information. In addition to the security organization, the committee should include representatives from CI, legal, public relations, and human resources.

3. *Define what information needs protection.* This is a fundamental piece of the OPSEC methodology described earlier. It can include proprietary information and trade secrets, but it also may include other information which serves as indicators and signatures.

4. *Establish levels of information importance.* It is recommended that no more than three levels (preferably two) be used.

Otherwise, the specific significance of each is lost. These are used to restrict access to the information.

5. *Develop guidelines stating what to protect and at what level.* This includes the corporation's general and specific policies on what to protect. This also includes what principles are used to determine protection levels and their relative importance to each other.

6. *Specify to whom the program applies.* This includes current employees as well as prospective employees, departing and former employees, vendors, suppliers, consultants, and others given access to sensitive information.

7. *Prepare and sign secrecy and associated agreements.* These should include agreements pledging no competition against current company programs for a specified period of time should the person leave, no raiding of the company's personnel to accompany a departed employee, and invention covenants.

8. *Establish a network of nonsecurity department coordinators throughout the organization.* These are administrative coordinators who process the paperwork necessary to run and manage the protection system.

9. *Appoint data custodians.* This means that the originators of sensitive data must also have people to classify and control the data.

10. *Define what constitutes a compromise.* People need to be trained to recognize when their sensitive information has been stolen, and it is also important to specify what procedures should be taken upon discovery, and what legal actions and remedies the company will take.

11. *Establish procedures for the control of information under a variety of conditions.* This involves setting up specific guidelines for communicating the sensitive information, whether it is verbally relayed over the phone or by fax or modem. It involves the public release of information, the presentation of information at conferences and exhibits, and the destruction of information.

12. *Maintain relevant and realistic security education and awareness programs.* Formalized classes, media presentations, circulars, and bulletin boards with security information related to the control of information must be furnished to the employees. They must be indoctrinated that security safeguards are an important part of their jobs, and this can be reinforced as a factor in pay raises, promotions, and bonuses.

13. *Document the program.* To be effective, policies and plans should be written. A keeper of the plan, perhaps the security director, should be assigned the task of making sure it is current and up-to-date.

The steps outlined by Pattakos become very important in light of the Economic Espionage Act of 1996 described later in this chapter.

John Nolan, Managing Director and Chairman of Phoenix Consulting Group and a former military intelligence and counterintelligence official, has developed a Corporate Competitive Intelligence Countermeasures Program (CCIM). It has many of the facets of OPSEC but also includes elements targeted against the competitor's intelligence organization and activities.

The CCIM examines intelligence being gathered to ensure that it is not misinformation designed to lead a collector down the wrong path. Nolan provides several case studies demonstrating the utility of CCIM.[50]

Deception and Misinformation Case Study 1

In the late 1980s, a new building control system called LOBA was under beta testing by Johnson Controls. Johnson had picked up some intelligence indicating that Honeywell was referring to their beta system as LOBO. At the time, Honeywell relied mainly on its sales force for intelligence gathering. To capitalize on Honeywell's misunderstanding, Johnson introduced a very conservative upgrade to an existing system and called it LOBO to conform to Honeywell's expectation. After examining LOBO, Honeywell decided to abandon their crash project designed to counter the product innovation which they had expected Johnson to bring to market. Johnson was able to bring their LOBA product (renamed Metasys) to market a year later, catching Honeywell completely off guard and unable to respond with a competitive product. This gave Johnson Controls a year to consolidate their dominance of the new product area.

Deception and Misinformation Case Study 2*

Allegro Aerospace was quite successful in their head-to-head competition against Zygote Technologies to win government contracts. Much of their competitive edge was credited to their proud CI unit, which was viewed as a strategic asset. As a major element of their competitiveness approach, Zygote took on a mission to neutralize Allegro's CI group. In effect, they put together a systematic OPSEC program. They postulated what information the Allegro CI unit would be after. They examined their own vulnerabilities and instituted various countermeasures. They put together an extensive employee education program. Zygote also set up a reporting mechanism for individuals who believed they were being elicited. A prepublication review program was set in place to screen the information disseminated in articles, papers, and presentations. They also tried to pinpoint likely sources that had been exploited by Allegro and cut off their flow of information. More important, Zygote instituted an aggressive deception and misinformation campaign in which they subtly leaked information congruent with the biases and expectations of the Allegro leadership. In some cases Zygote allowed some of their own people, thought to be sources, to believe and convey to Allegro's CI unit key information about price structure and personnel. Allegro priced their proposal accordingly, based on the faulty information. Allegro lost the next five head-to-head competitive procurements, valued at $325 million. The Allegro CI team's reputation was degraded as well. Upper management forgot their previous accomplishments and adopted a "what have you done for

---

*To ensure the confidentiality of the two companies, Nolan has given them the fictitious names of Allegro Aerospace and Zygote Technologies.

*me lately" focus. They reduced the CI unit from eight people to two
and shifted much of their information gathering from intelligence to
marketing research and librarian functions.*

There is a very thin line between issues management, which deals with
shaping and influencing the perceptions of decision-makers impacting
your product or program, and deception and misinformation. A company must be extremely careful that the public is not deceived and
misinformed and the laws and regulations of the Federal Trade
Commission are not broken. If a misinformation program is targeted
against a competitor, the company must also prevent the public and
government from being impacted by the deception. It is only with
reluctance that we would propose that companies engage in active
deception and misinformation efforts. It can easily backfire. Even in the
world of government, with national means, the greatest expertise, and
unlimited resources, such efforts often go awry. The damage that can
occur from a deception campaign if it is disclosed can far exceed the
benefits derived from its use. However, there may be a few select
circumstances which warrant their use. We strongly recommend that
the company's most senior management and legal department be kept
apprised of any deception and misinformation activities.

The Economic Espionage Act of 1996

A law signed by President Clinton in October 1996 caused much
concern and debate among competitive intelligence professionals. At
one extreme were those who claimed the "sky was falling" and that
competitive intelligence professionals and activities had become
illegal. On the other side of the fence were those who maintained
that the act was meaningless and would have virtually no impact on
the profession. As in most cases, the truth lay somewhere in between.

The Economic Espionage Act of 1996 (EEA) made the theft of trade
secrets a federal crime. Prior to its enactment, such crimes had to be
prosecuted under state statutes. For federal action to be taken,
prosecutors had to rely on the National Stolen Property Act of 1934.
This act required that the government prove that goods, wares, or
merchandise were transported across state lines or past the nation's
borders. In an age where someone can send a trade secret via the

Internet, such wording is archaic and irrelevant. Moreover, some courts did not equate intellectual property with goods, wares, or merchandise. The EEA makes it illegal to steal or "appropriate" a rival's proprietary information without their authorization. Violators could get up to 15 years imprisonment and fines of up to $10 million.

A *trade secret,* as defined by the EEA, encompasses all types of financial, business, scientific, technical, economic, and engineering information. These can take the form of patterns, plans, compilations, program devices, formulas, designs, prototypes, methods, techniques, processes, procedures, programs or codes.

There are two stipulations governing the enforcement of EEA:

- The owner must have taken "reasonable measures" to keep the information secret.

- The information's value must be derived from not being readily ascertainable through proper means, which is to say it is being kept secret.

These stipulations are somewhat broad and their interpretation is debatable.

Attorney R. Mark Halligan, Esq., maintains a running tally of recent decisions in trade secrets law.[51] Some of the more interesting recent trade secrets court cases are as follows:

Midgard Corp. v. Todd, 1977 U.S. App. LEXIS 3874 (10th Cir. March 5, 1997).
In 1991 and 1992, Paul Todd had discussions with Midgard's president about purchasing their waste recycling business. In these discussions Todd learned a great deal about Midgard's business, including information about suppliers, pricing, and purchases. Todd decided against the purchase of Midgard and instead entered into some business arrangements directly competing against Midgard. This harmed Midgard, and they had to file for bankruptcy protection. Midgard filed a trade secret misappropriation claim but lost in trial court. This was affirmed by the 10th Circuit Court of Appeals, which maintained that this was, in fact, not secret information, since Midgard had disclosed much of the same information given to Todd to hundreds of other individuals. A trade secret must contain elements which are unique and not generally known or used in the trade.

The message of this court case as conveyed by Halligan is that general business information relating to the possible sale of a business is not protectable as trade secrets.

Merkle v. Johnson & Johnson, 1997 U.S. Dist. LEXIS 5216 (D. N.J. April 15, 1997). *The pharmaceutical firm Merckle filed a suit against Johnson & Johnson and Ortho Pharmaceutical Corp. alleging that they had misappropriated trade secrets relating to their protein hormone called erythropoietin (EPO), which stimulates the formation of red blood cells. The defendants moved that the case be dismissed by arguing that Merckle had publicly disclosed information on its formula, that an identical product was publicly available, that Merckle failed to adequately protect the confidentiality of its clinical trials, and that the defendants made no competitive use of Merckle's trade secrets. The court ruled that the alleged secrecy of Merckle's formula would rest largely on the credibility of witnesses and that summary judgment was therefore inappropriate. The court found that the notion of whether Merckle took reasonable precautions to protect its secrets should be based on reasonable, not absolute, precautions. The motion for summary judgment to dismiss the case was denied.*

Blimpie International, Inc. v. ICA Menyforetagen, 1997 U.S Dist. LEXIS 3950 (March 21, 1997). *The sub sandwich food chain Blimpie International, Inc. sued the Swedish corporation ICA for trade secret misappropriation. The secret appropriated was related to Blimpie's "Grab 'n Go" concept. ICA was exploring the expansion of their fast food business in Sweden and had retained the services of the Swedish American Chamber of Commerce and two convenience store consulting companies based in the U.S. One of the firms arranged a meeting between ICA and Blimpie executives to discuss the Blimpie franchise system. During the discussion, the Blimpie officials maintained that they disclosed trade secret information in confidence to the ICA visitors, including strategic plans and marketing strategies related to their "Grab' n Go" approach. ICA indicated that they did not receive any trade secrets, nor did they give any assurances to hold Blimpie's information in confidence. After the meeting ICA formed a subsidiary patterned after the "Grab'n Go"* *concept and even filed a trademark application for the name. The trial court dismissed the case on the grounds of forum non conveniens. This meant that since the causes of action were related to the alleged use in Sweden, which has a well-developed legal system capable of hearing Blimpie's claim, and since Blimpie would be unable to enforce a U.S. judgment, as there is no agreement regarding the enforcement of judgments between the two countries, the case would be better to be held in Sweden.*

Baystate Technologies v. Bentley Systems, Inc., F. Supp. 1079 (D. Mass. 1996). *A six-count complaint was filed by Baystate Technologies against Bentley Systems, Inc. Baystate alleged that Bentley had misappropriated trade secrets, among a number of other infringements. After a three-day trial, the court ruled in favor of the defendant on all counts. The court found that there was a lack of reasonable measures to preserve any trade secrecy. For example, there was testimony that the Tool Kit source code that was allegedly stolen was distributed without restriction to requesting third-party developers.*

Individuals concerned with the legal ramifications of the EEA, and that should be just about everyone involved in competitive intelligence or corporate security, are advised to periodically visit Halligan's *The Trade Secrets Homepage* to keep current on the latest court cases. The 41 cases for 1997 and 1998 that were listed and described at the Web site as of early July 1998, demonstrate that it is very difficult to obtain a trade secret violation in court. In many cases the company alleging the information theft was found not to have installed adequate safeguards and preparations within their organization. The policies developed by Arion Pattakos and laid out above would certainly help your case should there be a need to go to court.

Even with the absence of major convictions to date, the EEA has impacted CI by causing many firms to reexamine and reassess how they conduct their programs and operations. Most companies are finding, however, that they are operating legally and ethically and that the EEA should not hinder how they collect intelligence.

The reality is that the reach of the EEA and how it may limit or hinder CI activities will not be determined until enough case law has been adjudicated. That will take a number of years. Clearly, the past two years have shown that it is being used and tested. A few companies, in a kneejerk reaction to the EEA, have eliminated or scaled back their CI organizations and activities. In the long term, this could be far more damaging to those companies and the U.S. economy than the impact of economic espionage.

Espionage Is Not CI

Guy Kolb, the Executive Director of the Society of Competitive Intelligence, makes a very important point in an recent editorial in SCIP's *Competitive Intelligence Magazine*.[52] He describes how another professional organization (ASIS, in the survey described at the beginning of this chapter) estimated the potential cost of intellectual property theft to be more than US$300 billion a year. Kolb also makes reference to government agents who investigate economic espionage and warn business travelers to be careful when visiting abroad. There is a major educational effort on the part of the government directed against economic espionage, which some may view as alarmist. Kolb does not argue that these activities do not occur, often on the behalf of foreign governments. Rather, his point is that the most competitive companies, the "eagles," to use The Futures Group's terminology, are operating effectively without resorting to economic espionage. Whereas it is important that companies employ the best security safeguards to protect themselves, measures such as breaking into hotel rooms, hacking into computer networks, and stealing information generally do not work well. These are poor substitutes for the collection and analysis tools and techniques that are the bedrock for legal and ethical competitive intelligence.

10

Protection from Cyber Espionage

The 1996 Information Systems Security Survey

In 1996, WarRoom Research conducted an information security survey of Fortune 1000 firms that produced striking evidence of serious problems in many commercial organizations. Nearly half of the 205 firms that responded admitted that their computer networks had been successfully attacked and penetrated by "outsiders" in the past year—with losses and associated costs of considerable proportions. The results of the 1996 Information Systems Security Survey were presented during a Morning Newsmaker press conference at the National Press Club in Washington, DC. The survey drew an unprecedented high rate of response from the estimated 500 corporate professionals surveyed. It was distributed through executives and staff from six prominent organizations. Among them were several leading vendors of information security technologies, who typically passed it on to senior managers who are clients and associates.

The objectives of the survey were twofold. The first was to better quantify the potential security threats to and vulnerabilities of these businesses, as well as to the national information infrastructure, i.e., vital computer systems such as banking, transportation, and telecommunications. It was also hoped that this research would foster a greater awareness of the need for joint public/private-sector initiatives to better secure corporate and government networks. The survey had another intriguing credential. The survey questionnaire was accompanied by a letter from Senator Sam Nunn's Chief Counsel with the U.S. Senate's Permanent Subcommittee on Investigations expressing their interest in the results and promising to respect the survey's guarantee of anonymity to all respondents.

Executives from 98 of the 205 firms that responded to the survey acknowledged that their staff had detected intruders who had gained unauthorized access to computer systems in the past year. But fully 27 percent of the respondents doubted their organization had the capability to detect illicit access attempts, or even penetration of their computers. The corporations surveyed were willing to estimate the losses and associated costs for each successful intrusion by outsiders. Costs per incident were estimated at over $50,000 by 84 percent (136) of the respondents. Moreover, 41 percent indicated losses of more than $500,000 per intrusion, with 36 of these companies estimating losses at over a million dollars.

The Manhattan Cyber Project

Our dependence on information technology for maintaining our systems and implementing key functions is steadily increasing. There is a corresponding growth in the vulnerability of such vital systems to the pervasive "cyber threat," which comes from the accessibility of these systems to both insiders and outsiders. Examples of this threat include malicious code (i.e., computer viruses, logic bombs) and an assortment of hacker tools and techniques that have the potential to impair or destroy the functioning of corporations.

There have been many government and private studies and pronouncements about the lack of security in cyberspace and the risks of an electronic Pearl Harbor, yet these warnings remain largely unheeded. The lack of reporting and documentation on cyber attacks also obscures what is really happening. There is no uniform method for measuring the value of data/information and assigning appropriate levels of security or safeguards. In short, the range of threats and vulnerabilities is broad, and the understanding of the cyber threat is small.

In 1996 in testimony during Senator Sam Nunn's (D-GA) hearings on security in cyberspace, former Deputy Attorney General Jamie

Gorelick stated that a Manhattanlike project was needed to deal with the cyber threat. A unique consortium organized by coauthor Gembicki, composed of industry, academia, and government, listened to this "call to arms" and decided to take a proactive stance with the formation of the Manhattan Cyber Project (MCP). The Manhattan Cyber Project became a voluntary no-profit partnership between academia and corporations united against the potential decimation of a computer-based national infrastructure by hackers. As in the 1940s, we are confronted with a threat to key institutions and infrastructures. Also like its namesake of the 1940s, the MCP seeks to engage the best and brightest of technical and managerial minds to address a formidable challenge. Unlike its predecessor, the mission of the MCP is focused on public awareness and the sharing of expert knowledge on the cyber threat in order to empower owners and operators of America's critical infrastructure. This includes improving on the availability and effectiveness of technology, people, and processes that safeguard critical infrastructure areas from the cyber threat. The approach to accomplish this mission is based on developing and facilitating a coordinated outreach program with industry, government, and academia. A core element of the MCP is an outreach program featuring participation in various conferences, trade association meetings, and special events around the country. A variety of cyber-related themes or topics have been presented in several formats, from lectures, seminars, and workshops to debates and hands-on demonstrations.

Corporate America's Competitive Edge: An 18-Month Study into Cybersecurity and Business Intelligence Issues

Following in the tradition of the prior research and collaborations with the U.S. Senate and the President's Infrastructure Protection Task Force and the Manhattan Cyber Project, WarRoom Research completed a comprehensive evaluation in late 1998 of cybersecurity and business intelligence issues. The report, "Corporate America's Competitive Edge," involved 18 months of in-depth information collection and analysis on 320 Fortune 500-ranked firms. The effort was motivated by the apparent lack of cooperation between industry and government to share incident data on cyber attacks as well as information on the true competitiveness of corporate America. The focus of the primary research study was on the current state of security and intelligence practices and how they affect corporate America's ability to compete and the stability of our nation's infrastructure. To protect the anonymity of participants, the project was a closely guarded secret for one year and operated under the code name Turning Point. Participants of the study were limited to executive management—CEO, CIO, CTO, CKO, CFO, President, VP, Director, and mid-level management who assisted staff in providing information for security and intelligence assessments. All were qualified in that they had intimate experience and/or knowledge in security, decision-making, and intelligence topics within their corporation. The study had a phenomenal response rate of 64 percent, which, in part, was due to the strict anonymity of participants as well as pledging not to exploit their cooperation by marketing products or services to them.

During the 18-month period of the project, over 150 questions from more than 36 core topics were posed to the Fortune 500 participants. Additionally, information security and business intelligence assessments were conducted to baseline the threat and vulnerabilities to corporate America and our nation's critical infrastructures.

Although some of the findings were expected, based on our experience with the 1996 Information Systems Security Survey and the Manhattan Cyber Project, others were truly startling. Examples include increased physical and cyber attacks across multiple industries with unprecedented losses of revenue, intellectual property, core talent, and market presence.

Specific questions were asked about instances of espionage and what actions were taken as a result. The following sample contains some of the more startling findings as well as a comparison to similar questions asked during the 1996 Information Systems Security Survey:[53]

Question 1: Has your organization been the target of information espionage?[54]

Answer:	69% yes	1996:	53% yes
	14% no		9% no
	17% unknown		38% unknown

Question 2: Of the "yes" respondents (Q#1), is some form of intrusion detection technology used to safeguard your computer networks?

Answer: 68% yes   1996:   27% yes

         25% no   51% no

           7% unknown   22% unknown

Question 3: Of the "yes" respondents (Q#1), have you brought these incidents to the attention of law enforcement?

Answer: 12% yes   1996:   9% yes

         86% no   83% no

           2% unknown   8% unknown

Question 4: Of the "yes" respondents (Q#3), do you believe law enforcement or private security/investigation firms are more effective in espionage cases?

Answer: 21% law enforcement 1996:   10% law enforcement

         79% private   90% private

Question 5: Over the past 12 months (1997) how many successful unauthorized accesses from outsiders have you detected?

Answer: 2% 1 to 10   1996:   42% 1 to 10

           13% 11 to 20   25% 11 to 20

           25% 21 to 30   16% 21 to 30

           52% 31 to 40   10% 31 to 40

            6% 41 to 50   5% 41 to 50

            2% over 50   2% over 50

Question 6: What would you estimate is the cost to your organization for each successful intrusion into your computer systems from outsiders (Q#5)?

Answer:	1996:
2% $1 to $10,000	4% $1 to $10,000
11% $10,001 to $50,000	8% $10,001 to $50,000
8% $50,001 to $100,000	6% $50,001 to $100,000
10% $100,001 to $200,000	9% $100,001 to $200,000
21% $200,001 to $500,000	19% $200,001 to $500,000
16% $500,001 to $1,000,000	15% $500,001 to $1,000,000
7% $1,000,001 to $2,000,000	6% $1,000,001 to $2,000,000
10% $2,000,001 to $5,000,000	8% $2,000,001 to $5,000,000
2% $5,000,001 to $10,000,000	3% $5,000,001 to $10,000,000
3% over $10,000,000	1% over $10,000,000
10% unknown	21% unknown

Further information on the 1996 Information Systems Security Survey, the Manhattan Cyber Project, and Corporate America's Competitive Edge reports can be found at: www.WarRoomResearch.com.

The Corporate America's Competitive Edge report serves to reinforce a major premise of this book: An organization's competitiveness is dependent on how well the distinct but interrelated areas of competitive intelligence, security safeguards, and decision-making support are coordinated and managed. One element of this "strategic triad" cannot be done well without a close involvement and synergy of the other two.

It is our hope that this book will serve as a catalyst for the professionals of each respective area to seek each other out, communicate, and establish methods and processes of working together. We believe that some of the techniques and approaches described in this book will provide a means to initiate this dialogue and working relationship. We also hope that this book will enhance the awareness of CEOs and other corporate leaders that through the synergy of competitive intelligence, security safeguards, and decision-making support comes an increased effectiveness of each area, as well as the corporation's overall competitiveness.

Notes

1. The Use of Spies, http://www.kimsoft.com/polward.htm.

2. Yves-Michael Marti of the French organization EGIDERIA benchmarked the intelligence system of the Roman Catholic Church. He found that although the Catholic Church features many of the same systems that exist in businesses, their management approach is very different. The Church focuses on doctrine and reporting rather than strategy and planning.

3. SCIP's Code of Ethics can be found at http://www.scip.org/ethics.html.

4. Information on the President's Foreign Intelligence Advisory Board can be found at http://www2.whitehouse.gov/WH/EOP/pfiab/index-plain.html.

5. The findings of the Ostriches & Eagles 1997 study can be found at http://www.tfg.com/pubs/docs/O_EIII-97.html.

6. Jan Herring, the former VP at TFG and the founder of their CI program, preferred the term *business intelligence* over that of CI, since it is more inclusive and has the connotation of collecting intelligence on the total business environment.

7. Schwartau is author of *Information Warfare: Chaos on the Electronic Superhighway* and several other books. Schwartau is also the founder and publisher of infowar.com, the premier Web site devoted to the subject. It is found at http://www.infowar.com/. Reto Haeni provides a comprehensive introduction to information warfare which describes Schwartau's schemata and furnishes examples. This can be found at http://www.seas.gwu.edu/student/reto/infowar/info-war.html.

8. This study can be found at http://www.mediasource.com.

9. Marcia Green, "Outside Allegiances Exert Lethal Force, Even Behind Bars," *The Washington Post,* Sept. 9, 1996, p. A-1.

10. World War II movies such as *Sink the Bismark* (1960), *Battle of the Bulge* (1965), and *Tora! Tora! Tora!* depict military planning occurring in war room-type settings. Futuristic war films such as *Fail Safe* (1964) and *WarGames* (1983) also present planning and decision-making within a war room facility.

11. Stafford Beer, *Platform for Change,* John Wiley & Sons, New York, 1975, pp. 447–451.

12. *The War Room* documentary was released in 1993 and was directed by D.A. Pennebaker. It focuses on the activities of political pros James Carville and George Stephanopoulos.

13. Ruth Marcuc and Howard Schneider, "Media Control Was Legacy of '92 Campaign," *Washington Post,* July 29, 1994, p. A7.

14. "War of the War Rooms," *US News and World Report,* Sept. 13, 1993, p. 12.

15. Jeffrey Birnbaum and Gerald Seib, "Beltway Bog—How Washington Frustrates Change," *The Washington Post,* Dec. 2, 1993, p. A-1.

16. Michael S. Arnold, "Espy to Ride the Crest of Flood Recovery Efforts," *The Washington Post,* Aug. 12, 1993, p. 25.

17. Michael Weisskopf, "Campaign '96—Small Business Lobby Becomes a Big Player in Campaigns," *The Washington Post,* Aug. 9, 1996, p. A1.

18. Jacqueline Mitchell and Neal Templin, "Autos: Ford Taurus Dethrones Honda Accord as Top-Selling Car in the U.S. during 1992," *The Wall Street Journal,* Jan. 7, 1993, Sec. 8, p. 1.

19. Cindy Skrzycki, "MCI's Alliance: Veddy British, But Really Rad: Forging of British Telecom Deal Required Crossing Cultural Gaps," *The Washington Post,* Sept. 5, 1993, p. H-1.

20. Mike Mills, "MCI Becomes a Broadcaster; $683 Millio Bid Wins Satellite TV License," *The Washington Post,* Jan. 26, 1996; A-1.

21. Caleb Soloman and Robert Johnson, "Scary Prosperity: Natural-Gas Prices Surge, and Producers Aren't Happy at All," *The Wall Street Journal,* Oct. 12, 1992, p. A-1.

22. Stephanie Wilinson, "Winning the War in the Mini-Storage Business," *PC Week,* Dec. 1, 1987, p. 64.

23. Bill Brubaker and Mark Asher, "A Power Play for Howard, in Many Acts; Bullet's Departure for Miami Set Stage for Agents, Owners, NBA and a Surprise Ending," *The Washington Post,* Oct. 27, 1996, p. D-1.

24. Peter Perl, "The Battle of the Airport Hilton; Management Shows Videos and Hands Out Cash Prizes," *The Washington Post,* April 6, 1997, *Weekend Magazine,* p. 10.

25. Certain sectors of the intelligence community refer to them as ECIs (elements of critical information), ECIIs (a Department of Energy acronym for elements of critical information and indicators), or EEFIs (an operations security term for essential elements of friendly information).

26. Steven M. Shaker and George Kardulias, "Quarterbacking Business Intelligence Collection at Conferences," 4th European Forum-Business Intelligence Practices: Key Factors to Success, Association Aeronautique et Astronautique de France, Paris, January 1996; Steven M. Shaker and George Kardulias, "Scoring at Conferences: The Quarterback Technique for Gathering Intelligence," *Journal of Competitive Intelligence Review,* v. 7, Nov. 4/Winter 1996, pp. 4–10.

27. John Nolan and William DeGenaro, two retired U.S. Defense Dept. intelligence officers, teach courses in elicitation techniques through the Center for Operational Business Intelligence (941 906-9244); WarRoom Research teaches elicitation techniques in its Quarterback training seminars.

28. Susan Roane, *How to Work a Room,* Warner Books, New York, 1988.

29. The following references describe the use of body language in business negotiations:

    Steve Miller, *How to Get the Most Out of Trade Shows,* NTC Business Books, Lincolnwood, Illinois, 1996

    Morey Stettner, "When Negotiating, Look for Nonverbal Cues," *Investor's Business Daily,* "News for You," Jan. 1, 1997 http://www.pcrsonal.engin.umich.edu/~tjjacobs/articles/bodylang.html

    Body Language, http://newciv.org/worldtrans/TP/TP1/TP1-57.html

    Lo and Behold, The Body Language Dictionary, http://el.www.media.mit.edu/courses/tft96/Students/coe/assignments/buildtool.html

    Anne Dudley, "Unspoken Words: Reading Body Language Proves Tough," Richmond Newspapers, Inc., April 1997, http://www.gateway-va.com/pages/talkbiz/apr/etiqqa.htm

    Donna Siegel, "Reading the Customer's Body Language," *SalesDoctors Magazine,* Nov. 24, 1997, http://www.salesdoctors.com/service/ser08.htm

30. How to plan for and collect from exhibit booths is discussed in the following references: Scott Hunter, "Trade Shows: Your Supermarket for Competitive Information," from the conference proceedings, The Society of Competitive Intelligence (SCIP), 12th Annual International Conference & Exhibit, San Diego, May 28–31, 1997, pp. 265–276; Michael Roney and Michael Utvich, *Guerrilla Guide to High-Tech Trade Shows,* Random

House, Inc., New York, 1965; Steve Miller, *How to Get the Most Out of Trade Shows,* NTC Business Books, Lincolnwood, Illinois, 1996.

31. This list is derived from Jean L. Graef's survey on CI professionals and their use of the Internet as reported in *Competitive Intelligence Review,* vol. 8, 1997.

32. This survey was published in the Winter 1997 issue of *Competitive Intelligence Review.*

33. Information on NERAC can be found at http://www.nerac.com/about/about.html.

34. Jesus Men's article on machine-learning and data mining in the Winter 1996 issue of the *Competitive Intelligence Review,* page 24, contains a list of the data-mining tools suitable for CI applications, their vendors, and their phone and e-mail addresses.

35. E-mail elicitation is described in an advisory notice of the Department of Energy's Information Security Resource Center dated Dec. 9, 1996.

36. Edward Tufte, *Visual Explanations,* Graphics Press, Cheshire, Conn., pp. 26, 38–53.

37. "Let's Talk," *BusinessWeek,* Feb. 23, 1998, pp. 61–72.

38. Benchtrending involves taking benchmarking and projecting it out into the future. Rather than comparing the companies' past and current performance, it benchmarks projected and possible performance.

39. Information on this merger and acquisition software can be found at http://www.moneysoft.com.

40. The crime visualization linking software can be found at http://www.harlequin.com.

41. These statistics were reported in SCIP's *Competitive Intelligence Magazine,* April–June 1998, p. 6.

42. The origin of OPSEC is described at http://www.nv.doe.gov/opsec/origin.htm, a Web site maintained by the Department of Energy.

43. The OPSEC Professionals Society Web site and membership information can be found at http://www.opsec.org.

44. The Laws of OPSEC are described at http://www.nv.doe.gov/opsec/understand.htm.

45. There may be organizations other than your competitor that may be harmful to your organization. It could be a special interest group or advocacy campaign that is trying to change the business environment in which you are thriving. It could be the media trying to publicize publicly

damaging information. It could also be the government zealously promoting regulations harmful to your operations.

46. Professionals can be found by contacting the OPSEC Professionals Society and SCIP.

47. Social engineering is a term used by hackers and information security professionals to describe the use of human weaknesses in order to trick people into revealing passwords or other information that compromises a system's security.

48. The Novell and PC vulnerability scanner and the Internet Security Scanner produced by ISS.

49. Pattakos details the steps required for formalizing an OPSEC/Counter Intelligence program in his article for the *Competitive Intelligence Review*, "Keeping Company Secrets Secret," vol. 8 (3), 1997.

50. Nolan's Web site at the Phoenix Consulting Group, http://www.intellpros.com/lib/dulledge.htm, contains several articles authored by Nolan that describe his approach to CCIM and some case studies backing up his approach. In his presentation, *The Emerging Role of Competitive Counterintelligence: Light Years Beyond Security,* at SCIP 10, Nolan described these case studies.

51. Halligan's Web site, The Trade Secrets Home Page, can be found at http://www.execpc.com/~mhalligan/new.htm.

52. Guy Kolb, *Competitive Intelligence Magazine,* April–June 1998, p. 56.

53. Conducted in collaboration with the U.S. Senate's Permanent Subcommittee on Investigations. The espionage responses contained in this document were *not* released in 1996.

54. WarRoom Research defines *information espionage* as a directed attempt to identify and gather proprietary data and information via computer networks.

Glossary

Approach: The first step in elicitation, which involves the first interaction and introduction between the source and the target.

Benchtrending: Projecting benchmarking into the future. Rather than comparing companies' past and current performance, it benchmarks projected and possible performance.

Collection Plan: A plan used to guide intelligence gathering, which consists of a structured, logical, sequential process in which the results of one CI step feed into the conduct of the next task.

Competitive Benchmarking: A method of comparing one company's CI organization and operations against those of a competitor.

Competitive Intelligence: A systematic, ongoing business process to ethically and legally gather intelligence on targets such as customers, competitors, adversaries, personnel, technologies, and the total business environment. It can be provided by any and all sources, and is disseminated to decision-makers at all levels in a visually effective, timely, and secure manner.

Data: The foundation, and lowest level, of information on the information pyramid. It refers to information which is typically quantitative and available to the general public through publications and on-line sources. It has not been analyzed and is of little value to decision-makers.

Defensive Competitive Intelligence: Monitoring and analyzing one's own business activities to determine intelligence vulnerabilities and activities competitors could utilize to learn about the company.

Elicitation: The technique of interaction a source uses to extract intelligence from a target. It is built on the use of social and psychological tactics which disarm the target's natural defenses regarding sensitive information.

Environmental Scan: A technique used to monitor the pulse of change in the environment by systematically reviewing published materials and interviewing knowledgeable individuals.

Essential Elements of Friendly Intelligence (EEFI): Those signatures or identifying characteristics that are exploitable by an adversary.

Essential Elements of Intelligence (EEIs): Further refinements of intelligence requirements that often are more quantitative and respond to analytical criteria.

External Sources: Individuals who seek to obtain intelligence from targets on a company's behalf, but who are not employees. They may be consultants, vendors, industry analysts, journalists, or others who can gain close proximity to a target.

False Flag: A technique in which a company sends a trusted employee to interview with a competitor in an effort to learn about the organization through the employment process.

Finished Intelligence: Intelligence which has been analyzed or has enough supportive information to make it credible so that it is deemed worthy to disseminate to senior decision-makers.

Flag: An unintended cue or action by a source which alerts a target that he or she is being elicited for intelligence.

Information: Information represents the mid-level of the information pyramid. It is data whose value is enhanced because it has been put in some analytical framework. It typically is qualitative in nature. It is of some value to decision-makers, but it is of more use to analysts.

Information Collection Process: The entry points for information into an organization from both internal and external sources.

Information Denial: Measures beyond normal protection to specifically target an adversary's collection systems.

Information Protection: Safeguarding information from information compromise and destruction.

Information Warfare: The offensive and defensive use of information and information systems to exploit, corrupt, or destroy an adversary's information and information systems while protecting one's own. Such actions are designed to achieve advantages over a business adversary.

Intelligence: A compilation and analysis of data and/or information provided by any and all sources, human or otherwise, that has foresight and can render an insightful picture of intentions, capabilities, or activities of a competitor, as well as their possible implications and consequences. It is the pinnacle of the information pyramid.

Internal Sources: Individuals from within the company who are used to elicit intelligence from targets. They are paid employees of the organization and have legal and emotional ties to the well-being of the company.

Logic Bomb: A type of Trojan horse used to release a virus, worm, or some other system attack. It's either an independent program or a piece that's been planted by a system developer or programmer.

Operations Security (OPSEC): A rigorous and structured approach to making the intelligence gathering of a competitor or adversary more difficult and time consuming.

OPSEC Assessment (OA): A critical analysis of a company's activities from the perspective of its competitors or adversaries. Activities are assessed to determine intelligence indicators or signatures.

Opsroom: A room concept developed by Stafford Beer in which computer technology graphically lays out information to facilitate decision-making.

Phantom Interview: Technique in which a competitor or a dishonest "headhunter" poses as a potential employer or executive recruiter, and makes inquiries to an organization's employees about their duties, functions, and programs.

Primary Sources: Providers who obtain their intelligence directly from the target. They learn their information from firsthand interaction and observation.

Raw Intelligence: Collected intelligence which has not been collaborated by other sources. It has not gone through an analytical framework, and its level of confidence is low. Its dissemination may be delayed because of the lack of collaborative information, or it should be noted as such in the intelligence report.

Requirements: Those questions whose answers are needed to support effective decision-making.

Reverse Engineering: Acquiring and closely examining a competitor's product, often by disassembling it to determine its subsystems and components, to enable a company to learn about its technology, quality, and cost. What is learned is often incorporated into the company's own product line.

Search Engine: A search engine is a utility that searches the Internet, an intranet, a Web site, or a database for terms the user selects. Search engines consist of three basic elements:

- A program that roams the area to be searched, collecting data and links to more data. There are different types of these programs, and they are often called spiders, robots, worms, or crawlers.

- An index of the data collected to enable fast access to terms being sought.

- A search interface, which is the form in which you enter your search terms and the software behind it, that queries the index, retrieves matches, ranks for relevance, and organizes the data for follow-on searches.

Secondary Sources: Providers of secondhand intelligence, who learned the information through someone other than the target.

Source: Individuals who are used to gain access to and elicit information from targets.

Subject Guides: Hierarchically organized indexes of subject categories that enable a researcher to browse the lists of Web sites by subject in search of relevant information.

Target: Those individuals who have the knowledge to answer your requirements, yet might be unwilling to talk with known collectors and analysts of your corporation. The targets are the custodian of the information sought by the source.

Trade Craft: Specialized skills and techniques, gained through training and experience, that are used to collect intelligence.

Trojan Horse: A code fragment that hides inside a program and performs a disguised function. It is a popular mechanism for disguising a virus or a worm.

Virus: A code fragment that copies itself into a larger program and modifies that program. A virus executes only when its host program begins to run. The virus then replicates itself, infecting other programs as it reproduces.

War Games: Scenarios relating to business situations and activities which are played out and evaluated in order to plan contingencies and decision options.

The War Room: A location optimized to facilitate team-based decision support through the collection, analysis, and dissemination of intelligence.

Worm: An independent program that reproduces itself in full-blown fashion from one computer to another, usually over a network. Unlike a virus, it usually doesn't modify other programs.

Bibliography

Achenbach, Joel: "Wire Me Up, Scotty; We Have Seen the Future, But We Still Can't Tell You What It Means," *Washington Post,* section W, Magazine, May 29, 1994, p. 10.

Barlow, Linda: "The Spider's Apprentice—Tips on Searching the Web," March 26, 1998 (http://www.monash.com/spidap.html).

Basch, Reva: "Find Anything Online," October 14, 1997 (http://www1.zdnet.com/complife/fea/9708/findny10.html).

Bates, Mary Ellen: "Emerging Trends in Information Brokering," *Competitive Intelligence Review,* vol. 8 (4), 1997, pp. 48–53.

"Battling Cyber Saboteurs," *Washington Post,* January 31, 1997, pp. G1, G3.

Bender, David, and Bruno Leone (eds.): *America's Future: Opposing Viewpoints,* Geenhaven Press, Inc., San Diego, 1990.

"Better Safe Than Sorry," *Home Office Computing,* October 1996, pp. 46–48.

"Body Language," http://newciv.org/worldtrans/TP/TP1/TP1-57.HTML.

"Businesses, Universities Team Up Against Cyber Threat," *Kiplinger,* June 9, 1997 (www.kiplinger.com).

Buzan, Tony: *Use Both Sides of Your Brain,* Plume/Penguin, New York, 1991.

Calof, Jonathan L.: "Home Pages: They're Saying More Than You Think," *Competitive Intelligence Review,* vol. 7 (4), pp. 84–85.

Cetron, Marvin, and Owen Davies: *Crystal Globe: The Haves and the Have-Nots of the New World Order,* St.Martin's Press, New York, 1991.

Cetron, Marvin: "American Renaissance in the Year 2000: 74 Trends That Will Affect America's Future and Yours," *The Futurist,* 1994.

"Coalition Warns of Cyber Threats," *News.Com,* June 9, 1997 (www.news.com).

Coates, Joseph: "The Highly Probable Future: 83 Assumptions about the Year 2025," *The Futurist,* 1994 (developed for Project 2025: Anticipating Developments in Science and Technology and Their Implications for the Corporation, sponsored by 18 large organizations in the United States and Europe).

Cohen, Laura: "Searching the Internet: Recommended Sites and Search Techniques," April 23, 1998 (http://www.albany.edu/library/internet/search.html).

"Companies Join Forces to Track Hackers," *Washington Technology,* June 20, 1997 (www.wtonline.com).

"Companies Team to Tap into Cyber Security Issues and Answers," *Contingency Planning & Management,* July/August 1997, p. 3.

"Companies Try to Secure Cyberspace," *USA Today,* June 9, 1997 (www.techweb.cmp.com/cwk).

"Competitive Intelligence: Using Advanced Technology to Support Strategic Planning," *Advance,* November 30, 1996, pp. 4–6.

Coplin, William D., and Michael K. O'Leary: *Everyman's Prince: A Guide to Understanding Your Political Problems,* Duxbury Press, North Scituate, MA, 1976.

"Corporate America Reluctant to Report Computer Attacks to Law Enforcement," *Defense Information and Electronics Report,* vol. 1 (9), November 22, 1996, pp. 1, 6–7.

Cramer, Myron: "The Information Revolution: Its Current and Future Consequences—Information Warfare," Dec. 21, 1996 (http://iw.windermefegroup.com/Papers/informer.html).

"Cyberspace Guards Quietly Snuff Out Hacker Attacks," *Washington Technology,* November 21, 1996, pp. 1, 37.

Didsbury, Howard, Jr.: *The Future Opportunity Not Destiny,* World Future Society, Bethesda, MD, 1989.

"Distributed Defense," *Computerworld,* December 2, 1996, pp. 81–82.

"A Do-It-Yourself War Room," *Intelligence Newsletter,* no. 281, February 8, 1996, p. 2. The Us http://www.scip.org/ethics.htmle of Spies (http://www.kimsoft.com/polward.htm).

Drucker, Peter: *Managing for the Future: The 1990s and Beyond,* Truman Talley Books/Plume (Penguin Books), New York, 1993.

Dudley, Anne: "Unspoken Words: Reading Body Language Proves Tough," Richmond Newspapers, Inc., April 1997 (http://www.gateway-va.com/pages/talkbiz/apr/etiqqa.htm).

"Escalating Computer Crime Fuels Demand for Security Experts," *Washington Post,* High-Tech Careers supplement, January 12, 1997, pp. 64–65, 67.

"Espionage Is Alive and Well," *World Trade,* July 1997, pp. 24–26.

"FBI to Open More Cybercrime Units," *Wired News,* February 27, 1997 (www.wired.com).

Fuld, Leonard, M.: *The New Competitor Intelligence,* John Wiley & Sons, New York, 1995.

Garrett, Laurie: *The Coming Plague,* Penguin Books, New York, 1994.

Hardy, Quentin: "Firms Are Hurt By Break-Ins at Computers," *The Wall Street Journal,* November 21, 1996 p. B4.

"Getting the High-Tech Bugs Out Can Be Big Business," *Register Star,* December 2, 1996, pp. 1C–2C.

Graef, Jean L.: "Using the Internet for Competitive Intelligence: A Survey Report," *Competitive Intelligence Review,* vol. 8 (4), 1997, pp. 41–47.

Green, William: "I Spy," *Forbes Magazine,* April 20, 1998 (http://www.forbes.com/forbes/98/0420/6108090a.htm).

Greenberg, Ross M.: "Parallel Search Engines: Seek, and Ye Shall Find," *Buyer's Guide,* November 25, 1996.

Grossan, Bruce: "Search Engines: What They Are, How They Work, and Practical Suggestions for Getting the Most Out of Them," February 21, 1997 (http://webreference.com/content/search/).

"Group Aims to Arm Businesses Against Cybercriminals," *Computerworld,* June 9, 1997 (www.computerworld.com).

Haeni, Reto: An Introduction to Information Warfare, August 1996 (http://www.seas.gwu.edu/student/reto/infowar/info-war.html).

Holden-Rhodes, J. F.: *Sharing the Secrets: Open Source Intelligence & the War on Drugs,* University of New Mexico Press, Albuquerque, NM, 1994.

Hunter, Scott: "Trade Shows: Your Supermarket for Competitive Information," Proceedings of the 12th Annual Society of Competitive Intelligence International Conference and Exhibit, San Diego, May 28–31, 1997, pp. 265–276.

"Industry Group to Examine Computer Security Threats," *Macworld,* June 6, 1997 (www.macworld.com/daily).

"Infectious Diseases Resistant, Study Finds," *The New York Times,* May 20, 1996, p. A3.

"INS Launches Security Outsourcing Service," *Communications Week,* December 2, 1996 (http://techweb.cmp.com/cwk).

"IT Looks to Fend Off Hackers Inside and Out," *PC Week,* January 27, 1997 (www.pcweek.com).

Jones, Gerald: *How to Lie with Charts,* Sybex, Inc., San Francisco, 1995.

Jones, Morgan D.: *The Thinker's Toolkit,* Random House, New York, 1995.

"K&R Coverage Can Apply to More Than Just Employees," *Business Insurance,* March 24, 1997, pp. 1, 16.

Kahaner, Larry: *Competitive Intelligence,* Simon & Schuster, New York, 1996.

"Lo and Behold, The Body Language Dictionary" (http://el.www.media.mit.edu/courses/tft96/Students/coe/assignments/buildtool.html).

Kolb, Guy D.: "The View From SCIP: Espionage Is a Poor Alternative to CI," *Competitive Intelligence Magazine,* vol. 1 (1), April–June 1998, p. 56.

Kriesel, Ronald W.: "Suggested Internet Research Strategies," March 1, 1998 (http://www.concentric.net/~Rkriesel/Search/Strategies.shtml).

Lake, Matthew: "Search Engine Shoot-Out," August 1, 1997 (http://www4.zdnet.com/pccomp/features/excl0997/sear/sear.html).

Lidsky, David, and Regina Kwon: "Your Complete Guide to Searching the Net," *PC Magazine,* 16.21, December 2, 1997, p. 227 (http://www.zdnet.com/pcmag/features/websearch/_open.htm).

Lynch, Clifford: "Searching the Internet," *Scientific American,* 276.3, March 1997, pp. 52–56 (http://www.sciam.com/0397issue/0397lynch.html).

Malhotra, Yogesh: "Competitive Intelligence Programs: An Overview" (http://www.brint.com/papers/ciover.htm).

"The Manhattan Project's Cyber Threat," *Communications Week,* June 16, 1997 (www.techweb.cmp.com/cwk).

Marti, Yves-Michel: "Benchmarking the Intelligence System of the Roman Catholic Church," Proceedings of the 12th Annual Society of Competitive Intelligence Professionals International Conference and Exhibit, p. 293.

Mathey, Charles J.: *Competitive Analysis,* American Management Association, New York, 1991.

Mendell, Ronald, L.: *How To Conduct Business Investigations and Competitive Intelligence Gathering,* Thomas Investigation Publications, Inc., Austin, Texas, 1997.

Miller, Stephen: "The Image Challenge for CI Professionals," *Actionable Intelligence Newsletter,* Society of Competitive Intelligence Professionals, December 1996, pp. 1, 4.

Miller, Steve: *How to Get the Most Out of Trade Shows,* NTC Business Books, Lincolnwood, Illinois, 1996.

"Most Large Companies Infiltrated in Past 12 Months, Survey Finds," *Kiplinger,* November 21, 1996 (www.kiplinger.com).

Mullaney, Timothy J.: "Busy Hackers Prove Costly, Study Finds," *The Baltimore Sun,* December 2, 1996, pp. 13c–14c.

Nasbitt, John: *Global Paradox,* Avon Books, New York, 1996.

Nelson, Scott Benard: "Countering Competitive Intelligence," *Kiplinger Online,* November 22, 1996.

The Newsletter of Environmental Scanning, Georgia Center for Continuing Education (http://www.gactr.uga.edu/Scanning/scan0196.html).

"1996 Information Systems Security Survey," Security in Cyberspace Hearings before the Permanent Subcommittee on Investigations of the Committee on Governmental Affairs, United States Senate, 104th Congress, 2nd Session, January 1997, pp. 596–604.

Nolan, John A., III: "Confusing Counterintelligence with Security Can Wreck Your Afternoon," *Competitive Intelligence Review,* vol. 8 (3) 1997, pp. 53–61.

———: "Is Someone Dulling Your Competitive Edge?" (http://www.intellpros.com/lib/dulledge.htm).

———: "Now That You Know How They're Getting It, What Do You Do Next?" *Security Technology & Design,* May 1996 (http://www.intellpros.com/lib/next.html).

———: "The Emerging Role of Counterintelligence—Light Years Beyond Security," Proceedings of the 10th Annual Society of Competitive Intelligence Professionals Conference, Arlington, VA, March 1996, pp. 467–499.

———: "What Is Competitive Intelligence and What Can It Do to Us?" *Security Technology & Design,* January/February 1996 (http://www.intellpros.com/lib/what.html).

Notess, Greg R.: "Comparing Net Directories," Database 20.1, February 1997, pp. 61–64 (http://www.onlineinc.com/database/FebDB97/nets2.html).

———: "Internet Search Techniques and Strategies," *Online* 21.4, July 1997, pp. 63–66 (http://www.onlineinc.com/onlinemag/JulOL97/net7.html).

———: "Measuring the Size of Internet Databases," Database 20.5, October 1997 (http://www.onlineinc.com/database/OctDB97/net10.html).

———: "On the Net: Internet Search Techniques and Strategies," *Online,* July 1997 (http://www.onlineinc.com/onlinemag/JulOL97/net7.htm).

———: "Search Engines Showdown," March 13, 1998 (http://imt.net/~notess/search/index.html).

———: "Toward More Comprehensive Web Searching: Single Searching Versus Megasearching," *Online* 22.2, March 1998, pp. 73–76 (http://www.onlineinc.com/onlinemag/OL1998/net3.html).

"Ostriches & Eagles 1997," The Futures Group (http://www.tfg.com/pub/docs/O_EIII-97.html).

"Outlook '94," *The Futurist,* 1993 (derived from various projections published in 1993 issues of *The Futurist*).

Pattakos, Arion N.: "Keeping Company Secrets Secret," *Competitive Intelligence Review,* vol. 8 (3), 1997, pp. 71–78.

Preston, Richard: *The Hot Zone,* Anchor Books, New York, 1995.

"Q&A: Cybercrime," *Pinkerton Solutions,* no. 7, 1997, pp. 6–8.

"Report Highlights Frequency, Cost of Computer Break-ins," *Computerworld,* November 22, 1996 (www.computerworld.com).

Roane, Susan: *How to Work a Room,* Warner Books, New York, 1988.

Roney, Michael, and Michael Utvich: *Guerrilla Guide to High-Tech Trade Shows,* Random House, New York, 1965.

Russel, Deborah, and G.T. Gangemi: *Computer Security Basics,* O'Reilly & Associates, Sebastopol, CA, 1994.

Sammon, William, Mark Kurland, and Robert Spitalnic: *Business Competitor Intelligence: Methods for Collecting, Organizing and Using Information,* John Wiley & Sons, New York, 1984.

Schwartau, Winn: *Information Warfare: Chaos on the Electronic Superhighway,* Thunder's Mouth Press, New York, 1994.

"Searching the Internet," January 6, 1998 (http://wwwscout.cs.wisc.edu/scout/toolkit/searching/index.html).

"Security Expert Bound for Cyberterra Incognita," *Wired News,* June 10, 1997 (www.wired.com).

"Security: It's Your Call," *Communications Week,* December 9, 1996 (http://techweb.cmp.com/cwk).

"Selling Security," *InfoWorld,* December 23, 1996, pp. 49, 51.

Shaker, Steven: "Competitive Intelligence: The Next Generation," Proceedings of the 10th Annual Society of Competitive Intelligence Professionals International Conference and Exhibit, March 27–30, 1996, Arlington, VA, pp. 500–519.

Shaker, Steven M.: "Setting Up Your Own Business Intelligence Arm," *Foreign Trade,* September/October 1991, p. 23.

Shaker, Steven M., and Theodore Rice: "Beating the Competition: From War Room to Board Room," *Journal of Competitive Intelligence Review,* vol. 6 (1), spring 1995.

Shaker, Steven M., and George Kardulias: "Scoring at Conferences: The Quarterback Technique for Gathering Intelligence," *Journal of Competitive Intelligence Review,* vol. 7, November 4, 1996, pp. 4–10.

Siegel, Donna: "Reading the Customer's Body Language," *SalesDoctors Magazine,* November 24, 1997 (http://salesdoctors.com/service/ser08.htm).

Stettner, Morey: "When Negotiating, Look for Nonverbal Cues," *Investor's Business Daily*—News for You, January 1, 1997 (http://www.personal.engin.umich.edu/~tjjacobs/articles/bodylang.html).

"Still at Risk," *Communications Week,* November 25, 1996, p. 10.

"Study: Majority of U.S. Firms Hacked," *Wired News,* November 22, 1996 (www.wired.com).

Sullivan, Danny: "Search Engine Watch" (http://searchenginewatch.com).

"Survey Reveals Computer System Break-Ins Are Common," *Merritt Risk Management News,* December 16, 1996, p. 2.

"Survey Reveals Security Fears and Vulnerability," *IEEE Computer,* February 1997, p. 22.

Tillman, Hope N.: "Evaluating Quality on the Net," November 13, 1997 (http://www.tiac.net/users/hope/findqual.html).

Tillman, Hope N., and Walt Howe: "Internet Tips and Tricks," November 16, 1997 (http://www.tiac.net/users/hope/il97/tips97.htm).

Toffler, Alvin, and Heidi Toffler: *War and Anti-War: Survival at the Dawn of The 21st Century,* Little, Brown, and Company, New York, 1993.

"Trouble from the Inside" *Infosecurity News,* January/February 1997, p. 9.

Tufte, Edward R.: *Envisioning Information,* Graphics Press, Cheshire, CT, 1990.

————: *The Visual Display of Quantitative Information,* Graphics Press, Cheshire, CT, 1983.

————: *Visual Explanations,* Graphics Press, Cheshire, CT, 1997.

Tyner, Ross: "Sink or Swim: Internet Search Tools & Techniques" (http://www.ouc.bc.ca/libr/connect96/search.htm).

"Under Attack—What Hackers Know Will Harm You," *Communications Week,* March 10, 1997 (http://techweb.cmp.com/cwk).

United Way Strategic Institute: "Nine Forces Reshaping America," *The Futurist,* July–August 1990, pp. 9–16 (adapted from the report by the United Way of America's Strategic Institute, "What Lies Ahead: Countdown to the 21st Century").

"A War Room to Clinch a Contract," *Intelligence Newsletter,* no. 302, January 2, 1997, p. 2.

"A Warning Shot," *PC Week,* January 20, 1997 (www.pcweek.com).

"Washington Draws Line Between Corporate Research and Spying," *Asia Times,* March 3, 1997 (www.asiatimes.com).

Westera, Gillian: "Using the Best Search Engine for Your World Wide Web Research," July 4, 1997 (http://www.curtin.edu.au/curtin/library/staffpages/gwpersonal/senginestudy /zindex.htm).

"When Knowledge Is Dangerous," *Computerworld,* June 30, 1997, p. 81 (www.computerworld.com).

Wighton, D.: "Searching FAQs," March 12, 1998 (http://www.cln.org/searching_faqs.html).

Winkler, Ira: *Corporate Espionage: What It is, Why It Is Happening in Your Company and What You Must Do About It,* Prima Publications, Arlington, VA, 1997.

————: "The Insider Threat or How I Stole $1,000,000,000," *Intelligence Online* (http://www.indigo-net.com/annexes/289/winkler.htm).

Zorn, Peggy et al.: "Advanced Web Searching: Tricks of the Trade," *Online* 20.3, May 1996, pp. 14–28 (http://www.onlineinc.com/onlinemag/MayOL/zorn5.html).

Zuckerman, M. J. "Cybercrime Against Business Frequent, Costly," *USA Today,* November 21, 1996, p. 1A.

————: "FBI Takes on Security Fight in Cyberspace," *USA Today,* November 21, 1996, p. 4B.

Index

About the Authors

STEVE SHAKER is a cofounder and vice president of WarRoom Research where he oversees business intelligence and decision support war room initiatives. A nationally recognized technology forecaster and futurist, he has over 18 years' experience working for industry and government, including serving as a CIA Case Officer. Shaker has appeared as a future technology expert on *Good Morning America, Nightline,* and *CNN.* Shaker is the author of *War Without Men: Robotics on the Future Battlefield* and also directs the marketing efforts for Intelligent Automation in Rockville, Maryland.

MARK GEMBICKI is cofounder and president of WarRoom Research. With more than 16 years' experience in technology management, intelligence processing, and security safeguards, he has worked with numerous government and commercial organizations. Gembicki was recruited by the National Security Agency at 17 and has since become a noted authority on information security, which is based largely on his leadership of the Manhattan Cyber Project, collaboration with the U.S. Senate on cyber threat issues, and directing the much lauded insider report "Corporate America's Competitive Edge." Gembicki is the originator of the Online or E-Quarterback approach to collecting intelligence on the Internet. Gembicki's body of work has been referenced in over 200 publications as well as featured on ABC, BBC, C-NBC, C-SPAN, Fox, and Radio Free Europe.